LOVE,
CHRISTOPHER
STREET

LOVE,
CHRISTOPHER
STREET

REFLECTIONS *of* NEW YORK CITY

edited by THOMAS KEITH
introduction by CHRISTOPHER BRAM

Chelsea Station

Editions

Published by Chelsea Station Editions
362 West 36th Street, 2R
New York, NY 10018
www.chelseastationeditions.com
info@chelseastationeditions.com

Manufactured in the United States of America

First published by Vantage Point Books June 2012.
Published by Chelsea Station Editions May 2013.

For information about the authors, readings, and permissions
contact lovechristopherstreet@gmail.com

ISBN: 978-1-937627-07-2

Library of Congress Cataloging-in-Publication data are on file.

0   9   8   7   6   5   4   3   2   1

Cover design by Victor Mingovits

CONTENTS

TO

MY BROTHER

MATTHEW KEITH

1970–2012

INTRODUCTION

I MOVED TO NEW YORK City from a small college town in Virginia in 1978, telling my friends (and myself) that I wanted to go to this big, noisy, dangerous, half-broke city only because I wanted to be a writer; I thought all writers needed to live for a year or two in the "Capital of the Twentieth Century." I was there to meet editors and other writers, and to take advantage of the culture: art museums, movie theaters, and the many, many bookstores.

Not until a few years later, after I was contentedly settled with a boyfriend, did I admit that I had moved to New York for sex and love. I had known unrequited love all too well in Virginia. I had needed to come here to meet real gay men who might want to go to bed with me as badly I wanted to go to bed with them. Which I happily did for two years, before I met Draper.

For a very long time now, I believed that my first set of reasons for coming to New York—work and culture—were lies, and that the second set—love and sex—were the truth. But after reading the wonderful assortment of stories in this book, I now see that all my reasons were good, and they were all true.

Thomas Keith has gathered together a remarkable collection of life snapshots, a constellation of different lives lightly held together by place—greater New York; time—1960 to the present; and sexuality. Sexual difference makes cities very important for anyone who needs to invent their own life. Before the Internet opened up the world for everybody, gay people needed to leave home in order to meet other people like ourselves, and we usually moved to the big city. Every queer New Yorker—every queer urbanite, for that matter—will see pieces of him- or herself reflected in the stories here.

SEX AND LOVE PLAY A big part, of course. How could they not? Brendan Fay comes from Ireland to study Catholic theology and ends up in bed with Jesús, a clerk at the Oscar Wilde Bookshop. Mark Ameen describes a five-year sexual tour that takes him through various bars, boyfriends, and boroughs. Aaron Hamburger comes here hoping for love, settling for sex, learning to enjoy the sex, then finding love—finally marriage—and worrying he's become *too* normal. Nicky Paraiso meets the Ivy League boy of his dreams in an East Village bar and follows him through love and addiction and death.

Culture is not just decorative, but an important part of who we are. Justine Saracen celebrates it in a delirious account of her obsession with trouser-wearing mezzo sopranos, a love she first experienced on television in Ohio and which deepened by coming to New York and arranging an interview with the mezzo of her dreams. Penny Arcade came to the city as a runaway, but was rescued from homelessness and drugs by a network of gay men who introduced her to the worlds of theater, film, and drag, and who shaped her gay sensibility.

Work, too, is hardly trivial. Look at Bob Smith's wonderful account of his life as a stand-up comedian, a world that includes a loyal family of other gay and lesbian comics. Smith makes clear how important performance is to any performer, like air and water, when his diagnosis with ALS—Lou Gehrig's Disease—means he can no longer get up on stage. Michael Musto tells how he did not find himself and his sexual politics until he began to work doing a column for the *Village Voice*.

Time plays a big role in this book. We watch the city (and the world) change over the years, growing more open. Felice Picano traces a history of Greenwich Village from the 19th century to the present. Val McDermid tells of repeated trips from Scotland from the 1970s to now, focusing in part on her visits to the lesbian bar that was first The Duchess, then The Grove, and is now a vitamin store. But the decline of lesbian nightlife is counterpointed by her own success as an out lesbian novelist. Time is also explored through friendships with people from older generations. David McConnell's wonderful memoir of artist/writer Joe Brainard includes glimpses into the gay New York of the 1950s and 1960s. The book is full of friendships: people meet in bars, at theaters, on jobs. Eddie Safarty takes a whole gaggle of gay friends—including more comedians—out to Long Island for Passover dinner with his mother and her friends, who prefer them to their more conventional families.

City is a state of mind as well as a geographical location. Several of the immigrants here were inner immigrants, growing up in Brooklyn (Musto and the Rev. Irene Monroe), or say, the Bronx (Charlie Vázquez, Charles Rice-González, and Thomas Glave), Queens (Nicky Paraiso), Staten Island (Michelle Karlsberg), Long Island (Andrea Myers and Eddie Sarfaty), or nearby New Jersey (G. Winston James) and Connecticut (Ocean Vuong). They need to leave the neighborhood to be free, but remain connected afterwards.

Many people don't even need to live in New York for the city to play a liberating role in their life. Its existence in books and movies and on television is like a star they can navigate by.

WEALTH IS NOW CROWDING OUT much of the scruffy life and art that first drew me to New York, replacing it with expensive shops and pricey restaurants, brand name goods that can be appreciated by the shallowest conforming consumer. Yet the ideal of old New York still exists, like a guiding star, in both memory and secret pockets, migrating to the outer boroughs and to other cities, like Vásquez's Portland, Martin Hyatt's rural Louisiana, Glave's Kingston, Jamaica, Fay's Drogheda, McDermid's Fife, Shawn Syms's Toronto, or the London of Shaun Levin or Thomas Glave. Real cities offer a place where all queer people, not just the sexually queer but the politically queer and the culturally queer, can find one another and find themselves and make a home.

"There is no place like home, there is no place like home," Dorothy chants at the end of MGM's *The Wizard of Oz*, taps her slippers, and returns to black-and-white Kansas. But for many of us, Oz is our home and always has been, even before we moved here.

CHRISTOPHER BRAM
JANUARY 2012

PREFACE

YES. ANOTHER ANTHOLOGY. FOLLOWING IN the series with his earlier collections about New Orleans, San Francisco, and Los Angeles—*Love, Bourbon Street*; *Love, Castro Street*; and *Love, West Hollywood*—Joseph Pittman invited me to edit this anthology about LGBT experiences of New York City. I declined, politely. Editing anthologies: *Too little money. Too much time. All those diplomatic refusals from talented writers.* And how would I prevail upon the kind of first-rate authors an anthology about New York City would require—willing to write original essays no less? Mr. Pittman asked me to think about it a bit more, so I did. While I was fretting, fussing, and earnestly making several druthers lists of possible contributors, my longtime partner Arturo (whom I used to refer to as my husband before it became legal) walked through the room and made a casual observation, "You're enjoying yourself. You ought to take that job."

As sort of trial balloons I thought I would ask one or two of the authors attending the upcoming Publishing Triangle Awards. I figured after a couple of people passed on the invitation, I'd have my answer. Before I finished the question, and without any details, Bob Smith said, "Yes!" So did Martin Hyatt, Christopher Bram, and David McConnell.

The most common response to the invitation continued to be "Yes," even after the details. So I called Joseph and told him I'd do it. And I'm glad I did.

Considering the limitations of space and my desire for a multiplicity of voices, I got lucky. Had I invited all those whose writing I admire to contribute to the conversation about queer New York City, this would have been a ten-volume set.

WHAT IS THAT APHORISM? "EVERYTHING is about sex except for sex." Sex. Whoever didn't come to New York for sex, raise your hand, please. (Many of us came to New York for sex but immediately fell in love with the city.) There are discerning accounts of sex in this book and of course very few of them are actually *about* sex. Like most of these narratives, in one way or another they are about love. The canard that the lives of gay, lesbian, bisexual, trans, or queer people are about sex *per se* is disproven throughout the essays. Are there books that disprove that same idea about the lives of straight people? Probably.

A thread of life—freedom, individuality, community, self-determination, whatever, I won't quibble—runs through all of these essays. Dark corners and dark days are there, as they have been and will be, but the overwhelming trend is toward "Yes."

Something else woven into most of these essays is empty space.

The space of the missing: the space where people might have been, the space where they were, the space where they still are—in our minds. For the future of every Charles Ludlam, Derek Jarman, Essex Hemphill, Michael Bennett, Ron Vawter, Ian Horvath, Vito Russo, Paul Monette, and Keith Haring lost to AIDS, there are thousands whose lives form part of that space, that gap, those things that are not.

Arriving in New York City from Cleveland in 1985 was, for me—to steal Mark Ameen's metaphor—arriving in the middle of a storm. Along with all the excitement of the East Village and working in Off-Off-Broadway theater, there was an awful surprise waiting: the deaths, often weekly, always monthly, and the succession of funerals and memorials. How many years will it be before a book about LGBT experiences in New York will not be laced with the pain and loss of the AIDS crisis and the ongoing hazards of HIV? A lot.

Is CHRISTOPHER STREET THE MOST famous "gay" street in the world? It doesn't matter. It is a ready emblem for the queerness of Gotham. An unscientific, informal search through these essays offers other NYC icons that are meaningful to this eclectic group of writers: The Oscar Wilde Memorial Bookshop, The Duchess, The Bar, The Lesbian and Gay Community Center, ACT UP, Julius, the Christopher Street Piers, The Stonewall Riots, Greenwich Avenue, The Marriage Equality Act, Central Park, and Andrew Holleran's novel, *Dancer from the Dance.*

Contrary to the experiences of most of our parents and of people from earlier generations with same-sex orientations (not necessarily separate groups), we now know that queer people are everywhere. Everywhere. Yes, I'm stating the obvious but it has only been obvious beyond a gut level for the fifty-or-so-year span covered in this book. The jig is up. Everywhere. And everyone you know is related to one of us. In addition to *everywhere,* in this volume LGBT people can be found in comedy clubs, schools, department stores, hospitals, rooftops, subways, offices, churches, synagogues, beaches, factories, onstage, backstage—gossiping on stoops in Brooklyn, huddled, homeless in Penn Station, meeting someone's parents in Queens, fooling around in Central Park, dancing on Staten Island, falling in love in the Bronx, driving in from New Jersey, and on their way home from a Seder on Long Island.

So, does New York City hold a unique attraction for lesbian, gay, bisexual, and trans people? Yes. In the same way that it is a world leader in the areas of finance, media, technology, fashion, entertainment, international trade, and fine arts, New York has long been a leading global producer of the most undomesticated, domesticated, accomplished, ordinary, radical, ambitious, funny, passionate, compassionate, brilliant, out, sexy, beautiful, queer people.

These are a few of their stories.

THOMAS KEITH
FEBRUARY 2012

"The moment I actually saw New York, I wanted it."
—QUENTIN CRISP

SILENCE = DEATH: THE EDUCATION OF A COMEDIAN

BOB SMITH

"LOU GEHRIG'S DISEASE? I DON'T even like baseball!"

My best friend and fellow stand-up Eddie Sarfaty claims that was my initial reaction when he accompanied me to Columbia-Presbyterian Hospital in 2007 to receive my you're-gonna-die-agnosis. I don't remember saying it, but I'm convinced one of the reasons I'm still alive is that good comedians naturally respond to Pain and Death as if they're hecklers trying to ruin our shows.

Many of my oldest and closest friends in New York are accomplished and brilliant stand-up comedians, but we've made each other laugh harder offstage than with anything we've ever said in our acts. The morning after my sister Carol committed suicide, comedian Judy Gold, another dear friend, called to see how I was doing. When I broke down crying uncontrollably, Judy matter-of-factly inquired, "Bob, don't you think you're overreacting? It's been almost twenty-four hours."

I didn't stop crying, but I did laugh. I've known Judy for twenty-five years, and our friendship has no boundaries. One time, Judy called about forty-seven times, badgering me not to be late picking her up at the airport. To get even, I stood among the limo drivers waiting at the gate holding up a sign that said: BITCH. I ignored the stares and whispers about my sign until I finally heard Judy laughing while simultaneously telling me to go fuck myself. Judy accusing me of overreacting is the perfect example of my belief that comedy is not frivolous, but one of the most vital and serious aspects of being alive. Her making me laugh the morning after my sister's death was like lighting a candle in a coffin.

I've often been asked, "What stand-up comics influenced your work?" and I've always cited Woody Allen and Lily Tomlin, but once you start performing, your major influences are your friends who are also stand-up comics. Your influences get you to step out on a stage, but your friends help you develop into an artist who actually deserves to have a microphone. The friends who have most influenced me are Jaffe Cohen, Danny McWilliams, Eddie Sarfaty, Judy Gold, and Elvira Kurt.

Not that my initial influences weren't important. Woody's stand-up act is a fictional autobiography, as is mine. Lily Tomlin is a more surprising influence since she's primarily known for her characters, and I'm the only character in my act. But I've always responded to Lily's poetic precision, best illustrated by what I regard as the perfect joke: "The other day I bought a wastebasket and I carried it home in a paper bag. And when I got home, I put the paper bag in the wastebasket."

Lily was also instrumental in my realizing that I was gay. When I was thirteen, I read a letter about homosexuality in Dear Abby's advice column and thought, *That sounds like me.* I had recently begun masturbating with the fervor that makes every teenage boy a willing victim of the most enjoyable Obsessive-compulsive disorder. While patting myself on the front, I always thought about my classmate Kirk Gunsallus's muscular arms, but decided to test my heterosexuality by thinking about a woman. But which woman? By chance, there was a magazine article about Lily Tomlin in our house. I headed to the bathroom with magazine in hand. A half-hour later, my gayness was confirmed. If Lily Tomlin couldn't get me off, then no woman could.

Thirty years later I performed at an AIDS benefit in Palm Springs with the dream team for Palm Springs' old queens: Lily Tomlin, Carol Channing, Lorna Luft, JoAnne Worley and Sally Kellerman. After the show, all the performers took a bow on stage and I felt a hand on my shoulder. A voice I recognized immediately said, "Bob, you're really funny!" After all that time, Lily Tomlin finally got me off.

A great stand-up comic's voice is as distinctive and unique as any great singer's voice. Joan Rivers is our Maria Callas and Rodney Dangerfield is our Frank Sinatra. It took me ten years to find my voice, and I discovered it by moving to New York. In the summer of 1976, at age eighteen, I started performing in Buffalo and immediately got laughs with jokes like: "Last year my family fought for weeks over whether to buy an artificial or natural Christmas tree. Finally, we reached a compromise. We bought an artificial tree, but we're going to throw it out each year."

I was an English major in college but stand-up appealed to me because there is no director or editor weighing your every word. It's the most immediate of all literary art forms—and all great jokes are very short stories. Your work is judged by the audience; their silence is your rejection letter.

In July of 1986, I made my Manhattan debut at a comedy club in SoHo called Comedy U. A few weeks earlier my best friend Michael Hart looked through a stack of my 3 x 5 joke cards. "You know, these jokes about being gay are funny. You should do them."

At the time, there were no out gay comics in New York, though I'd read in the *Advocate* about a handful in San Francisco. But minorities and outsiders—Jews, African-Americans, Latinos, and women—have always dominated stand-up comedy, so I figured it would only be a matter of time before gay and lesbian comedians broke through.

I also knew I could soon be dead from AIDS.

1985 was the year Rock Hudson died and the year the family of Ryan White, an HIV-positive hemophiliac, began an eight-month legal battle when his elementary school refused to let him attend school. 1986 was the year before ACT UP was founded, and I, like most gay men, was angry about our government's indifference and disgusted with the *New York Times* printing the word gay in quotation marks as if it were the final arbiter of our identity. I was also livid that at twenty-eight, I was dwelling on my mortality before I'd even decided what I was going to do for a living.

In 1986, an "inconclusive" result on my AIDS test frightened me so much that when I was retested, I never picked up the results. I was determined to be an out comic in New York since it was the right thing to do, both artistically—a closeted artist is still an oxymoron to me—and politically.

A month after moving to New York, I was walking down 3rd Avenue when traffic suddenly disappeared due to President Reagan's motorcade. What fixed that moment in my memory was that people on the sidewalk—men in suits, women pushing strollers—stopped walking and booed as the President passed. I happily joined in. Our collective response made me truly love New York. I already loathed

Reagan for willfully ignoring AIDS and for initiating the Republican-led assault against our nation's environment. Standing on a comedy club stage as an out gay man, during the era when gay was synonymous with AIDS, was another way of razzberrying Reagan.

I came out onstage at Comedy U. with four gay friends in the audience: Michael, Sean, B.J., and Bruce. Within two years, Sean would die of AIDS. Back then, my friends were all young, handsome, and thickly muscular. The emcee that night proved my thesis that those who can't do stand-up usually emcee. The nerdy comic focused on my friends—his eyeglasses outweighed his biceps—and actually remarked on how they weren't laughing at his often-homophobic jokes.

Bruce said loudly with his very deep voice, "When you say something funny, we'll laugh." The audience chuckled, and the emcee shut up. It reminded me of the moment I lost my fear of homophobic bullies.

In high school, I went to watch my friends play hockey. After the game, I was bantering in the locker room with my jock pals when someone I barely knew said loudly, "Smith, you are such a fag."

There was a hush, and everyone stared at me. Pat Connolly, the porky, moon-faced "athlete" with the big gut, waited to see how I'd react. It surprised me that I didn't feel intimidated, just furious.

"Yeah, Connelly, well, there's a three-letter word that starts with an f that describes you, too." I puffed out my cheeks in case the lummox couldn't figure out what word I was talking about. The locker room erupted with laughter. Even the lummox laughed. I could see the joy, pride, and relief on my friends' faces that I hadn't backed down. Bill Silecky, the tall, handsome captain of the football team said, "I could see the wheels turning and knew you were thinking of something good."

It was the first time I realized that getting the last laugh can triumph over the first insult. At Comedy U., I had prepared a line in case of homophobic heckling. If someone shouted "Faggot!" I would calmly respond, "Ex-boyfriends can be so bitter!" I never used that line because Manhattan audiences weren't homophobic, which I regret somewhat, since it would have gotten a big laugh. All comics have bad nights performing, but I always observed the other comics were also having a bad night, so I never blamed my lack of laughs on homophobia.

The emcee introduced me, and I told a few jokes to establish credibility with the crowd before I said, "I come from a very conservative family—my dad's a state trooper—and it wasn't easy telling my parents that I was gay. I made my carefully worded announcement at Thanksgiving. I said, 'Mom, would you please pass the gravy to a homosexual?'" (Years later when I appeared on *The Joan Rivers Show*, she added the brilliant tagline, "She passed it to my father.") The entire room laughed. I followed with another gay one-liner, "My high school had a Head Start program for homosexuals; it was called 'Drama Club.'" The room laughed louder, and I ended my set to enthusiastic applause. When I walked offstage, the two owners of the bar, both straight guys, came over and complimented me. They'd never done that before.

I became a regular performer at Comedy U., and it was there that I met Danny McWilliams. While Danny wasn't officially out, his signature bit was an impression of Bette Davis as Dorothy in *The Wizard of Oz*. His opening line, as he mimed taking a drag on a cigarette, was, "Toto!" each *o* elongated. "I have a feeling we're not in Kansas anymore!" Danny spoke with Bette's signature staccato pronunciation where each word sounded as if she bit it out of a dictionary.

In 1987, Danny and I began performing together at gay and lesbian shows in the East Village (put together by a self-proclaimed straight comic) along with lesbian comics Reno and Sara Cytron.

I'd heard about Jaffe Cohen from Danny and first met him on the night of the stock market crash of 1987 at the Crow Bar in the East Village. The show was cancelled. No one wanted to splurge on a three-dollar cover during a financial calamity, but Jaffe and I were curious about each other's material and performed for each other in the empty club. Later, we admitted we were relieved that each of us found the other funny. It was the first indication of how being funny was always the priority for Danny, Jaffe, and me.

Over the next year, the three of us performed at occasional East Village gigs with terrible names like "Fruit and Fiber," until the summer of 1988, when Jaffe was approached by Helene Kelly, the manager of the Duplex, about putting together a show for two weekends in September.

Jaffe wanted to do an all-guy bill with Danny and me. We immediately agreed but needed a name for our show. Since personal ads were a big phenomenon then, one of us suggested parodying Single Gay White Male with Funny Gay White Males. (We quickly dropped white when we realized it sounded racist.)

The Duplex, at 55 Grove Street, had been a cabaret since the late fifties—Woody and Joan had both performed there—but by 1988, it had the battered appearance and aroma of an ashtray full of cigarette butts floating in spilled beer. There was a dingy piano bar on the first floor and a dank sixty-seat cabaret on the second where we performed. It had a tiny, narrow dressing room (ironically the size of a closet), and the two of us who weren't performing would wait and listen while the third did his set.

Our first shows got a rave review in *Back Stage*—getting an unsolicited review in New York was as rare then as it is now—and the Duplex booked us for four weeks in November, then for all of February. Laurie Stone of the *Village Voice* did a full-page profile and review of our show, which resulted in us being booked every weekend for the next three years. We became a minor—but real—phenomenon in New York, attracting audiences that included gay celebrities such as Vito Russo, David Feinberg (he interviewed us at his apartment), Charles Ludlam, and Quentin Crisp. Laurie had noticed something significant during our interview: "The guys effortlessly finish each other's sentences."

Our close friendship developed slowly. At first, Jaffe annoyed me. In restaurants he'd pester our waiter to change his order, bring him more water, or ask if the chef could chew his food because he was tired. Meanwhile, Danny cursed with a vehemence that I found poetic and shocking. One time, when we were discussing the "God Hates Fags" Reverend, Fred Phelps, Danny burst out, "With all his bad karma do you know what he's coming back as? He's coming back as a turd dropping from a fucking rat's ass. No. You know what? He's going to come back as a crab crawling on the balls of a cockroach! No, wait a minute. This is better. No, for his next one thousand incarnations that sick fuck will come back as a fucking dingleberry piece of shit, hanging from a crab's ass, while the crab is sucking on a rat's balls. That's what he's coming back as!" (This is a verbatim quote as it's the one time I immediately wrote down one of Danny's rants in my writing journal.)

Later, Jaffe admitted that he didn't know how to behave in restaurants since his family never ate in them, and Danny soon completely converted Jaffe and me into believing that his foulmouthed diatribes were actually the most courteous responses you could make to assholes like Reverend Phelps.

It soon became apparent that the three of us shared an identical comic sensibility and also shared the same values. One time at a sketch comedy show, we quickly discovered the group onstage wasn't funny except for one woman who was hysterical. Watching in the dark, I noticed she made all three of us laugh out loud at exactly the same times. I also fondly remember a party where a gay Republican defended George W. Bush in front of Danny, Jaffe, and me, days after the House Republicans voted to drill in the Arctic National Wildlife Refuge. The host came running out of the kitchen shouting, "No politics!" because the three of us had ganged up on him. It's the only time in my life when I've been proud to be a horrible guest.

One of the benefits of being among the first dozen or so openly gay stand-ups was that our lives were virgin territory; it was like discovering that you were the first person to tell a mother-in-law joke. Eventually we all developed material about being gay kids: Jaffe performed a brilliant bit about how to be a sissy in gym class; I did jokes about gay boys playing with dolls. "Bobby, don't play with Barbie. I want you to play with blond, rippling, muscular Hercules!" And Danny did a hilarious book report bit about being a fifth-grade queen reading a biography of Judy Garland: "...they gave her pills to wake up and pills to sleep! What they did to her!"

We always went out to dinner after our shows, and while eating we frequently said something funny. There was a mutual competitiveness, aligned with a shared drive to make a good show better.

One night, Danny told us how he'd witnessed a fan approach Lauren Bacall, who was starring on Broadway at that time. "Oh, Miss Bacall, I'd love to see more of you!" To which she barked, "Come to the show!" Then Danny ad-libbed, "Can you imagine her answering machine, 'Hello, this is Lauren Bacall. HOW THE HELL DID YOU GET MY NUMBER?'"

That was the first of many times when I said, "Put it in the act." We repeatedly proved Picasso's maxim: "Good artists copy. Great artists steal," which means that great stand-ups gladly accept a better punch line for a joke.

We also ran new bits by each other, and when something got two thumbs-up, it usually worked. We each had our strengths. Jaffe was a genius in using his body to sell a joke. His sissy-in-gym-class routine included a reenactment of a bored gay nerd staring at his fingernails during a volleyball game, momentarily distracted as the ball sailed over his head. I especially loved the joke about a friend who was so gay that his driver's license picture was taken over the shoulder. Jaffe would sharply twist his head to illustrate the hilarious posture of the big queen. Danny was brilliant at bringing comic characters to life. He had worked at a deli counter as a teenager, and his portrayal of an imperious New York City harridan demanding that he slice her ham order thinner was Lily Tomlin sharp. "I'm next! I'm next! I'M NEXT!" she shouted viciously, elbowing her way to the counter, before muttering, "Now what do I want?"

Danny was also gifted in mimicking vomiting cats, squeaky clotheslines, and vacuum cleaners. My strength was my ear for a punch line. I believe a joke should be subject to the same rules of all prose writing, no wasted or imprecise words. One example from my act: "In college, I experimented with heterosexuality. I slept with a straight guy. I was really drunk." Setup, punch line, and tag. Jaffe and Danny played around with their punch lines, and I would browbeat them into doing what I regarded as the correct version.

Danny and Jaffe's artistry changed my act. Danny's characters made me add a quick one-paragraph portrayal of a gay priest—Father Mary Louise—hearing confession: "...for your penance, watch *The Ten Commandments* ten times. Wasn't Anne Baxter terrible?" Jaffe's mugging inspired me to physically act out a punch line. I do a joke about how my partner Michael is Jewish, and we celebrate both holiday traditions. "At Christmas, we set up a Nativity scene, but all the figures look skeptical." Then I mime Joseph and Mary's manger postures of total disbelief.

As a boy, Danny revered Lucille Ball and *I Love Lucy* was his daily half-hour sanctuary from a brutal childhood—Danny once rendered a roomful of comedians speechless when he casually mentioned that his father once pissed on him for wetting the bed. When Lucy was hospitalized in 1989, Danny shared his genuine concern with Jaffe and me, and talked about her so much at the law firm where he temped that on the day she died, his supervisor called and told him not to come in, while assuring him that he'd still be paid. I believe that was the first-and-only case of gay bereavement leave in history —when your diva dies, you're given time off from work.

Danny especially loved tough, old gravelly-voiced Lucille Ball, and he regaled Jaffe and me with stories about her later years. Lucy gave seminars about her career around the country, and she could be brutal during the Q&As. One woman reportedly asked, "Miss Ball, could I come up onstage and give you a big hug?"

"Absolutely not! Next question."

Danny also recalled some young sitcom star was in the audience and kept interjecting her own performance anecdotes during Lucy's seminar. Finally Lucy snapped, "Look, I've seen your show, you're not that funny. Sit down! You might learn something."

These phrases became the first of many "Dannyisms" that became a private Funny Gay Male language. While we watched unfunny, aggressively annoying comics perform, Jaffe would whisper, "Sit down! You might learn something," and I'd crack up. When someone suggested doing something we were vehemently opposed to—supporting Republicans, for instance—we replaced "No" with "Absolutely not! Next question."

Danny also told us about a woman from Queens who became angry with him after she said, "I got the call," and Danny logically asked what the call was about. The woman snapped, "My Archie died!" Soon, "I got the call" became our synonym for death, and after the loss of my father, Danny's mother, and Jaffe's father, one of us invariably used the phrase.

In 1991, we became the first out stand-ups to appear on national television on *The Joan Rivers Show*. Before the taping, Joan turned to us and said, "All right, fellas: give me a few serious answers; then, Funny, Funny, Funny!" This became a performing mantra that Danny often said to us in Joan's voice before shows to calm our jitters. Danny did a brilliant impression of Joan in his act and after my sister's suicide, he called and left me a serious condolence message followed by Joan referencing her husband's suicide, "Edgar, Edgar, why? WHY?!" Danny added, "Mrs. Smith, that's so wrong. But I think you'll get it." Danny made me laugh at a time when I never thought I'd laugh again.

At the time we did Joan's show, I made most of my income from stand-up, but still cater-waitered to pay my rent. Two months after our taping, a caterer asked if I was available to work Christmas Day. I had just purchased a Mac Classic computer and wanted to buy Microsoft Word. Since working holidays meant double pay, I agreed. "Before you say yes," the caterer warned, "the party's at Joan Rivers's house." We discussed the possible embarrassment at being recognized, but I decided to forgo wearing my usual contact lenses in favor of my glasses, delusionally thinking my Clark Kent "disguise" would work.

Before the party began at Joan's palatial Fifth Avenue condo, which was part of a converted 1903 mansion, she gave the staff a short pep talk. I was relieved when she didn't seem to recognize me.

Later, as I passed a tray of champagne, a guest asked me, "Hey, weren't you on Joan's show?" I nodded yes. "Does Joan know?" I shook my head no. A half hour later, while passing hors d'oeuvres in the library, I felt a hand on my elbow. "Excuse me, everyone!" Joan shouted to the entire room. Conversation stopped. "This is a wonderful comedian. He was a guest on my show!" Joan then said in a low voice, "Isn't this horrifying?" which made me laugh. "Don't let it bother you. You're just starting out. One time, I did a show with Jack Lemmon; then two weeks later I waited on him."

Her gentle mocking reinforced my belief that making a joke in a difficult situation can be an extraordinary act of kindness.

Danny, Jaffe, and I did go through a period where, when one of us was missing, the other two talked about him. I was an angry shrew about the always-late Danny and Jaffe when we traveled, and we performed all over the country, plus Canada and Australia. When we flyered the beaches in Provincetown, Jaffe thought nothing of plopping down on a fan's blanket, leaving Danny and me to cover the rest of the beach, which pissed us off.

But we grew to accept each other's personal foibles, since our friendship had been tested by numerous professional ordeals. There was a manager who booked us for five grand but paid us three. (To get out of our contract with the scumbag, we had to pay him three grand.) We also had to contend with a continually drunken publicist whose press contacts seemed limited to wine magazines. The only benefit of these ordeals was laughing at Danny's truly obscene, half-hour long monologues about the manager and his dead-on impression of the tipsy publicist.

In each city, we'd rent a car on our day off and take field trips, during which we discovered that all three of us liked to smoke a joint, crack jokes, and appreciate nature. I saw my first redwoods with Danny and Jaffe at Muir Woods, my first bald eagle with them on Whidbey Island in Washington and enjoyed my first earthquake—the Northridge quake—with them in Santa Monica. After the first violent tremor, Danny cracked from his bedroom that an overweight actress we all knew must have fallen out of bed. We laughed until the equally violent aftershock scared the shit out of us.

And, yes, fat jokes are wrong, but anyone who knows comedians quickly learns that professional boundaries are not the same as our personal boundaries. I would never refer to any woman as a bitch or fat onstage, but I stood in an airport with a sign saying, BITCH because my audience was Judy Gold, another comedian. It was wrong, but I didn't care since I knew Judy would laugh.

One of our field trips was to the Franklin Roosevelt estate along the Hudson River in Hyde Park. We were on a guided tour of the main house and Roosevelt's wheelchair was displayed. We stood in the back of the group and Danny said, "Oh, Eleanor, you wouldn't treat me this way if I wasn't in this wheelchair." Then switching to Bette Davis's voice in *Whatever Happened to Baby Jane*, he sneered. "But-cha-aar in that wheelchair! But-cha-aar!" It was an example of perfect timing and the three of us became so hysterical we had to quit the tour.

When I met Steve Moore, the first comedian to do jokes about being HIV-positive, he mentioned being ten years older than I, and I cracked that he had "Model-T cells." Our friendship was confirmed by his almost spitting out his orange juice.

AIDS and AIDS benefits were an unfunny, ever-present part of the Funny Gay Males' careers. Several times after shows, guys told us, "I just found out I was HIV-positive today, and I didn't think I could laugh, but I did." One night at the Duplex, a gaunt young man and his mother came to the show. He was in his early-to-mid-twenties and used a cane. The young man laughed loudly and repeatedly, but his mother was inconsolable. Afterward, she told us that he had really wanted her to see our show, and she thanked us—although her pain was palpable. It wouldn't be the last time real life entered a comedy club.

The most harrowing show I ever worked was Frank Maya's last performance at Carolines, a comedy club on Broadway, in 1995. It was a benefit with an all-gay-and-lesbian lineup. Jaffe and Danny were there, and I was asked to emcee. (This is what stand-ups call a "callback," when you refer back to an earlier joke. It doesn't usually bite you in the ass.) Frank had always been muscular, but his sunken cheeks told me he was sick. It was a moment that happened repeatedly in the eighties and nineties, but the social convention was to behave like nothing was wrong. We were all members of a gay men's chorus whistling in the dark. There was also a manic gleam in his eyes I'd never seen before. Frank opened his set by declaring, "This is my farewell to comedy."

I'd first met Frank at one of our East Village shows. He was a well-known performance artist who talked to us about coming out in his work, and a short time later he did. (It still seems unbelievable that there was a time in New York when shoving yams in your cooch onstage was permissible, but admitting you were gay was going too far.)

Frank was a pro and had a classic bit about how as a New Yorker he was envious of Anne Frank's hiding place in Amsterdam: "It had a skylight..." But that night Frank rambled, and the audience wasn't laughing. Comedy slang for bombing is "dying," and the term had become literal. One asshole shouted, "Get off!" as Frank's fifteen-minute set stretched to over a half hour. The comedians in the room knew he should wrap it up, but there was none of the usual whispered griping that he had gone over his allotted time, a comedy faux pas that is inexcusably rude to the other comedians on the bill. Everyone in the room was transfixed by the stand-up tragedy. For the comedians watching, he was also a piercing reminder that just because you're funny, it doesn't guarantee that you'll be happy. Finally, the manager of the club suggested I stand near the stage and signal to Frank that his time was up. In comedy clubs, there's a small red light that goes on when your time is up, and until that moment I had never considered it to be a metaphor for death. Frank saw me and asked from the stage, "Bob, should I get off?" I nodded my head. It was an agonizingly sad moment and, to this day, I regret not shouting, "NO!" Within a short time, Frank was dead.

One night, a major talent manager had seen me kill. Afterward, he took me aside and said, "You're funny, but why do you have to do the gay stuff? Why can't you just be 'Bob Smith from Buffalo'?" I replied, "Because I'm not ashamed of being gay, but I am embarrassed about being from Buffalo." (That was a joke because I'm actually a booster of my hometown.) The manager added, "They're never going to have anyone gay on *The Tonight Show*."

I immediately knew he was an idiot. There was no proof then that I was ever going to succeed on a big level, but I had worked around New York for over two years, and straight audiences liked my comedy. My first paying gig in New York had been for a Conservative synagogue's singles night. The rabbi had told me how much he enjoyed my set. Of course, I didn't know then that I would become the first out gay stand-up on *The Tonight Show* in 1994.

As Funny Gay Males' reputation spread, we worked all around New York. At Dixon Place with the fledging Blue Man Group, back when Dixon Place was in an apartment, I suggested onstage that Funny Gay Males should be called "Blow Men Group." At La MaMa, we met the legendary Ellen Stewart. We also did numerous benefits at places like the Rainbow Room at Rockefeller Center, hosted by people like Harvey Fierstein—who is as charming and friendly offstage as on. I also worked solo, including one night at the Pyramid Club, where the stage was made up to look like a vagina, and I passed through the birth canal at 1:00 a.m. to do my set.

I knew Judy Gold from Comedy U., but we really became friends when she came to see Funny Gay Males perform in Provincetown. The next day we went to the beach, and Judy and I bonded comedically when the two of us spent several hours loudly repeating variations of the phrase "I make the muffins," in the most annoyingly nasal voices we could create. Judy and her then partner, Sharon, were staying at a guesthouse owned by a wealthy gay guy whose penniless partner constantly claimed in his nasal voice that he put the Breakfast in their B&B because he made the lousy muffins (from a mix).

We mined every possible comic twist on "I make the muffins," mimicking his whiny honking endlessly: "I make the sand"; "I make the lesbians"; "I missed the Kadima ball." It was an experience that was enjoyable for comedians but excruciating for anyone else. Finally, Sharon screamed, "Will you two shut the fuck up about the fucking muffins!" People we didn't know on a nearby blanket applauded when they heard her, which only made Judy and me burst out laughing at our own obnoxiousness.

The week after Judy and Sharon left Ptown, I received a call from Sharon telling me Judy's father had died unexpectedly. I immediately called Judy to offer my condolences. She was understandably teary until she angrily mentioned that she had received a "condolence" call from a comedian acquaintance of ours, a gay man who is one of what I call the Johnny-Come-Out-Latelys, as he came out onstage in 2000, long after the moment of courage had past. He had asked Sharon, "Has Judy had to cancel any gigs for the funeral? Because I'd be happy to fill in."

This became a reflexive joke Judy and I still share. Anytime a famous movie star or celebrity died, one of us would immediately call or e-mail, "You know he's calling the widow." In fact, when I told Judy that I was diagnosed with the motor neuron disease ALS (Amyotrophic lateral sclerosis, also known as Lou Gehrig's Disease), she immediately said this comic would soon call to say how sorry he was and ask if I had any gigs I needed to cancel. I laughed, but part of my pleasure by then was that every time we came up with a new twist on that joke, we celebrated our long friendship.

When Judy gave birth to her son Ben in 2001, I was living in LA, and she left a message so suffused with radiant happiness that I didn't erase it for months. A week later she invited me to visit. "If you don't fucking come, I'll fucking kill you!" It was right after 9/11, and Judy was working at Rockefeller Center as a producer on *The Rosie O'Donnell Show.* I visited the same week an NBC News worker tested positive for anthrax and they closed several floors of the building. The following week, Judy was returning to work and she asked if she should be worried. Her question wasn't a joke, and I could see she was anxious.

A few hours later her neighbor knocked on the door and handed me Judy's mail. Judy was changing Ben, and I shouted, "Margery brought the mail. There's an envelope with white powder in it."

Without missing a beat, Judy shouted, "Would you mind opening it?"

"No problem," I replied.

We've been through terrorist attacks, the deaths of our fathers, breakups for both of us, a suicide, and the loss of beloved pets. Judy once called and told me her cat had cancer, and my response was, "Was she a smoker?" She laughed and then called me an asshole. She liked my joke so much that she repeated it to all our friends. It would be inappropriate to make such a comment to anyone else, but comedians are artists who intimately face pain in their work. We try out jokes that bomb and know immediately that we've failed.

One thing I admire about Judy is that I've never seen her give a lousy performance. She gives it her all, no matter how bad the audience seems. Emulating her perseverance is how I got my HBO special. In 1993, Madonna's production company flew Funny Gay Males to LA to audition for an HBO gay-and-lesbian comedy special.

The audition was at Igby's, a shabby comedy club, on a rainy Tuesday night. The room was nearly empty, with fifteen customers and a row of HBO big shots sitting in the back. By then, we were friends with several wonderful gay and lesbian comics who weren't part of the lineup, but some of the worst comics I'd ever seen auditioning were there. Several of them had no gay material, clearly they weren't out yet, but they apparently would come out for HBO. One guy did hacky airport jokes that caused Danny, Jaffe, and me to wince during his set. I watched in horror as every comic bombed—including, unfortunately, Danny and Jaffe. For big shows, I always planned my set order in advance, but watching this dreadful train wreck inspired me to open with a different joke and basically wing it. I was incredibly nervous, but from my first joke I got huge laughs and kept making the audience roar. After my set, Danny and Jaffe were incredulous. "Where the fuck did that come from?" Jaffe asked.

I had no idea, but I was thirty-five, had been working as an out comic for seven years, and was impatient for some sign of mainstream success. I had also worked diligently on my act over the past three years in Provincetown, adding signature bits such as declaring why the Catholic church shouldn't be homophobic: "They should give us credit. We started the Renaissance. It was probably two gay men talking during a party: 'Wouldn't it be fun to sell paintings of hot, muscular, naked guys to churches?' 'Oh, that would be a hoot!'"

After the show, Chris Albrecht, the head of HBO, came over to say how much he enjoyed my set while pointedly ignoring everyone else.

The next day, I got a phone call saying HBO didn't want to do a group show, but they did want to give me my own half-hour special. Then, they gave a lesbian comedian her own special—Suzanne Westenhoefer, a good friend of mine.

Our HBO specials were favorably reviewed by the television critic of the *New York Times*. It was strange and gratifying to see my name in the paper I'd been reading every day for almost ten years.

After my move to Los Angeles in 1996, Eddie Sarfaty assumed my spot in Funny Gay Males with my blessing. Eddie's ten years younger than the rest of us, muscular and handsome, and I joked with Danny and Jaffe that people would see the Funny Gay Males poster and say, "The other two have aged horribly, but Bob looks great!"

All four of us eventually performed together, and Eddie became part of our brotherhood. We bonded with him because he's smart and funny, but also because he's an unhappy hunk, prone to depression, and so possesses a great heart and a genuine sense of empathy for others, qualities often lacking in more self-contented hotties.

In 2005, I decided to move back to New York and became Eddie's roommate in his two-bedroom apartment. My return to New York as a stand-up after nine years away was a revelation. There were queer comedy shows all over Manhattan and dozens of gay and lesbian comics. I loved being back in New York, and also fell in love with someone I'd known for twenty years, a sexy writer named Michael Zam, an old friend of Jaffe's. Michael eventually introduced me to the other crazy love of our lives, our dog Bozzie.

New York also seemed happy to have me back. I was thrilled when *Back Stage* magazine awarded me their Best Comedian of the Year award in 2006. I also auditioned for the reality show *Last Comic Standing,* and made the cut. But I had foolishly stopped dyeing my hair—I went gray in my early thirties—and was eliminated before the show taped, I'm sure due to my looking forty-nine when their prized demographic was 18-48.

One of my proudest moments being back in New York was after Proposition 8 passed in California. The vote to deny marriage equality was heavily backed by the Mormon Church. I was furious that the church founded by Joseph Smith, who married a fourteen-year-old girl when he was thirty-eight, and Brigham Young, who clearly liked to fuck 'em young, since he married a fifteen-year old when he was forty-two, had the gall to claim the marriage between two consenting gay or lesbian adults was immoral. Judy called me up and said a demonstration was going to be held in front of the Mormon Temple at 66th Street and Columbus Avenue. She really wanted to go since her two sons, Henry and Ben, were old enough to understand that this bigotry was directed against their family. Eddie and I made signs for Ben and Henry to carry. We all marched, and seven-year-old Ben carried the sign with my joke, "My 2 Moms Can Beat Up Your 14 Wives!" The next day on *The View*, Whoopi Goldberg quoted my joke, and *Salon.com* also mentioned it. Ben giggled as he marched, and I felt a sense of solidarity with Eddie and Judy, knowing we all understood that sometimes a breezy joke conceals furious contempt.

I was working on my Alaska novel at my desk in Eddie's apartment in May, 2006 when Eddie noticed a muscle twitching on the back of my left arm. It turned out to be an early symptom of my ALS. The twitching didn't go away, and I began a long series of medical tests.

That autumn, after I performed for the Human Rights Campaign in Boston, I received a phone call from my agent. She first told me she heard the show went well, then she asked, "Did you drink before the show? Because they said you sounded drunk."

I was horrified and assured her that I never drank or smoked a joint before any performance. Stand-up requires my complete focus and has always been too important to me. My slurring was due to the ALS. I hadn't noticed any problems with my voice, but other people obviously had. I began to start my sets by explaining I wasn't drunk, but had a neurological problem.

My explanation worked for a long time, but I have the bulbar variant of ALS that first preys upon the muscles of the tongue and throat. I could still do stand-up and even appeared on a Canadian gay comedy special, broadcast from the Winnipeg Comedy Festival. I killed but have never watched that performance. It would be too painful to hear my jokes delivered sloppily.

It was fittingly in a small East Village comedy club in 2010 that I decided to stop performing. There were only ten people in the audience, but I had lost my fear of small audiences back when I auditioned for HBO.

I hadn't performed for several months and immediately noticed how difficult it was to pronounce my jokes, lines I'd done hundreds of times. Jokes that always killed were garnering looks of incomprehension. I apologized and repeated a few lines again. Something I'd never had to do before. After the show, I apologized to the host, who graciously said there was nothing to apologize for. I was in a state of shock.

I had always thought I would perform stand-up for my entire life. When Funny Gay Males performed in Montreal at the Just For Laughs comedy festival, one of the headliners was Milton Berle. He was eighty-three and had made thousands of people laugh, including us. We had followed Milton as we went through Canadian customs and overheard him cracking a joke about the cigar dangling from his lips. "It's a Lawrence Welk cigar," he said. "A piece of shit surrounded by a band."

I envisioned myself cracking jokes at his age.

Of course, the one benefit of having ALS is that whenever my comedian friends vent about their problems—unemployment, relationships, possible eviction from their apartments—I can always trump them by saying, "three to five years," which is the Google life span of people with ALS. Now when they discuss their problems, they always jokingly preface them with, "I know I don't have ALS, but..."

I am proud to have achieved the two biggest goals of all stand-ups: appearing on *The Tonight Show* and having my own HBO special. I also don't feel I've given up comedy since I can still write novels and essays. But it takes so long to become a good stand-up that giving it up was deeply painful; it's even more agonizing when I watch comedians perform who aren't nearly as funny as I am. I'm also incredibly proud of Funny Gay Males. We had the guts to be out when even Judy was afraid of coming out.

We performed at the first-ever Gay-and-Lesbian Inaugural Ball at President Clinton's inauguration in 1992, along with Kate Clinton and Suzanne Westenhoefer. We also performed at the LGBT March in Washington in front of half a million people in 1993. I wrote a new joke for the event: "I think we should have a gay agenda. It would be limited to two things: Number One—Full civil rights. Number Two—We want our national anthem to have a twenty-five-minute dance version." It got the biggest laugh and most thunderous applause of my career. I'm also proud that on Ellen DeGeneres's historic coming-out episode, someone on the show gave a nod to Funny Gay Males, by featuring the immediately recognizable purple-and-yellow cover of our book, *Growing Up Gay*, in a bookstore scene.

My only regret in my stand-up career is that I wish Funny Gay Males hadn't just mimicked the toughness of old showbiz pros like Lucille Ball and Lauren Bacall and had, instead, become as indomitable as they were.

In the mid-nineties, we were offered the chance to do a six-week Off-Broadway run of Funny Gay Males by the prestigious Atlantic Theater Company. We were eager to move beyond our loyal LGBT audience, but our manager at the time insisted we should turn down their offer and let him raise the money to produce us Off-Broadway. He clearly implied he would be deeply hurt if we accepted the

Atlantic's offer. (Performers quickly learn that agents and managers have touchier egos than almost any entertainers.) Why we had to be nice guys and didn't stand up for ourselves mystifies me still.

Our weakness was that we lacked Lucille's balls. Show business produces tough cookies because performers have to make every mistake to learn anything. I know now that we made a colossal error, but it did teach me an invaluable lesson.

For the past six years, the Angel of Death has become my stalker, following me around from gig to gig, scaring my friends, showing up at my apartment to pester me.

"Mr. Smith, I'm a big fan and wondered if I could hug the life out of you?"

"Absolutely not! Next question."

AN OLD QUEEN'S TALE

PENNY ARCADE

GROWING UP IN NEW ENGLAND, New York didn't figure in my landscape. There were occasional references to New York by my mother, about the carefree, single days of her 20s, attending Radio City musicals with her unmarried girlfriends. A coven of first-generation Italian American women, my mother the only Italian immigrant among them, traveled every few months to New York by train. All of them sweatshop seamstresses with the glamorous aspirations that the films of the 1930s had left them with; hats and gloves and red lipstick. Later, much later, when I was twenty-one, I interviewed these women—all of them unmarried—trying to unravel the mystery of my mother; the boxes of photos they had taken in the '40s proved she had once been happy.

To me and the kids I knew, Boston, an hour and a half away, was the city. Closer to home, forty miles away, Hartford, Connecticut—with its tall buildings and in late 1959 a building made of blue-mirrored glass—to me and the factory-town kids like me, it was the future.

It was the gay bars of early 1960s Hartford that I was sneaked into as a fourteen-year-old. Sneaked in is an exaggeration, really, because Natalie, the transsexual at the door, had never stopped me, not even on my first visit, accompanied as I was always by Larry Buscaino. Tall, skinny, as charismatic as he was alcoholic, Larry Buscaino was three years older than I. Obsessed with The Rolling Stones and Bob Dylan, he carried a guitar most places, and would play outrageous, percussive solo versions of Rolling Stones or Dylan songs anywhere he felt like it. In his unruly Beatles mop top, wireless eyeglasses, and mod suits he purchased in New York on visits to "the Jewish side of the family," Larry was always dressed to the teeth, as we used to say back then.

Larry ruled Hartford's only gay bar and the all-night coffee shops on the Berlin Turnpike, with an élan never before or after experienced in our nearby factory town, New Britain, Connecticut. On the streets of New Britain, Larry stood out like crazy—high on the diet pills he pilfered from his mother, silhouetted by that grey, bleak, brick town, shouting back at the passing, taunting cars, whose pompadoured occupants shouted out, "QUEER!"

"That's right I'm queer!" he would shout back. "What about it?"

When we left the bar the first time, Larry had turned to me and asked, "What do you think of Natalie?"

"She's very nice," I said. "She let me in!"

"Anything else?" Larry pressed on.

"She's very pretty," I replied.

Then laughing at what he perceived as my coyness, Larry growled the next words that signaled that we were entering into a verbal duel.

"Notice anything else?"

"Well, she's a boy."

"And?" he rose to his full height and danced around me waiting for my next remark chanting, "AND? AND?" in an exaggerated way.

"And," I replied in a half swoon, "She looks like Elizabeth Taylor!"

Larry gave me Genet's *Our Lady of the Flowers*, the book that was the Bible for certain gay men in those days—actually for all the gay men and boys I knew—and it became a Bible for me too, till I replaced it with Genet's *Thieves Journal*. Genet's writing spoke directly to us. When I met Andy Warhol in New York much later, it was clear that he had patterned his look—black leather jacket, Marseille-striped sailor jersey, and jeans—on Genet, so great was the iconic criminal artist's influence on the gay demimonde of the 1960s.

LARRY TURNED ME ON TO the thrift stores he frequented. It was because of him I started to understand why my mother had saved all her 1930s and '40s clothes for me in neat garment bags in the back hall closet. I started to wear them to the bar in Hartford and soon, everywhere. Later, it was this extensive wardrobe of 1930s and '40s vintage clothes and shoes that prompted New York Underground star Jackie Curtis to close every discussion about costumes in my plays with, "Penny Arcade has her own clothes."

My mother was mortified when I started to bring home vintage dresses I picked up for nothing in the second hand clothes stores Larry took me to. We went thrifting nearly every afternoon but when I started to buy black old ladies' shoes with big stacked heels, my Italian mama became really upset. "Somebody else's shoes!" she would moan. "Old lady shoes! Dead lady's shoes." It was further proof to her that there was something really not right with me, something really wrong with me.

As we devoured *Vogue* and *Harper's Bazaar*, Larry would offer suggestions on what Ma could sew for me. My taste expanded, and through Larry I saw that my long attempts at self-definition were not so unique, not as weird as they had seemed in that factory town with collegiate aspirations, and I stopped asking Mama to copy the John Norris of Norwich preppy, heather-colored clothes I saw the richer girls in my school wearing. Instead we copied clothes I loved in *Vogue* but rarely saw in any store, not that I could have afforded them. Ma made all my clothes. The only store-bought clothes I owned I shoplifted; an ability I showed prodigious talent for long before I met Larry, but further developed under his tutelage.

My mother could make any pattern out of newspaper. This process of pattern-making was one of the few ways I could distract her from what she felt was my intrinsic badness, my difference, my otherness. It always amazed me when I would see her drop her defensiveness towards me as she figured out how to make a pattern from a magazine photo and she would happily add my ideas to the patterns. Then there was her delight in choosing the material from her vast stores of fabric in our cellar.

Larry and I made quite a spectacle of ourselves without opening our mouths, although our mouths were rarely shut—not with Larry's endless supply of diet pills pilfered from his mother's medicine chest. Soon he introduced me to Aggie, a slight, first-generation Ukrainian-American guy, a little older than Larry, who lived with his widowed mother in the new suburbs that had started to spring up around New Britain in the early 1960s. Aggie had a car and he would pick Larry up each night and together they would drive to my house and turn the lights on and off to signal their arrival. I would climb out of my third floor bedroom window as everyone in my house slept. Eventually, one night, a few months before my seventeenth birthday, while all the factory workers in my neighborhood were fast asleep, Larry and Aggie, high on pot, pills, and whisky, showed up with a carload of queens we knew from Hartford, and pulled up in front of my darkened house. I climbed down the fire escape only to be told by Larry that there was a change of plans for this particular evening.

"Pack your drag. We're going to Ptown!"

"What's Ptown?" I asked

"Gay capital of America," Larry hissed. "Gay capital of the world," Aggie tittered, and I climbed back up the fire escape, threw a few things in a brown paper bag and left that town where I was born and where my difference had made me a public martyr since I was twelve years old.

In 2009, in San Francisco, I booked two performances at odd times over a weekend— 5:00 p.m. on Saturday and 3:00 p.m. on Sunday—to develop a new performance through improvisation called *Old Queen*. As the audience showed up I noticed an elderly man shuffling on a cane and I introduced myself, asking what had brought him to see me. He pointed to a younger man in his early 60s and said, "My friend read about you on the Internet." I excused myself and went over to the younger man.

"Hi I'm Penny Arcade, thank you for coming and bringing your friend. What enticed you into coming?" I was really curious.

"Well, I read you had hung out in the gay bars of Hartford, Connecticut in the early '60s. I did too. So I was intrigued."

"I met your friend George," I said, gesturing back to the older man, now seated, whose name was George.

"That man happens to be George Birisma, one of the greatest gay playwrights America has ever produced. He is my friend and my neighbor." He took his seat next to George as I told George it was an honor to meet him. The younger man scanned my face and we spoke about Hartford's gay scene in the early '60s and he asked, "Did you ever know Inga? She was a transsexual. She was my best friend. She died seven years ago."

Quietly, I said, "No."

His face filled with sorrow. I didn't know what to say, his pain was palpable, and the performance, which I was about to improvise, was about to start. Desperate, I blurted, "Did you ever know Billy Hansen?"

His eyes widened and he replied, "Inga *was* Billy Hansen."

For years I had tried to find out the whereabouts of Billy Hansen, a Hartford hairdresser, who was quietly androgynous with a self-confident, casual, easy grace. Billy Hansen had earned my early devotion by walking in the big drag pageant barefoot, in blue jeans. The goal was realness and the queens spared no expense in devoting weeks of preparation to wigs, frocks, and extensive makeup.

The beauty pageant drew participants from all over the tri-state area of Connecticut, Massachusetts, and Rhode Island. Where the other queens walked on in bouffant wigs, heavy makeup, and elaborate gowns, Billy had brought the crowd to silence as he crossed the stage barefoot, in blue jeans, a loose white T-shirt, no makeup, not even lipstick, in his own pale blonde hair, holding a ladies' wallet like he was walking to the corner store. Everyone knew Billy Hansen was the realest one of all.

I was stunned as this younger man, Richard, who had left Hartford for San Francisco forty years before, with sadness in his blue eyes told me the story of Billy/Inga. How she had died of "women's cancer" years after her sexual reassignment. I was speechless, amazed, and grateful that I was finding this out at this moment. It made me feel so right about my instincts for this new show I had set out to create for Hot Fest at Dixon Place in just two weeks time.

"Well, " I replied, hardly able to contain my elation, feeling Billy Hansen's presence as palpably as Richard's, "Billy Hansen has a big role in the story I am about to tell."

Minutes later I was onstage telling the audience how it had

come about that, unbeknownst to me as a fourteen-year-old girl, I had set out on a trajectory to become an old queen. How every night in those gay bars of my teen years, my goal had been to sit with the old queens, a very difficult invitation for a teenaged girl to get. The old queens knew everything about life, history, and culture. The old queens understood the human condition, something that baffled me, and I needed the comfort and the understanding that lay beneath their cruel barbs. The old queens recognized me by my curiosity, by my wit, by my recognition of them as superior to me. As I told my story on the bare stage that afternoon in San Francisco, each time I mentioned a name from long ago, Larry Buscaino or Aggie, this man Richard, from Hartford, Connecticut, sitting in the front row, would shout, to George Birasima's growing delight, "Larry Buscaino! Oh no! Aggie! Billy Hansen!! Oh MY GOD!!!"

After my performance ended, I walked over to them and Richard looked at me hard. "I remember you now," he said. "You had dark brown hair then. You were very young. I didn't like you."

I gulped, trying to remain poised. Frightened, I asked, "Why didn't you like me?"

"You were very obviously underage, the only girl in the bar, late at night, wildly dancing and carrying on. I was afraid that you were going to get us all arrested."

THE WEEKEND IN JUNE OF 1967, when I left New Britain, Connecticut, the queens—Larry and Aggie and I—terrorized Provincetown, Massachusetts.

All of us had sneaked into the room Aggie rented at The Crown and Anchor and crashed there. I was a little shocked on Monday when they prepared to go back to Connecticut. "Why? "I asked Larry. "Why go back?" Larry and Aggie took the news that I was staying put in stride and piled into the car and waved goodbye with

Larry yelling out the window, "Where are you going to sleep? How are you going to eat?" I smiled and shrugged my shoulders. I wasn't thinking about any of those things.

So it came to be that I spent the 1967 Summer of Love in Ptown. It was during that summer I got to know Billy Hansen a little bit better, because Billy spent the whole summer there every year. One afternoon, I ran into Billy right in front of the Meat Rack and, not knowing what to say after "Hi," I held up the ends of my long hair and said, "Look, my hair is a mess! " Billy laughed and said, "Come with me. I can fix that up," and we walked to his house. In his tiny kitchen Billy lit a joint and started to cut my hair. I was in a glorious trance, happy to be sitting so close to Billy Hansen. I was trying to memorize Billy's cheekbones and—between the weed and Billy Hansen inches away from me—I was in a swoon. I didn't realize till afterwards that the drone I heard in the background was Billy Hansen buzzing off all my hair! "All done!" Billy said with satisfaction in his voice, a satisfaction that I interpreted as approval of me. Running my hand up the back of my head, it felt a little boy's buzz cut! I was speechless. "Go wash your head," he eventually said. He didn't say hair, he said head. I went to the bathtub and, kneeling under the faucet, I found that I had no hair left!

"This is so much chicer on you than Mia Farrow," Billy said, slouching in the doorway of the bathroom, puffing on another joint. "I cut it shorter, much more radical." I believe that was the first time I heard the word "radical" spoken out loud. The Summer of Love was The Summer of Hair, but I turned seventeen that July in Ptown with my head shorn like Joan of Arc. It was a small price to pay for being close to Billy Hansen.

It was also in Ptown that summer that I met Jaime Andrews, who would change my life forever. One day, as I tried to cross Commercial Street in the butt-to-bumper traffic, a new sedan gunned its engine and jumped forward, just grazing my thigh. But there was no escape for him because the traffic wasn't moving and I felt evil, so I draped myself into the empty passenger side window and crawled along with the car saying, "Very tacky to be killed by a 1967 Chevy, thank you very much!" The "very much" lasted about nine syllables. Victorious, I strode off, but I was followed by cackling laughter. I didn't look back right way. The merry cackling continued to follow me. I turned on my heel and stopped, and what a sight: a beautiful man in a white linen suit. My eyes trailed him down and up. White shoes, three-piece white linen suit, white Panama hat, and white, white teeth, twinkling and laughing in a big smile. Big brown, twinkling eyes in the white, whites of his eyes.

I surveyed him, cocked my head to the side and haughtily spat out, "I need *your* elegance?" And the elegant one laughed more and I jumped, jerk-turned around, and then turned back because he was amazing to behold. But I was intimidated so I kept walking fast and he strolled, la-di-da, behind me, still laughing, and called out, "Hey, Miss Thing! Who writes *your* material?" And I slowed down thinking, *Hmm, maybe he has a place to stay*, and we walked and talked and he told me his name is Jaime Andrews. He's half-Italian, half-Portuguese, from Lawrence, Massachusetts, a factory town like mine. He's twenty-seven years old and he'd just graduated from RISD with a double major in photography and architecture. He said, "RISD" like I'm supposed to know what that means. "What's RISD?" I asked and he replied, "Art school," somewhat incredulously and went on to explain art school to me. We walked all the way to the house where he was staying and he went immediately to the record player and put on the Four Tops. "Bernadette" filled the living room and we danced all afternoon and smoked pot. He told me I made him think of a seventeen-year-old boy he had a crush on, Mark McCarthy. He asked me where I was staying, but I chickened out from telling him I was homeless and I made something up, and before I knew it I was back at the Meat Rack, looking for a place to crash. I was crashing in hallways and on back steps and, when I was lucky, in some vacationing fags' hotel room. The boys came and went from all over the country and lots of them let me share their room for a night or two. I often went to parties where I was the only girl. One night I was at The A House with Jaime and the crowd he hung out with, which included a tall, thin man with a pencil mustache named John who stuck out in my mind because he was the only person in Jaime's group not going to New York at the end of the summer—he was going to Baltimore to make movies. John was often with a beautiful dark haired girl named Marina who I thought was the most glamorous creature on earth. Later that night we went to someone's house after the bars closed. I was, as we used to say back then, "carrying on for days," and a young Asian queen hearing me talk asked Jaime earnestly, "Is she real? How come she talks like a queen?" Before Jaime could open his mouth I turned, one hand on my hip, and said, "I didn't spend $25,000 and *six* months in Casablanca to have you ask if I am real!" Jaime just shook his head and crowed, "Miss Thing can out-dish us all! Is she not divine?"

The next night or soon after, I was at the Meat Rack wondering again where I was going to sleep and some skinny queen with bad skin from Milwaukee ran by yelling, "Queens from New York, Andy Warhol queens from New York!" and everyone followed him down the street, including me.

Jaime had given me a raccoon fur coat to wear, and even though it was summer I wore it. Feeling very fabulous, I followed the pack of fags to The Terrace where I never went because I had no money. But I was there in my glory until "Babbo," the gigantic queen who ruled Ptown from his table at The Terrace, called out to me, "Careful, daughter!! That animal wasn't trapped—it was beaten to death." And everyone laughed, even me, because funny is funny no matter who says it. The place was packed and *tres gay* with the lights, and the night, and the laughing.

Then Babbo stood up and announced, "Those queens from New York look evil and dangerous."

The skinny queen with the bad skin tittered, "Dangerous but glamorous like thugs with make up." Then suddenly it was very quiet. Everyone looked at the gate and there they were, just two of them, and I thought, *Wow! That's a lot of drama for just two queens!* But they were like no queens I had ever seen. They were wearing tight, tight black leather jackets, tight, tight. No, I mean like painted-on tight black jeans, and super mean, pointed-toe, Puerto Rican shit-kicker black boots. They were very, very butch but only up to the neck! The taller, skinnier one was blonde, more than blonde, platinum, with bouffant hair like Marilyn's. The other was a bit shorter, a bit stockier, with black hair in a fabulous upswept French twist and looked like Suzanne Pleshette. Both of them had on full makeup. Pretty makeup with at least three pairs of false eyelashes each and big, red, pouting, lipstick mouths. They were in Technicolor from the neck up and black leather, butcher than anything, from the neck down. No one moved, no one said a word; everyone was holding their breath.

I walked over to get a closer look at these New York queens, surprised that no one else was talking to them. Up close they looked like well-groomed horses in a Memorial Day parade. "Are you from New York?" I asked the blonde one. He glanced down at me, and murmured, "Uh huh." Glancing back at the wave of crowd in front of him he said to the dark-haired queen, "This child is the only one who has the nerve to speak to us," indicating me with his chin.

"Everyone thinks you're dangerous," I blurted out.

And he purred, "We are dangerous," through a smile, but his eyes, ice blue and cold, didn't smile. I checked out his makeup and it was flawless. Perfect false eyelashes marched across both eyes. His cheekbones looked like war monuments, lit at night from below. He turned to me and ran his index finger along the end of his eyebrow and softened slightly as he asked, "How long have you been here?"

"Most of the summer," I replied.

"Do you have room for us where you're staying?"

"Well?" I braced myself and said, "I'm not staying anywhere." But this was not a bombshell, not to them.

The other queen, Suzanne Plushette, spoke for the first time, "Most of the summer? I wouldn't give this town two days. We're going back to New York tomorrow. I'm Randy by, the way. He's Johnny."

Johnny rocked back on his Cuban heels. "Lets blow this joint. Care to come along, hon?" I glanced around but there was nothing to hold me there and I walked out the gate with them.

We walked along Commercial Street and Johnny turned to me and asked, "Have you been to New York?"

And I said, "Not yet."

And he said, "You're a natural for New York. Believe me, you are wasted here. You can come stay with us." And I couldn't believe my luck!

We stopped at the dark edge of a driveway and Johnny let air out softly through his lips and said, "Ooh, Look at that bus." I looked in the driveway and there was a big beige luxury tour bus parked there, dark inside as the night itself.

Randy walked alongside it. "Hey, I guess we found tonight's digs."

That made me nervous. It was a bus. Busses have drivers. I preferred porches, hallways, and back steps for passing the hours between 2:00 a.m. when the bars closed and 11:00 a.m. when it was okay to be seen back at the Meat Rack without calling into question your living arrangements.

I braced myself and said, "I don't think this is a great idea."

"Why not?" demanded Randy, kind of meanly.

"Well, for one thing it's...." I drifted along, trying to think of something to say, dragging on the last syllable.

"It's what?" demanded Randy, losing patience with me, along with one false eyelash that drifted to the ground.

"Well it's...too beige," I blurted out.

Johnny, who had been pulling on the door handle of the bus, started laughing " Too beige!! Too beige!! *Touché! Touché!*" Randy bent down to lift the eyelash off the tarmac drive and Johnny pulled the door open.

"Oh my God, it's open," Randy screamed and all three of us scrambled inside. It was plush, clean and soft. We lay back in the rosy interior and I sank deep into sleep.

The next day Johnny and Randy headed for the bus back to New York and we stopped in the middle of the meat market. With everybody looking, Johnny stabbed his index finger into the watch pocket of his jeans. But the pocket of his jeans was so tight he could hardly get the top of his index finger in. He stretched up, arched his back, and leaned back further and further and wiggled his finger around like he was baiting minnows and finally he pulled out a matchbook. Then, with his eye on the crowd, he pulled out a yellow stub of a pencil from the inside pocket of his motorcycle jacket. He scrawled his number on the matchbook and had me read it back to him, out loud, and then he said, loud enough for everyone to hear, "You better get out of this hole as soon as possible, or you'll end up boring...like them." He pointed to everyone on the Meat Rack, turned on his heel and they walked away without looking back once. Then everyone turned and stared at me as if they were seeing me for the first time.

Two months later—in a story that is too long to go into here—I found myself in a telephone booth on the corner of Bleecker and Thompson Streets, with Mark McCarthy, a beautiful blond boy from

Worcestster, Massachusetts. Mark was seventeen, too. Yes! It was the same Mark McCarthy that Jaime Andrews had told me about in Ptown. I had met Mark in a crash pad in Boston when I left Ptown. We left Boston because, as young as we were, we both hated living in a student town. The matchbook Johnny Pepin had given me was in my hand and I called that number, holding my breath, hoping that the number was still good.

Johnny answered the phone completely unsurprised that I was calling, then asked, "Where are you?" I asked Mark and repeated Mark's words into the phone, "Bleecker Street and Thompson Street."

"No! No! No!" He said, "All wrong! Get into a cab and come to the corner of East 7th Street and Avenue C. Call me from the corner when you get here."

THIS IS HOW I CAME to fall in with the most infamous set of criminal, intellectual, psychedelic queens. Soon I was living in shooting galleries and hotel rooms populated by what was called the "A Set." A for Amphetamine.

These shooting galleries floated between apartments and different hotel rooms around the city. One early morning I was alone in a room in the Broadway Central Hotel, known locally as the Heroin Hilton, when I saw someone climbing into the window. He had long brown hair and a hooked nose of some architecture. "Don't worry," he called out as he folded himself under the half-open window from the fire escape, "I'm Joel. Everyone knows me." He pronounced it Jo-ell. He was Joel Markman, famous from Jack Smith's *Flaming Creatures*, considered by many to be the true star of the film because of his infamous lipstick scene. It was Joel who had brought amphetamine to Warhol's Factory and, as any student of things Warhol knows, The Factory, along with Andy Warhol, was fueled by Amphetamines in the early years. Through Joel I came into contact with the anarchist speed freaks and junkie queer artists who roamed the East Village intent on "A and art," as they put it, including the great Ondine, subject (and only subject) of Warhol's infamous *A*, a book-long document of one of Ondine's Amphetamine fueled rants. Instead of coffee klatches, there were Amphetamine and Methadrine klatches that lasted whole days, if not weeks, without sleeping. I spent long hours listening to these singular, extraordinarily larger-than-life queens, whose values had been formed at the outskirts of humanity, when homosexuality was still a way to differentiate yourself from polite society, when homosexuality was still part of the criminal demi-monde. They spent hours elucidating different operas, opera singers, movies and actors, and the lives of artists and poets from long ago, centuries ago, whom they seemed to know in intimate ways. I was given a context for a greater cultural world that dwarfed the world that had rejected me. Most days I would walk from the East Village to Christopher Street: one never knew who one would meet up with there, and one day Larry Buscaino reappeared. Christopher Street was the first place anyone went trying to find their friends—for decades it has been the crossroads of the gay world. Larry and I took up with one another again without missing a beat. He was crashing at the apartment of a male nurse who had painted his two-room East Village, bathtub-in-the-kitchen slum tenement to look like Versailles, all pale champagne and ivory moldings, and every stick of furniture in the sparsely furnished apartment was white and gilt French provincial. This thin-lipped, prissy queen worked nights at Beth Israel Hospital, but his good will towards Larry soon evaporated when Larry moved me and then a boy, another seventeen-year-old runaway, there to crash, sleeping, when we did, on the bare floor. Still, we managed a couple of months there, eating mayonnaise sandwiches with the refrigerator door open for the cool air, and clearing out before the nurse got home. We'd head for the West Village, where Larry played his guitar and sang on the stoops of Christopher Street and we carried on as we always had; then at night we would repair to The Stonewall and dance the night away smoking cigarettes and joints in the very back corner of the bar with the Black transexual street whores like Marsha P. Johnson, who everyone called Black Marsha in those days. Then the next day we would start all over again, walking to the West Village to sit on those Christopher Street stoops and wait for our friends to show up. Eventually Larry replaced speed and booze with heroin. Soon after, the nurse demanded his keys back and Larry and I went our separate ways, finding new places to crash. And one day, just as he had appeared, Larry disappeared. It would be forty years before I heard from him again.

ONE AFTERNOON, MONTHS AFTER ARRIVING in New York, crashing from speed, hungry from not eating for days, and worn out from late night wrestling with sex-hungry guys in the crash pads where I passed the nights, I wandered along 2nd Avenue, and there under the marquee of the St. Marks Movie Theater, a voice called out to me. It was Jaime Andrews. His eyes searched me up and down. Taking in the tracks on my arms and my exhaustion he declared, "You don't look so good. I think you need to come and live with me." I demurred, embarrassed. I was not used to kindness, but I walked away with his phone number in my pocket. I fought my way through another sleepless week, fending off unwanted sexual advances that were the price of being a homeless girl in New York's East Village, before I finally called the number Jaime had pressed into my hand. Soon I found myself ensconced in Jaime's one-room studio on East 9th Street between 1st Avenue and Avenue A. He pointed out his sleeping loft and offered me his drawing table for my bed. "You are small. You fit there just fine." And I began yet another orientation, drugless except for LSD and the pot plants Jaime grew on his windowsill.

Jaime's phone book was filled with the names, addresses, and phone numbers of famous artists he hadn't yet met.

"But why do you have their phone numbers?" I'd ask.

"Well, how do you expect to meet the people you want to know if you don't know who or where they are?" he would answer. Jaime worked in market research and left each morning at 7:00 a.m. I would slowly wake up and make the pilgrimage across 8th Street to Christopher Street where I would meet up with other queer kids, and spend the day knocking around, slowly meeting the people I would come to know for the rest of my life. Jaime worked with John Vaccaro, whose Playhouse of The Ridiculous was the other game in town besides Andy Warhol's Factory. It was at Jaime's one night, coming down from LSD and desperate to entertain my patron, that I named myself Penny Arcade. Jaime brought me to John Vaccaro's loft on Great Jones Street. John had amazing parties attended by the brightest and the best of downtown New York's art world as well as by some of the most notorious members of the queer underworld. One night after Jaime told John Vaccaro I had changed my name to Penny Arcade, John asked me to join the Playhouse of The Ridiculous on the strength of my having changed my name alone!

"You know," John whispered to me conspiratorially, "I read a chapter of *Moby Dick* before I go to sleep every night without fail."

I didn't understand where Herman Melville fit in with drag, theater, and the best pot, LSD, and music collection in the East Village, but I was completely seduced by his statement. Jaime was delighted when John told him I was joining The Playhouse.

"Fabulous!" Jaime said. "Now we are going to channel all that talent."

Today when I speak to young queers who want to know the differences between today and back then I say quietly, "Show me one twenty-seven-year-old queer guy who is going to take in a homeless seventeen-year-old girl. Back then we knew we had to take care of each other. You didn't have to be a card-carrying homosexual. It was beyond identity politics. It was humane and inclusive, not exclusive. Everyone recognized their people intuitively. We knew how to form community."

For many years the trek from Avenue A across East 8th Street, then St. Marks Place, then East 8th Street again, then West 8th Sreet to Christopher Street would be a daily pilgrimage. Even now, on days when I awake and don't know what to do with myself, I find my feet leading me there. Christopher Street, the great queer Rialto of my youth, is no longer populated by the greats that once cruised there, lingering on those stoops. No more the eye-opening conversations, no more the bent-over doubled-up laughter. No more Harry M. Koutoukas, Jackie Curtis, Candy Darling, Robert Beers, Marsha P. Johnson, International Chrysis, Douglas Fisher, Ritta Redd, Tony Ingrassia, Jack Smith, Charles Ludlam, Bunny Eisenhower, Frances Francine, Taylor Mead or the others—many others whose names even I have forgotten—names once famous in gay circles. They are mostly gone now, but I walk with them still and I know I always will. I know what Walt Whitman was talking about when he spoke to us across the great distance of time, "If you want me again look for me under your boot-soles."

A few years ago, my phone rang and a muffled voice asked, "Do you know who this is?" The voice sounded very familiar but blurred in a way I couldn't really make out completely.

"You sound so familiar," I said. "But it is hard to understand you. I think we have a bad connection."

"It's because my jaw is wired shut!" he shouted.

"Your jaw is wired shut?" I asked, not quite sure that was what I heard.

"Yeah, I fell down, face-first on the glass coffee table, Marilyn Monroe-style."

"Larry Buscaino!" I cried out. No one else phrased a sentence like that! It could only be Larry.

"So, you remember me?" he asked.

"How could I ever forget you?" Then Larry told me a long saga of being a male nurse in Florida, of alcoholism and jail, with many repetitions made necessary by his wired-shut jaw. "Jail?" I asked him. "Five years. I just got out. There were some misunderstandings with my employers," he laughed.

"Do you remember all those days and nights on Christopher Street?" he asked eventually.

"Oh yes, Larry, I remember us on Christopher Street."

"Do you ever walk over there now?" He asked.

"Yeah, Larry, I still do."

"I suppose the scene has moved somewhere else," he said, a bit mournfully.

"Not really, Larry," I replied. "All the homeless, queer kids are still on Christopher Street, that hasn't changed—only now there aren't any cheap diners for them to go into."

ON THE NIGHT OF ACT UP's twentieth anniversary event in 2007, I walked up toward the LGBT Community Center and saw a bunch of kids huddled outside the front door. As I got closer, I saw they were all girls, mainly black, a few Latinas. They were smoking cigarettes and laughing and screeching as I approached them.

"Hey! Could I get a cigarette off one of you?" I ventured.

There was something feral in the way the girls turned towards me. "Are you gay?" the girl closest to me asked, as a challenge, waving her cigarette in my face.

I froze. But then a rage whipped up my spine. "Do you know that people fought and died so that question, 'Are you gay?' would never matter?" I wasn't sure what the response would be and I sucked in my breath, but then the whole crowd seemed to suddenly see me as one of them. The energy shifted and a cigarette was offered and we started laughing and hanging out there on the street in front of The Center.

It turned out their weekly dance party had been cancelled to make space for the ACT UP benefit. I asked them if they knew about ACT UP, but they shrugged their shoulders. I said, "Come with me." Eight street kids and I went inside The Center and I asked the doorkeeper if I could bring them in. "It's $20 a head," he said, unmovable. I spotted Bob Kohler, the sage, handsome warrior and lifelong advocate of queer youth, ran over to him, and explained the situation. "Ridiculous!" Bob exploded, walking to the front desk. "Of course! These kids have to come in." And in they came, but the energy of the evening didn't reach them, and to the older gay men who made up the bulk of the evening's audience, they were invisible. After forty minutes the kids left, before I even performed. Tahesha, who had given me the cigarette, waited for me by the door as the rest poured out. I went over to her.

"I want to stay but my peeps want to go up to Christopher Street," she said. "Can I have your digits? I want to call you sometimes, run my shit by you. Okay?"

"Sure," I said giving her my number, "remember to call me."

Tahesha was seventeen then. She lives in a group home in Brooklyn. Sometimes she calls me. Sometimes she texts me. Sometimes she emails me. Sometimes I run into her and her peeps on Christopher Street. It's nice to run into people I know there again.

THE ISLE OF STATEN
40° 35' 0" N / 74° 8' 59" W

MICHELE KARLSBERG

IT WAS LATE DECEMBER BACK in... Oh wait, wrong story.

Once upon a time, on the twenty-sixth day of February in 1965—
in a hospital that overlooked the water in Bay Ridge, Brooklyn—
this Pisces was born to swim through the waters of life. Little did I
know there was no better way to navigate that journey than to be on
the Isle of Staten. Shore Road Hospital has since been replaced by
senior housing. I must admit, for many years I did not believe that
this hospital even existed. My parents had always told me that I was
found in Macy's window and I learned to accept that.

I don't remember much of the first five years of my life, although
I am reminded of one thing for sure. Each time we drive through
the "old" neighborhood, my Mom makes it a point to show me the
building where I was conceived. Today I continue to ask questions,

wanting to know about those early years. I seek to know what set my biological and psychological foundation.

My father is a Russian Jew and my mother is an Italian Catholic. I understand that my paternal grandparents weren't quite happy when they heard their first grandchild was being raised Catholic. I actually don't think they were very happy when the Jew *married* the Catholic, although, in time, the family came together. I always looked forward to visiting my grandparents in Brighton Beach, where we strolled along the boardwalk and then headed to the kosher deli with my grandmother to buy that freshly made gefilte fish. I must admit, to this day I have never been in a synagogue. When I am asked about Judaism my reply is, "All I know is matzah balls, jelly rings, and that you get multiple gifts during Hanukkah." I wear a pendant around my neck of a Jewish star with a cross on top of it, which symbolizes my "biological makeup." In catechism class, I was asked to remove the pendant. I was told, "How dare you wear a Jewish star in a Catholic institution." I refused to remove it and kindly reminded them that Jesus was a Jew. I can't say much about Catholicism, either. When I attended church service, the one part of the service I know I looked forward to was the "Peace be with you" part, hoping that an attractive woman was close by that I could wish peace to with a handshake or a hug.

While growing up, my house was number 173. Each "Mother/ Daughter" home (a two-family house) looked exactly the same. The only way I could tell my house apart from the others was by the black-and-white vertical aluminum siding at its peak. Other than that it was a carbon-copy row of houses that in 1970 each cost $41,000. My neighborhood, known as Ocean Breeze, was filled with Brooklynites who had made their way over via the Verrazano Bridge in 1964. Native Staten Islanders weren't happy then about the incoming, and to this day we Brooklynites still hear their gripes as the population of the most suburban of the boroughs has grown to over 500,000. Perhaps it was an abundance of elderly Italian women all dressed in black that became too overwhelming. These women arranged beach chairs on their stoops and sat there for years on end, mourning the loss of their husbands. Is this what traumatized the natives? It sure left an impression on me.

Staten Island is still one of the most mysterious boroughs to many people. Interestingly enough, people still ask me, "How do you get back to Staten Island when the ferry stops running?" I kindly remind them that a bridge does exist. As a matter a fact, four bridges connect to the Island. And if there were no bridges there would be no worries, because the ferry runs all night long. It still makes me chuckle that people actually think this Isle is like Gilligan's. Our neighborhood was a quiet one, filled with families raising their children. The two-and-a-half mile long FDR board-walk, the fourth longest in the world, was less than a mile from our home. The fresh ocean breeze that swept through our block was breathtaking. Knowing that the South Beach Amusement Park was only a hop, skip, and jump away made it feel like we lived in a resort town. At my fingertips daily were Skee-Ball, photo booths, carnival games, and rides. At one time Staten Island even hosted the San Gennaro Feast at the beach before it made its yearly trek into Manhattan. At this feast I would hope to win those pin-up posters of Farrah Fawcett, Cheryl Ladd, and Diana Ross—and once I did, and they were hung in my bedroom, it was obvious that my pin-ups were quite different from the Rob Lowe, Leif Garrett, and Ralph Macchio posters which hung in the other girls' bedrooms at that time. The best part of Saturday morning chores was playing Diana Ross continually on my record player. I couldn't help myself. I held that invisible microphone as I sang proudly with each chorus of "I'm Coming Out."

Staten Island holds so much history—so much history that, after living here forty-two years, I have still not visited all of the historical sites on this Island: from Sandy Ground, which is the oldest community established by free slaves in North America, to the Conference House, the only pre-Revolutionary manor house still surviving in New York City, where notables like John Adams and Benjamin Franklin spent time. As a Staten Islander and an out lesbian, I enjoy looking into the LGBT history that this island holds. When I first discovered Alice Austen and made numerous visits to Clear Comfort (a.k.a. The Alice Austen House) I felt like I was reunited with an old friend. Although Alice Austen was certainly not the first lesbian photographer, she was the first who is known to have photographed lesbians who could be recognized as lesbians. Her oceanfront home, with the Verrazano Bridge as a perfect backdrop, is where Austen photographed her friends and her lover in a way that seems remarkably conspicuous for the time—around 1900. Only 13.9 miles long and 7.3 miles wide, the island holds a rich tradition of gay and lesbian life. Notable inhabitants of the island have included Audre Lorde, Langston Hughes, Henry David Thoreau, Ralph Waldo Emerson, and Joan Baez, among others.

IN 2010 I MADE A personal LGBT historical contribution to Staten Island. I was given the opportunity to produce *Back to Back*, starring Lily Tomlin and Kate Clinton, at the landmark St. George Theater—the very same theater where I tapped and glided across the stage as a young dancer. Each week for three years I took dance class with Mrs. Rosemary, a Staten Island dance icon who taught tens of thousands of children the arts of dance and music for over fifty years. She rescued the padlocked St. George Theater in 2004, and if it weren't for Mrs. Rosemary, this little gal's dream of being back on the stage that I had danced on so many years ago would not have come true. It was an extraordinary full-circle event for me and for the community.

Growing up, it was my five childhood friends on our block, all female, who brought me joy. We walked to and from school each day. We hung out on the corner; we enjoyed afternoon cookie and milk breaks; in the wintertime we trekked into the swamp to the pond where we ice skated; we wrote and performed plays together in our basements; we smoked our first cigarettes together. But most of all, we protected each other. One outing I always looked forward to was skating at the roller rink, because it was there at the rink that I got to hold hands with the girls as we choreographed movements to the music. And we had a special camaraderie, one where we found joy in singing, "I'm on the top of the world looking down on creation..." from atop dirt mountains on the undeveloped land across the street from our homes.

It was a much simpler time, when hanging out after school each weekday was always fun. Kickball games, wiffle ball, tag, bicycle rides, hopscotch, stoopball, and making macaroni art were some of the activities that we indulged in. We created our entertainment. We only had two choices—inside or outside—not the deluge of electronics we now have to keep kids from innocent childhood exploration.

Weekends were spent playing with our Barbie dolls. We had it all—the Barbie Dream House with furniture sets for each room that included bedrooms, kitchens, dining rooms, living rooms and more. But my favorite was the Barbie Convertible. As Ken (I was always Ken when we played—wink, wink) I would pull up to that Dream House and get that kiss from Barbie and then she hopped right in. And off we went on our date. One day I think I went a little too far as I was playing Barbie and Ken with one of the neighborhood gals. As Ken was trying to get to first base with Barbie, I tried to get to first base with my playmate. That ended quickly as her mother opened that bedroom door and caught us. As I recall I was not allowed to play with her for some time. As adults all five of us are still in communication, reliving our childhoods through each other, reminding each other of the best of times and the worst of times. My childhood friends now speak about knowing that I was a lesbian, and how they saw it no differently than their heterosexual lives.

Folks ask me all the time if I was born this way—a lesbian. My reply is always, "Yes, this is the way I was created, and I am proud of that." I am quite happy that I am what I am and never at any time have I regretted who I am. I can remember admiring the other gals as far back as when I was in kindergarten. Truly paying no attention to the boys. I think the only real attention I paid to the opposite sex in my youth was when I was beating them up. Their parents were constantly knocking on our front door so they could show my parents what I had done to their sons. I cannot remember what the reasons were for beating them up but I am sure they did something cruel that egged me on. It wasn't easy being a menstrual nine-year-old who was already wearing a bra and eyeglasses.

One keepsake, among others, that forever lives in my memory was dinnertime. You knew it was *that time* when you heard your mother yelling your name out the kitchen window with the message, "Get home now."

I sat with my family and we ate well-rounded meals and held conversations. Praying I would not be tormented by carrot and beet side dishes yet again—which I refuse to eat as an adult—we indulged in our delicious home-cooked meals as we caught up on the day and discussed the next one. For many people this simple pastime is gone. After dinner I headed back outside to await the arrival of the Good Humor man. I always wondered why he was called the Good Humor man—I never found him funny. He was just a man dressed all in white whose truck full of candy and ice cream arrived at the same time each evening. I could not wait to get my hands on the Chocolate Fudge Bar.

House 173 is still in the family. My younger sister purchased the home from my mother and grandmother in 2004. My visits there prompt my memory back in time to grasp the moments I long to relive with two of the most significant people in my life, my maternal grandmother and my great aunt. Along with my mother and two sisters we were a house of strong opinions, intelligence, and courage. My mom, who was divorced from my dad, raised us, and at the same time looked after her mom and her aunt who lived in the downstairs apartment. Saturday mornings were not only chore days, which included ironing, cleaning, and a trip to the corner deli to get cold cuts for lunch, but a day in which we got to enjoy Grandma and Aunt Jay to the fullest. We woke up to blueberry pancakes, enjoyed afternoon rummy games, and savored the smell of Grandma's Sunday sauce on the stove. There were six women in that house and that house was six-women strong. Growing up in that house taught me to lead, not to follow. It taught me that women are sensitive, beautiful, and caring. It taught me to never give up. My grandmother had solid beliefs and to my benefit she believed that her granddaughter—her lesbian granddaughter—deserved the same human rights as the next person. She made it clear that marriage between two women shouldn't even be an issue. I know she would have been rejoicing on that day that Marriage Equality in New York was passed. I also know that the day after she would have probably given my partner and me an engagement gift. That's just how she rock-and-rolled.

Aunt Jay also knew of my sexuality, though we never spoke about it. She knew who my partner was, she spoke about women to me and let me know whom she thought was attractive—but we never spoke about anything in detail. Aunt Jay was a quiet woman. Although it might not have looked like she knew all that was going on, she knew everything, and once it was discussed Aunt Jay unfailingly had a definite opinion. Her life always sparked my curiosity because she remained unmarried. She had told me that she was engaged at one time but when she cut her long hair off her fiancé broke their engagement. His loss. I admired her oomph and strength. One day, while accompanying Aunt Jay for her yearly doctor visit, we were sitting in a waiting room full of patients. She was telling me about a book she was reading, and in one breath she had an outburst about the main character in the book, "She is a lesbian, you know, just like you." Shocked but so happy that my ninety-one-year-old great-aunt even said that, I looked around the room and with a big smile gave everyone a royal wave.

Throughout my elementary and junior high school years I just went with the flow. I had my teacher and schoolgirl crushes, and onward I went, keeping it all to myself. But when I entered high school it was the dawn of a new day, a new time, and finally Michele became Michele.

My coming out to the family was not exactly by design—love letters from my first girlfriend, hidden in my bedroom closet where I thought no one would ever find them, were discovered. This led to some unsettling times. It was 1982 and my girlfriend worked at a local straight bar. As a matter of fact, that bar is where we first met. As quickly as I entered the bar was as quickly as our relationship began. We are still friends to this day, and she says that it was my outfit that sparked her interest in me. I just happened to be wearing the same color coordinates as she did that very evening we first met. If only it had been that easy to attract women after our breakup. This rocker bar, an old eighteenth-century inn located on Staten Island, very conveniently still had rooms on the second floor that we used during her breaks for some quick intimate moments. Then one stormy Saturday night a knock at the door announced my parents. My first thought was "Who died?" Little did I know what was to confront me. My first thought was "deny everything." And deny we did as my girlfriend and I sat as far away from each other as we could in the red-leather back-seat of a huge black Cadillac. My parents questioned their eighteen-year-old daughter and her twenty-six-year-old girlfriend relentlessly. Even though the proof was in the pudding (since they held the letters my girlfriend had written to me), we still stood strong together deny-ing it all. This of course angered them more.

I can remember my father saying later that evening, "I would have rather found out that you were pregnant." He then proceeded to grab his gun and head to my girlfriend's house. Thank goodness his friends stopped him, because if they hadn't this would have been a whole other story. I recently reminded him of his words and actions. His reply was, "I was young and crazy then. I am old now." Looking back I think my mother was just going with my father's flow so that she didn't have to fight with him about it. My mother has become quite accepting of me and of my sexual-ity. Actually I feel as if she doesn't even blink an eye about it. She shares with relatives who fret over their children being gay that her daughter is and to have no worries. I find it entertaining that she now makes sure she tells me further details about women I intellectually and physically admire and that she enjoyably attends various LGBT events.

The initial discovery of my sexual orientation by my parents led to a strict curfew, monitored phone calls, and a visit to a therapist who would help me with my "disease." Never having been to a therapist before, and knowing only what I had watched on television about ther-apy visits, I asked the therapist where the tape recorders and camera were hidden in his office. I asked him to make sure all of them were turned on so that I could be quoted correctly by him after my session.

I explained to the therapist that I was not the one with a disease. Nor was it a phase that I was going through. It was indeed a disease that affected my parents. Their understanding of my sexuality was influenced by the ignorance spread by others that homosexuality was harmful to society. I closed my session with the therapist by reminding him that in 1973 the American Psychiatric Association declassified homosexuality as a mental disorder. The American Psychological Association Council of Representatives followed in 1975.

After the unproductive first therapy session my parents never took me back. Today we laugh at the fact that my relationship and life is at times more stable then those of my two heterosexual sisters.

My youngest sister is ten years younger than me and my other sister is three years younger. When they learned of my sexuality they were actually quite supportive. They just wanted their sister around and to continue on as if Mommy and Daddy were the ones going through a phase, not me. My sisters have given me the gifts of both a wonderful loving niece and a nephew. They love their two aunts unconditionally and it is so precious to me that they are lucky enough to grow up with two aunts they adore and that gender makes no difference to them—love is love. It makes me melt when my nine-year-old niece asks "Auntie M, do you have a date set for your wedding yet? What shall we wear? Will it be on a golf course or beach? And can I set the menu?" To know that these two will grow up on Staten Island with same-sex role models is comforting.

This island is a very conservative one. Staten Island is the only Republican stronghold in New York City. In my youth I had no clue how intensively conservative it was. In 1994, Staten Island Borough President Guy Molinari announced that Karen Burstein, a judge, was unqualified to serve as attorney general because she is a lesbian. For reasons like this I never hid or denied the fact that I am lesbian— I actually believe the opposite—that it is of utmost importance to demonstrate that I am just the same as the next person. There is no difference. I can raise a child, I can love my partner till death do us part; I can read, write, hold a job, help someone in need...well, you get the point. LGBT Staten Islanders work hard to educate our families and friends. Just recently, The Staten Island LGBT Center, an initiative of Community Health Action of Staten Island (CHASI) was opened. The Center provides lesbian, gay, bisexual, and transgender individuals and their family members with direct local access to culturally competent, gay-oriented, LGBT-friendly services, programs, events and activities that promote their overall physical, mental and emotional health and well-being. In 1973 the first LGBT college courses were taught at Richmond College. Staten Island Community College and Richmond College (which merged in 1976 as the College of Staten Island) both had significant gay and lesbian organizations. Dorothy Riddle of Richmond College developed the Riddle Homophobia scale as part of the American Psychological Association Task Force on Gays and Lesbians. The College of Staten Island still offers their LGBT curriculum and has a very active gay-straight student alliance.

We no longer have any surviving gay or lesbian bars here. From 1958 to the early '70s gay men and lesbians could socialize at the Mayfair Bar. Soon followed by the opening of two other gay and lesbian bars on Staten Island: The Sandcastle (LGBT) and The Beach Haven (Lesbians Only). To my advantage both of those bars were located in my neighborhood and were my gateway to freedom. One was a stone's throw away, located right down the block from my home. The Beach Haven was a nondescript cabin facing the ocean and the front door had the only window, which was the size of a cereal box. You had to know the secret knock that allowed you to enter and once inside you were a world away from home. All it took was a dimly lit room filled with women who played pool and swayed with each other to a jukebox's music. It was paradise.

WE HAVE COME A LONG way on this island. We now host our own LGBT Pride Parade, we have elected our first openly gay official in the 61st district, we have one of New York City's two LGBT bookstores, the LGBT community marched in our local Columbus Day Parade, and local high schools have created gay-straight alliance groups to help eliminate hate through education and create safe spaces for the LGBT youth.

SO HERE IS WHERE THIS island dweller remains—my island—my Isle of Staten. Life on the Isle of Staten has shaped me and it is the many elements of this Island that bring me peace. I am grateful that my experiences have allowed me to have an open mind and become friendly with others from different backgrounds and family structures—I look at it as a huge accomplishment when living on an Island where people truly try to corrupt your thoughts of what is right and wrong. I have made and maintained many relationships here with friends whom I consider my extended family, from my high school physical education teacher—who to this day is my best friend—to others who always have my back. I treasure my relationships with all of them, and without them my life experiences here on Staten Island would have been quite different: they are a support group the likes of which I can only wish each person is lucky enough to have in their lives. After many years in search of the perfect partner, I have spent the last fourteen incredible years partnered with another native and proud Staten Islander. Together we all continue to live happily ever after.

POSTSCRIPT

IN NO WAY COULD I have known in 1989 when Stan Leventhal asked me to partner with him to create Amethyst Press, a small gay men's publishing company, that LGBT literature would become a prominent part of my life. After twenty-three years of publicizing, marketing, editing and coordinating I have now, for the first time, contributed my own writing to a collection that includes an amazing array of writers. I am quite honored. I would like to dedicate this piece to Stan who appropriately resided on Christopher Street.

FINDING JESÚS ON CHRISTOPHER STREET

BRENDAN FAY

AUGUST 1984, SCARLET STREET, DROGHEDA, Ireland. It's early in the morning and the sky is a gorgeous bright blue. I am aware of unwelcome and unexpected feelings. An unusual longing to leave is accompanied by the loneliness of knowing there is no turning back. I glance around the room, look at the icon of Mary from Sister Regina in Siena Convent, the photographs of family and friends, the poster of Archbishop Oscar Romero of El Salvador, the old picture of the Drogheda quays, the threadbare donkey Da gave me in Harcourt Street hospital when I was two, and Campaign for Nuclear Disarmament stuff. I grab the letters from St John's University professor Mike Warren. I'll never forget their impact and how much they meant to me; the long airmail envelopes from America with letters to a youth in Scarlet Street, Drogheda. Mike and Connie's typed letters to me told about their program of Youth for Peace and MA degrees. They quoted Dorothy Day and Thomas Merton—ideas that seemed from another Catholic world. They urged me to apply and come to St John's University, New York! On the Drogheda dole queue, I used to dream about what to do, I'd reread their letters, and look at the stamps and the New York addresses on the airmail envelopes. As I write today I'm filled with gratitude for the New York teachers who reached an Irish fella, and they remind me of what Graham Greene said: "There is always one moment in childhood when the door opens and lets the future in."

Time to go. I tell myself it's only for a short time in America. I'll be back—in a year. I couldn't imagine staying too long in Reagan's America. That's for sure. But I definitely need to get out—out of Scarlet Street, out of Drogheda, out of Ireland, out of the closet.

So here I am to the neighbors: young Fay off to America. The lad from Scarlet Street. Pete's son.

"He's off to study religion or something."

"The Fay lad is shockin' religious, so he is."

"He's off to be a graduate student in St John's University in New York."

I don't say much—my head is swirling with delight and with doubt. The begrudgers have their say and remain like a chorus in the mind. *Wait till they find out who you really are! Ye mad head banger, who the fuck do you think you are?*

OH YEAH, THE BAGGAGE. THE *other* baggage: fear, anger, longing, silence, shame, guilt when I look in the mirror, hatred for my body, hatred for the person I was becoming.

I go into the parents' bedroom. Tears threaten to well up as I enter, I hug and kiss Mam goodbye. She makes the quick sign of the cross on my forehead.

The Da drives. I sit in the front seat the other side. We don't say much, we never did anyway. He drives by Joe the Barber's and Campbell's shop, down past the medieval Lawrence's Gate, St. Augustine's on Shop Street. Just before we get to the airport we pass the Balheary—St Mary's Christian Brothers—for four years my home, from September 1972 to June 1976. Age fourteen to seventeen, going to be a Christian Brother—give my life to God. Then, in the distance, I see the towers of Dublin Airport.

Goodbye Ireland. *Good friggin' riddance Ireland.* Did I just think that? I need to leave whether I want to or not. Most leave Ireland for economic reasons. Immigrants have left Ireland fleeing persecution or poverty, in the pursuit of dreams, or on British prison ships. And there are the artists who made their way to Paris or London or Florence—and the thousands of nuns and priests who left for religious reasons, centuries of missionaries.

So why am I leaving? I'm leaving to find a place where I can be myself. Sex. It's a huge factor with me. I never read about anybody leaving for sexual reasons. I want to go where I can breathe. I want to breathe. I want to be.

Where do you go if you're a gay queer, a fairy, a faggot—the river, the seminary, the pretend marriage, or the boat. Well, for me it's the airport.

The turbulence outside the plane, nothing like the turbulence inside. I can't wait to see New York with the Statue of Liberty, Liberty Island. Ah, yes, land of the free: Fifth Avenue, St John's University, Washington Square, Peter, Paul and Mary, Simon & Garfunkel, Bette Midler, the Flintstones, the Waltons, and Batman and Robin.

They warned me about America at Maynooth College. One said, "Beware. Don't become like the Americans, so open minded that your brains fall out!" *I'll be all right; they love the Irish in America.*

MIKE AND CONNIE'S HOUSE IN Jamaica, New York, not far from St. John's—the car seemed huge, the yellow taxis just like in the films and the *News from America*.

That night, lying on the bed in their guest room, everything is so bright. Night drifts in but I can't sleep: nerves, doubts, and excitement and soon after, the sounds begin—and they go on all night! They sound like the croaking of frogs. *Must be a pond near here.* Turns out to be cicadas. There's a clean smell and look of American orderliness. *Spic and span. I am here in Amerikay.*

Next day walking to St, John's, I love the heat—the sunshine, the bright and warm weather—feels nice. Students everywhere seem so big and bright and young and good-looking and going places. Many drive big cars.

Also I can't believe the men wearing shorts—nearly every one of them. I never saw such a thing—I was out of shorts soon after I made the Holy Communion; getting into long trousers is a rite of passage for a young fella becoming a man. But here—even the old men are wearing shorts. Can't help but notice the legs, the shapes, the muscles. I feel overdressed, and my legs look like Gandhi's.

And the colors—you wouldn't believe fellas wearing lime green and yellow and pink. And there's me in the white, brown, and grays. Even the nuns and the religious are dressed in more color. Soon I discover second hand shops in New York, and people take pity on me and give me stuff.

Mosquitoes. They come out at night. I am eaten alive. Barely visible, I hear them at night buzzing around my ears, I dream of them flying into my ears, and I wake up covered. Now I understand why they have what they call the screen doors here and in Ireland we have the half-doors to keep the chickens outside.

At the admissions office I fill out forms, including one that asks about race, ethnicity, color. What I want is to put Irish as an option—I don't feel white—I've never been asked "What color are ye?" before. The only reference I ever heard in Ireland to color was, "Ye look pale," or "Ye have a grand color, ye must have been in Bettystown, Torrimolenos, or Annagasan!"

Overwhelmed by the lists of courses, the libraries full of students who read and can type away—I can barely write, but I'm here. And the library, inspiring and intimidating: books, floors and floors of them. I can sit in the aisles reading for days: liberation theology, Irish history, saints, nuns, Vatican II, catechesis, youth ministry. I love the smell of the library and the quiet hum of students whispering loudly—"You've a brogue!" they say to me.

Mass in the chapel and the gorgeous men, so many well-scrubbed, well-polished, they are gleaming. Priests are all tanned here—I'm pale in comparison. After the mass, college types all go for coffee. Nice, very nice coffee people. And their teeth so white, the diction so confident, and they greet me with, "The top of the morning to you." They like the brogue. They annoy with their, "Are you a leprechaun?" —No, I'm an Irish fairy, actually.

Reading sex notes on bathroom walls and doors reminds me of the dark world of prejudice. *"The words of the prophet are written on the bathroom stalls."* Before long—slowly, surely—I become more adventurous, wandering around the New York City wilderness asking questions, living with doubt, embracing the dark, trusting the dawn.

"KNOW ANY GAY BARS AROUND here?" I ask a police officer. (They carry guns here.) He points me to the Magic Touch in Jackson Heights, near Roosevelt and 74th Street. So I stay in Queens, going between the Liffey Bar, which is Irish, and the Magic Touch, which is gay.

In the Liffey Bar immigrant construction workers sit on bar stools, Guinness is on tap, the juke box plays Dolores Keane, Christy

Moore, Mary Black, Paddy Reilly—sounds to make me proud, homesick, and sad. I drink Guinness and dream of my mother in Scarlet Street, Drogheda. I try to repress the mood and pretend it's great here. So who am I—what am I doing here—is this the tribe? I don't fit in here.

So over to the Magic Touch to try there: a bejeweled fella named Buddha serves bar, disco sounds, drinks and small talk, the glance of the eye, and the touch of the hand above the knee. More, "Love the brogue." I don't quite fit here, but it's more comfortable.

Sure it's not a village at all, Greenwich Village. I come in at the weekend on the subway. I'm here. I've arrived. I light up a Marlboro Light.

Washington Square is full of music, homeless buskers, and peddlers freely pushing Jesus Christ and pot. The pigeons and squirrels—lovely like the Dublin Zoo never saw—are playful, "cute," as they say here. People are hugging, holding hands, and making love. I circle and watch and feel warm inside at the wonder of it all.

I love the way people walk in the City—with a spring in their step, going places—there is a New York energy—a swagger. I hope I catch the wave. For all the mad problems here, there is an energy like nowhere else.

The men of New York are gorgeous—so beautiful to look at, to listen to, so fearless and loud, and brazen. The exhilaration. The anxiety. The fright of AIDS is on the front pages of newspapers here. I look. I gaze. The faces of the men. Their eyes are beautiful, their lips and the way they talk and move and sit and shift in their shorts or levis—I hope they don't see me seeing them, I hope they don't notice me noticing those legs and how sexy they look, how sensuous. I crave and long to touch and be touched. Not necessarily to have sex—sometimes it ends up that way—too nervous. AIDS is a deadly wrench in the works.

One thing is for sure though—I'm so glad to be out of Scarlet Street with the damp days and depressing nights. Distant from family troubles and squabbles. At times there's a rush of guilt at having fled and left my sisters to care—I wonder if I will ever be able to be like these gay men of New York, who sit so confidently and yak away so unconsciously to their hearts content. *Hey! I could be denied entry at JFK and sent back to Ireland—it's a criminal offense in Ireland, and a sin there, and they want to cure me. I would have to face friends and the Charismatics and Father Enda and listen to my poor mother, depressed in the bed and reading who died and what horses were running, and my father on the chair in the corner by the fireplace.* Traveling back and forth through Dublin and JFK airports between 1984 and 1992 always brought on the fit of anxious nerves, always the possibility of being sent back. I'm so glad I'm here in New York…

A NUN IN THE GRADUATE program suggests I visit a gay and lesbian Catholic group called Dignity. I go there for Mass on a Saturday evening. Hope and hospitality is was what I find. Going up the steps of old Saint Francis Xavier Church in Greenwich Village reminds me of the churches in Ireland. I walk inside to find familiar sights and smells. In the dim light, candles flicker before side altar statues, old and worn from fervent faithful touching. The Church smells of wooden pews, candles, and incense. To step into a church is to be invited to another place. Dignity was Alan Royal and others who restored hope and laughter in the darkness of AIDS. They helped me not to take it all too so seriously, to laugh a bit; the pain of it all and the innocence gone forever.

Dignity. Someone with the oversized American smile and handing out the leaflets says welcome—greeters they call them here—I know, the hymns, and the prayers. And here they are, gay men and women—over 300 of them—in a church and the lights are on. They proceed with candles, cross, book of the Gospels, and the rainbow flag. These people come as they are, most ordinary looking or some in leather, a few in drag, old and young, All smile and sing and hug and seem so confident of their faith, the love of their God and glad to be gay. They speak about justice and equality. They pray for those who have died from AIDS. *Jesus help me*. God have mercy. I can't stand the battle in my heart—it's a wrestling match. I'm not sure about anything other than I'm glad I found this place/city and these people. It is here that I later meet Tom and marry him in 2003.

So what if I have a masters in theology—I know less about God than when I was able to rattle all the answers in the catechism in Sister Clare's Holy Communion class, or the Confirmation classes in St. Michael's Athy, where I had all the answers and was safe in God's hands. That was when the Bishop came to St. Michael's to confirm us all with the chrism oil and a slap on the cheek.

At Dignity and in the University I hear people inviting each other to brunch. I always wanted to get invited to brunch, a mix of breakfast and lunch. They love to eat out in New York. The brunch crowd in the diners are telling their stories, making plans, talking about work, life in the Catholic closets, the ways of the world, and the great sex lives they're having—roars of laughter. At times they'll camp it up, call each other "Mary." I was in the Legion of Mary in Ireland and so they get really hilarious and tell me I am now an official member of the "Legion of Marys" in America. I join the laughter. I often would look at these men and women in Dignity—hugging and embracing and holding hands, and going out for burgers to Julius's, and then on to sing Broadway tunes in Marie's Crisis—and begin to think, *I like the gay world. It breaks open so many doors and walls, opens me to religions and ethnicities, and dozens of Broadway show tunes.*

FROM WEST 4TH STREET I walk till I discover Christopher Street. I have arrived on Gay Street America. But it is number 15 Christopher Street—home of the Oscar Wilde Memorial Bookshop—that changes everything. Up the couple of steps and turn left into the shop, small, warm, cozy, welcoming sounds, music playing in the background.

Books. I always loved books—God, the books, the authors, the shelves filled to the brim: Oscar Wilde, Walt Whitman, Christopher Isherwood, there's the Catholic priest John McNeill, David Leavitt, Armistead Maupin, Audre Lorde, Carter Heyward, *Giovanni's Room*, James Baldwin, John Reid and Andrew Tobias's *The Best Little Boy in the World*.

Craig Rodwell, the owner, seems a little cranky initially; sort of busy, he hears my accent and asks if I know my gay Irish heritage. "No," says I, "not really." *If I was terrified about my own being gay why would I know about my gay Irish heritage?* Unimaginable and impossible.

Soon Craig pulls out from under the counter a thick black book, a copy of *The Black Diaries of Roger Casement*. There's a shamrock inside, dried like a page holder. Roger Casement gay? And then he told me about his naming the shop after Oscar Wilde. Craig made me rethink being Irish and gay, and ever since I think differently about Oscar Wilde.

And then I met the other worker at the store, Jesús Lebron. "What's your name? Jesus, yeah, right." My life is never the same—people do that to each other—why, I don't know. The gift of it really is all that matters.

He looks so gorgeous, so beautiful; brown skin and hair, and the shorts, and the torso tugging his shirt. I get the look. He's interested in me. He wants to see me after he closes the shop some day. *What?* Well I could have done summersaults up and down Christopher Street.

This good-looking, beautiful, attractive Puerto Rican New Yorker falls for me—the short, unfree, gay gobshite from Scarlet Street?

Some nights later we are dancing around the bookshop to the upbeat rhythms of Cris Williamson's "Song of the Soul"— "Truth will unbind you, then we can sing for a long long, long time."

"Why don't you sing this song?"

I sing with the record, "Come to your life like a warrior—you can be happy. Let in the light it will heal you." I am dancing. "Dancing along in the madness," I roar.

Where to go and be together is a challenge. A few times Craig Rodwell gives Jesús the keys to his Bleecker Street apartment. One night we lie on the bed and watch Jesús's favorite film, *West Side Story*. We just lie on the bed together—this is new—something I have been waiting for all my life. The chorus goes, "There's a place for us—somewhere, we'll find a new way of living…" Arms touching, holding, caressing…I fall asleep.

I wake up. The lights are out. I'm in bed in New York with Jesús—he is touching me and I am touching him and I like it and my body likes it and the guilt is nowhere to be found.

Rolling in sheets with no clothes on. Naked. Starkers. Sweat. Friction. I come so quickly. I want to say, "I couldn't help it. I'm sorry."

I think he is asleep. I'm not. I can't believe his name is Jesus. How will I tell them in Ireland that I'm gay, "Oh, and I met someone, and his name is Jesus." That's a far cry from your Liam, Mick, Sean, Paddy, and Willie Joe. But he doesn't say Jesus the way we do, he says, "Hay-Soos." I want to pinch myself.

GAY PRIDE, MY ARSE. I could barely whisper I was gay in the confession box and here we are on 5th Avenue with thousands dancing, leaping, hugging, and roaring for rights. At first Jesús coaches and coaxes me out of the closet. He also gets me to rallies against violence and to ACT UP. He tells me about Audre Lorde—"Your Silence will not protect you." I am with Jesús in Washington for the National March. We silently weave among the quilts—like walking around a graveyard where everyone died in the past six months. So AIDS becomes part of our reality, the language of the infected or affected. *I want to live before I die*—that's what I take away.

We march against AIDS—he shows me how to take passion and love from the sheets to the streets. It's the same love flow—politics, feminism, the personal is the political—he has that activist edge. I can be passionate about apartheid, El Salvador, Nicaragua, nuclear disarmament—but gay rights? I'm more at home with shame and guilt.

Jesús also tells me about counseling and therapy. I have the Irish view: I could talk to someone in the pub on the bar stool. Or else I'll talk to the priest in confession. In America you get three things after a while: allergies, a therapist, and a green card.

Shortly after we meet, Jesús says, "No taxi will pick me up. Brendan, you go ahead and get one." I'm puzzled. He's the citizen and I'm the foreigner. Bouncers check him at bars. He opens my eyes to color prejudice, raw racism, and the difference differences make.

I GO THROUGH THE SEASONS with Jesús. I hear of his Puerto Rican parents making their way to New York after the war. His mother brave and abandoned by an alcoholic father. Poverty grinds down, the projects come up. Italians and Irish move to the suburbs. She learns English, becomes a seamstress, and, with help of welfare, puts all the six kids through Catholic school. She goes to college. She is Catholic and Puerto Rican and loves her two gay sons.

Jesús listens as I tell stories of being a Catholic schoolteacher on the Lower East Side. I tell tales of nuns in Athy, Drogheda, the nineteenth-century Nun of Kenmare, and my father's work in the asbestos factory. I tell him that my mother called and asked, "Do you have a woman in America?" And my answer: "Ma, the only women in my life are you and the Blessed Virgin."

Christmas Eve 1987, the elevator is broken and the smell of piss is strong as we walk up the stairs to the LeBron family's apartment in the South Bronx.

Inside there is a miracle occurring. Not for them, but for me. Like a candle can light up dark peace in a shadow world, they give me something that Christmas to change my life again. Much of it unspoken. In the midst of all the music and pastellas and pork and laughter and poverty, they have each other. (And of course they all seem to have the great teeth.) And here is the familia—mother, daughters, sons, sons-in-law, kids, friends—they are dancing together and I am in the middle. We dance to salsa and Christmas tunes—*Feliz Navidad*, percussion instruments, güiros, maracas, bongos, conga drums, the jíbaro, and a cowbell. This family in the Bronx has embraced me as one of their own.

They make me feel the possibility of coming out of hiding—the Lebron family is showing me how to do it. I leave there a freer man. I want what Jesús Lebron has.

EVENTUALLY I TELL MY SISTERS.

Mary says to me, "God help ye it's not your fault if ye were born that way."

Joan is insistent, "There must be a woman out there somewhere in America that could get it up for ye."

Carmel tries to reassure me, "Well at least you're in America—it could be worse. Whatever ye do, Brendan, don't tell the mother or father—we're the sisters, we can handle it."

So it's done. I'm out—sort of. Now the parents.

SUMMER 1989. I'M HOME IN Scarlet Street for the holiday. There are just two days left before I fly back to New York. I'm in the sitting room, The da is in his usual armchair. It's a bright evening. The only sounds are the pages of the Sunday newspaper turning and the ticking of the clock on the mantlepiece.

Da turns the pages, the glasses on his nose, and looks up every now and then from the page—his huge eyebrows are so prominent, his thick head of white wavy hair—we catch a glimpse and few words are exchanged. I'm sweating. And then I do the unimaginable.

Dad knows something is going on. I never just sit anywhere that long. I'm sitting in the armchair opposite. I look at him, he at me. I say, "Da, there's something I have to tell you." I speak about going to America to do the masters in theology. "Well, there's another reason I left. Da, I'm gay..." My body temperature changes—I feel a rush of heat, blood swirling, mind racing, heart thumping and jumping. Da looks at me.

"Brendan, I been around the world. I've traveled a bit," he says, referring to his time in England and his stint in the RAF in Libya and the Suez. "I've seen a lot in my time. But, knowing you, Brendan," says he, "I see trouble down the line." It's 1989 and we both know he's referring to my health and my activism.

"No, Da. Not at all—thank you, Dad."

He goes back to his paper. I can say no more. The sisters said not to tell the da or he might have a heart attack. Right now I'm feeling like I'm the one having the heart attack.

That's it. Bells ring out. It's Christmas, my birthday, and the New Year all in one. I am present with my da and he accepts me. I am out. I did it. We did it. Me and the da. I feel the tears well inside. I don't want the da to see me. I run out the back door past the mother's rose bushes towards the garden residence, the tears well and flow and will not stop. I look up at the sky. I am happy.

THE N TRAIN. ANOTHER HOT summer's day in 2011 on my way from Astoria to Times Square where I'll change for the 1 train downtown to Christopher Street in Greenwich Village. I have a cup of coffee from Maussaud's in one hand and the paper in the other. Across from me sits a young Mexican couple with a child and a stroller. They smile a lot—eyes to eyes. Then I see his hands waving and her hands waving back. Fingers and hands dancing, guttural grunting sounds, sounds that begin to sound as beautiful as speech. They are deaf. They are communicating with hand waves and finger movements. The child between them stands on the seat, gazing delightfully out the train. They touch her. She looks about five. The cheap stroller is a pink color. I sip the coffee.

My gaze travels from subway ads above their heads to the rows of seated humanity and faces of the world that make New York home. Beside me a woman reads a book in Japanese. On the other side is a Bangladeshi man, Muslim. Opposite a fella in hugging jeans fashionably ripped here and there. He simply looks forward. I see someone reading *Nowy Dziennik*, the New York Polish daily. These N train riders clutch coffee, Bibles, iPods, iPads, novels, Spanish novelettes, Catholic prayer books, and the New York dailies. Here we are, humanity pressed together upon each, snaking our way through tunnels, borough to borough. I let go with the rhythm and hum and daydream, sip coffee, plan events, gaze admiringly at men, and wonder, and wish I got more done in the day, in life.

I reflect on the city I have grown to love as it loves me back, shaping who I am. There is beauty here amidst the fierce, rough edges, where illness and poverty and struggle are in plain sight. Ah, yes, New York, since I first laid the immigrant eyes on you for real I smelled your smells from sidewalk food carts, coffee shops, and diners. With time you slowly seduced me and webbed my gay Irish immigrant heart till one day I declared I am neither Irish nor

American. I'm now a New Yorker. New York's my hometown! I see disease, and poverty to make me weep and despair. I join defiant protests—against war, injustice, and violence—that make me proud. Here, street theater, puppetry, subway singers, dancers, and gymnasts make me pause even when I'm in a mad rush. Sounds of Shakespeare in the park and opera in the subway send me soaring. In New York streets, shelters, and soup kitchens I have seen the capacity of the human heart for terror and tenderness, unimaginable greed and utter goodness. But here, too, I have seen and come to know firsthand a wild embrace and cheering and celebration of the mad diversity and adventurous human imagination that is this rare and queerest piece of earth.

DIS-REMEMBERING STONEWALL

REV. IRENE MONROE

"By institutionalizing memory, resisting the onset of oblivion, recalling the memory of tragedy that for long years remained hidden or unrecognized and by assigning its proper place in the human conscience, we respond to our duty to remember."
—UNESCO Director-General Koïchiro Matsuura[1]

FRIDAY, JUNE 27TH, WAS THE last day of school that year. And with school out, my middle-school cronies and I looked forward to a summer reprieve from rioting against Italian, Irish and Jewish public school kids for being bussed into their neighborhoods. However, the summer months in Brooklyn's African American enclaves only escalated rioting between New York's finest—the New York Police Department—and us. During this tumultuous decade of Black rage and white police raids, knee-jerk responses to each other's slights easily set the stage for a conflagration, creating both instantaneous and momentary fighting alliances in these Black communities— across gangs, class, age, ethnicity and sexual orientations—against police brutality.

That night of June 27th started out no differently than any hot and humid summer Friday night in my neighborhood. Past midnight, folks with no AC or working fans in their homes were just hanging out. Some lounged on the fire escapes while others were on the stoops of their brownstones laughing and shooting the breeze. Some were in heated discussion of Black revolutionary politics, while the Holy Rollers were competing with each other over Scripture. The Jenkins boys were drumming softly on their congas to the hot breezy mood of the night air. And directly under the street lamp was an old beat-up folding card table where the Fletchers and the Andersons, lifelong friends and neighbors, were shouting over a game of bid whist.

The sight of Dupree galloping up the block toward us abruptly interrupted the calm of the first hour of Saturday, June 28th. Dupree stopped in front of the gaming table and yelled out, "The pigs across the bridge are beating up on Black faggots—right now!"

Cissy Anderson, who was just moments from throwing in her hand to go to bed, let out a bloodcurdling scream that shook us and brought a momentary halt to everything.

Nate Anderson grabbed his wife to comfort her and said, "Cissy, calm down."

Those of us not still paralyzed by Cissy's scream quickly gathered around Dupree to hear more.

"The motherfuckers are taken to going after the weakest among us. The pigs busted into this bar and started beating on them."

"Nate," Cissy cried out to her husband, "what we gonna to do?"

Someone from the crowd shouted, "Let's go whip their flat

white asses!" Laughter erupted from the crowd, but so too a volley of humorous and heated insults about the NYPD.

"WE GOT TO ACT. DAMNIT! We got to act—right now!" Dupree stomped his foot and gave a Black Power fist salute.

Heads nodded in agreement as noisy anger rose from the crowd and fighting alliances formed. More people poured onto the street as news spread. The Jenkins boys pounded their drums in a whipping beat, raising a fierce rage and collective resolve.

"Where in the fuck is this bar?" someone else from the crowd shouted.

"Some place called Greenwich Village," Dupree shouted above the noise.

"You mean upstate New York?" someone questioned.

"I ain't got no car," another voice shouted.

"Ain't that Connecticut?" someone else shouted

"I still ain't got no car," shouted the familiar voice.

"No, dumb ass. It's someplace in lower Manhattan," Dupree, annoyed, shouted back to whomever asked the question.

Less than twelve hours ago was the last day of school and none of us school kids could have expected to be in another riot so soon, and especially outside of Brooklyn. Very few of us that night would have known of Greenwich Village, not only because of the insularity of our neighborhoods, but also because of our undisclosed history and impermanent residency in the Village.

GREENWICH VILLAGE IN THE 1800s had housed the largest population for former slaves in the country. "Little Africa," the area around Bleecker, MacDougal, Sullivan, and Thompson Streets established the country's first Black newspaper, *Freedom's Journal* (1827-1829), and first Black theater, the African Grove (1821-1823).

But gentrification forced racial relocation and led to Harlem becoming the Mecca of Black America.

On the surface, the Village appeared then and appears to this day to be a site of easy racial and social coexistence. Its worldly reputation as an artists' enclave, a Bohemian hot spot, and a gay refuge of progressive thinkers and cultural tolerance already attracted people worldwide. And for African Americans running away from the stinging indignities of Jim Crow America and the religious homophobia of the Black Church, it brought hope. But the Village's entrenched milieu of race and class elite liberalism relegated Blacks to the margins of the community.

For lesbian, gay, bisexual, transgender, and queer (LGBTQ) African Americans, our presence in the Village by the 1960s had less to do with the white LGBTQ community's marginal tolerance of us than it had to do with our permanent eviction from Harlem. As a Black cultural and social Mecca, Harlem was home and refuge to New York City's Black population beginning in the early 1900s. And within Harlem various groups of African Americans found their specific niche of self-expression and acceptance. By the time of the Harlem Renaissance, roughly from 1920–1935, LGBTQ African Americans, too, carved out for themselves a queer space of self-expression and acceptance.

During the Harlem Renaissance, a subculture of African American LGBTQ artists and entertainers emerged. Rent parties, speakeasies, sex circuses, and buffet flats were places where many of the major gay and bisexual male literary figures like Alain Locke, Countee Cullen, Langston Hughes, Claude McKay, Wallace Thurman, and Richard Bruce Nugent met, and many of the major bisexual and lesbian blues singers like Bessie Smith, Ma Rainey, "Moms" Mabley, Mabel Hampton, Alberta Hunter, and Gladys Bentley performed. The renowned Savoy Ballroom and the Rockland

Palace hosted drag ball extravaganzas with prizes awarded for the best costumes. Langston Hughes depicted the balls as "spectacles of color." George Chauncey, author of *Gay New York*, wrote that during this period, "perhaps nowhere were more men willing to venture out in public in drag than in Harlem."

Harlem was both a complicated open and closeted queer social hot spot. The annual Hamilton Lodge event openly referred to the drag ball extravaganzas as the "Parade of the Pansies," "Dance of the Fairies" and "'Faggots' Ball." These balls were wildly popular and growing among Harlem's working class, but the constant harassment by white policemen patrolling the neighborhood made the trans community a conspicuous target along with public denouncements of them by Black ministers like the famous Adam Clayton Powell, Sr. of the Abyssinian Baptist Church.

By the '50s, the country was on a campaign to restore traditional gender roles that had been disrupted by World War II, and McCarthyism was its policing mechanism. Special attention was given to LGBTQ Americans because J. Edgar Hoover's FBI and the police department kept a running list of us. Many of Harlem's prominent LGBTQ denizens, who enjoyed a relative openness about their sexual orientation from the 1920s through the 1940s, were driven into the closet. By the 1960s, known queer spaces in Black urban communities like Harlem had for the most part disappeared. With the early part of the 1960s shaped by the Black Civil Rights Movement that was led by homophobic African American ministers, and the latter part of the '60s shaped by the Black Power Movement that was built on the most misogynistic and homophobic strains of Black Nationalism, Black LGBTQ sexualities were perceived as a threat, not only to Black male heterosexuality, the Black Church and community, but also the ontology of blackness itself.

WHEN DUPREE STOPPED IN FRONT of Mr. Fletcher's game table, he was signaling to his aunt and uncle that their son Birdie, who sang like a beautiful songbird, was more than likely in the melee across the bridge. Everyone knew Birdie was gay, and we wondered where he and his "brother-girls," as he dubbed them, had gone on the weekends when they laughed and spoke in code on Sundays about their exploits while robing-up for choir.

CISSY DETESTED THAT HER ELDEST, Nate Turner "Birdie" Anderson, Jr., went outside the community to a white neighborhood to be himself. As it was, Cissy felt she had no control in protecting her children. Her youngest children were ensnared in the ongoing bussing debacle where the court mandated they attend school outside of their neighborhood; and now Birdie went out of the neighborhood to Greenwich Village. She worried about cops killing him, or a gang of white thugs chasing him to his death.

And her fears were not unfounded. That's what had happened to her middle brother, Herndon, twenty years before, in 1949 in Lynchburg, Virginia. He was gang-raped, but his death was reported as a lynching. Herndon was gay, an effeminate and slight man, no more than five feet seven inches tall, weighing roughly one hundred forty pounds, like his nephew Birdie. When he went to visit friends on his own while strolling down dirt roads in Lynchburg, rednecks— a bunch of them together—would try to catch him. When they did they would tie him to the back seat of their pick-up truck and take him into the woods to gang-rape him, and make Herndon perform fellatio on them. On the day they killed Herndon, he'd refused to give them the satisfaction they demanded. The men mutilated Herndon, vying for his genitals as souvenirs to sell; but they eventually divided the pieces among themselves and kept them.

Nate, Sr., too, worried about his eldest son. When Birdie told his dad he was gay, his father asked him if he understood that he didn't know how to keep him safe, especially if his son wandered out of his purview. Mr. Anderson took great pride in keeping his family together and safe, which is why he had hightailed it up North to Brooklyn, bringing his childhood sweetheart Cissy with him after he'd shot dead two of Herndon's rapists—and turned Bo Milt, the third rapist, into a quadriplegic by repeatedly running him over with his truck while Bo Milt yelled, "Nigger, stop!"

NATE TURNER ANDERSON SR. WAS a race man: like the African prince High John the Conqueror, he was handsome, charming, beguiling, and not to be messed with. At six feet eight inches tall, Nate, Sr. was barrel-chested and a blue-black complexioned man of few words with a distinctive bass voice that commanded attention. When his voice rose above Dupree's and the crowd, we were as shocked to silence as we were by Cissy's bloodcurdling scream.

"My son is somewhere there and I need you all to help me find him and bring him home safely to his mother and me."

The charge to find Birdie trumped, for some, our rage to fight cops. Rechanneling our energy around Nate, Sr., groups of us hopped the IRT 7th Avenue subway line to the Village.

Coming out of the subway station at Christopher Street we could hear the commotion. The shoving and pushing by both protestors and police yanked three of us away from the core group; we were left to fend for ourselves. When we made our way into the crowd swarming the front of the Stonewall Inn, we too threw bottles, garbage, and anything we could get our hands on. In the midst of the riot I realized the moment looked and felt similar to the Martin Luther King riot. But this time I knew who the LGBTQ folks fighting along with us were.

AS THE MOMENTUM OF THE crowd pushed my small group to Waverly Place, a block away from the Stonewall, we witnessed two white cops pummeling a Black drag queen. "I should shove this stick up your ass," said one of the cops as he pulled up her dress with a nightstick in his hand. The taller of the two cops yanked off her wig and laughingly tossed it to the other cop. In spotting us, the cop who caught the wig threw it at us yelling, "You nigger fags get away!"

The wig missed and landed about a foot away from us, but the cop's words hit, striking fear. And with just the three of us traveling together—the boys were high school football linebackers and me, a middle schooler—and being the youngest and only girl with them, I felt vulnerable after having lost Nate, Sr. and the group. Witnessing the beat-down and disrobing of the drag queen made me want to cry, but I fought back the tears and ran, following the boys down the block.

When we came home the night of June 28th, we still had no idea of Birdie's fate. Throughout that day and the night before we had witnessed so many Birdies beaten badly. We stopped by the Andersons to convey our concerns and that we had looked for Birdie. Cissy told us that he was safely home, having sustained a number of blunt trauma injuries—a black eye, assorted bruises, broken ribs, a sprained ankle, and a busted lip. None of us know how Nate, Sr. found Birdie in the riot, but he did—we assumed parental instinct trumped the seemingly impossible.

When I look back at the first night of the Stonewall Inn riots, I could have never imagined its future importance. The first night played out no differently from previous riots with Black Americans and white policemen. And so too, it being underreported. But I was there.

ON THE FIRST NIGHT OF the Stonewall Inn riots, African Americans and Latinos were the largest percentage of the protestors because we heavily frequented the bar. For Black and Latino homeless youth and young adults, who slept in nearby Christopher Park, the Stonewall Inn was their stable domicile. The Stonewall Inn being raided was nothing new. In the 1960s gay bars in the Village were routinely raided, but, "Race is said to have been another factor. The decision by the police to raid the bar in the manner they did may have been influenced by the fact that most of the 'homosexuals' they would encounter were of color, and therefore even more objectionable." [2]

Although, today, African American and Latino trans communities are relegated to the margins of Greenwich Village, if not expulsed from it, these communities, nonetheless, force their way into being a visible and powerful presence in our lives, leaving indelible imprints while confronted with not only transphobia but also "trans-amnesia." The inspiration and source of an LGBTQ movement post-Stonewall is an appropriation of a Black, brown, trans and queer liberation narrative and struggle. The Stonewall Riot of June 27-29, 1969 in Greenwich Village started on the backs of working class African American and Latino queers who patronized that bar. Those brown and Black LGBTQ people are not only absent from the photos of that night, but have been bleached from its written history. Many LGBTQ Blacks and Latinos argue that one of the reasons for the gulf between whites and themselves is about how the dominant queer community rewrote and continues to control the narrative of Stonewall.

1. The UNESCO Slave Route Project, "Lest We Forget: the Triumph Over Slavery," that marked the United Nations General Assembly's resolution proclaiming 2004 "The International Year to Commemorate the Struggle Against Slavery and Its Abolition."

2. T-Vox contributors, "The Stonewall Riots," T-Vox, Wikimedia Foundation Inc., http://www.t-vox.org/index.php?title=Stonewall_riots (accessed December 3, 2011).

BEFORE I BEGIN

DAVID McCONNELL

JOE BRAINARD LIVED IN A loft on Greene Street. Long ago, when white Akitas were the fad dog in New York, Chris Cox took me over to meet him. I was going to sublet the place for the summer. As we climbed the usual kilometer-long SoHo flight of stairs, Chris, a writer and editor who'd admitted he was a "talent snob" and all of whose friends, to hear him tell it, were legends (I was starting to think this might be true), quickly narrated Joe's life with the cheerful coldness I was still young and suburban enough to find amoral, a bit frightening. As if my family's cooing caveats of niceness when gossiping constituted morality!

"Well, he was Frank O'Hara's boyfriend. Until Frank got run over by the dune buggy on Fire Island. But he knows everybody, and everybody loves him. He wrote *I Remember*, but he was mostly famous for his collages. He was a complete speed freak for years, so it sort of made sense that he was always cutting up these tiny pieces of paper and putting them together. And he used to stutter so badly you'd have to write your whole dinner conversation on the napkins. Then he quit speed and just stopped making art. It's kind of a mystery. Actually—" Chris stopped me. His balding forehead came toward my chin. "The big mystery is nobody knows how he gets his money. People say his friend Kenward Elmslie gave him all this money—just decided one day that Joe should never have to work."

Joe nodded us into the loft bashfully, laughing at himself in a soft pant for no reason whatsoever. He immediately removed his glasses after looking at me. He wore jeans and a white shirt open over his grizzled chest. He was slender, curly-haired, homely, and vaguely Italian-looking, like a high-end cobbler, except he wore black Keds.

Repetition—it shouldn't be surprising in a stutterer—had a magical quality for Joe. Since "the ear likes repetition," you could say his life was more like music than narrative. Whenever I returned to Greene Street after that first visit he would answer the door with exactly the same soft self-conscious laughter, wearing exactly the same clothes, taking the same stiff waltzing steps of welcome into the loft. The apartment, mostly empty, never changed. It smelled of him. He was there all day. His routines, the magazines, the books, the eye drops, the dinners, the summers in Vermont tanning in a black Speedo, the way he wrote LOVE JOE in block letters at the end of every note, were all unvarying. But you never thought "boring" about Joe. Joe's routines seemed honed, meticulously aware, and were as delightful to observe as glass-covered clockwork.

Still, the words Chris had used burned my ears: "He just stopped making art. It's a mystery." Even before I made it to the top of the stairs, I started to feel disappointment and pity for the man I was about to meet. I was young. I had a plan. It's hardly an exaggeration to say the only thing I thought about in those days was how not to give up making art. I thought about it so obsessively I wasn't able to make much art to speak of. A "stopper" was a figure of horror and fascination. (Another great stopper, Rimbaud, probably fascinates ambitious young artists as much for his stopping as for his jerky genius.)

Like a wizard waving the sleeve of his houppelande, Joe dissipated my pity the instant he opened the door. Almost the first thing I thought was, *Oh my god! This guy really is an artist!* I don't know what made me think it (quite possibly Chris's legend-spinning), but I was certain I was right and that my rightness in using that particular word, "artist," mattered. It didn't and doesn't, of course, but I'm describing a youthful state of mind as characteristic as love and not so different. I seemed to recognize Joe as soon as I met him.

The lives of many interesting people in New York appear pretty uninteresting. Joe wasn't alone. There's chat, drinking, smoking (not quite so much anymore), going to restaurants, and either actually attending shows, exhibitions, and performances or just boning up on what's out there. Even Truman Capote erred by introducing an absurd bit of action—a runaway horse—into his portrait of New York in *Breakfast at Tiffany's*. Because there is no real action here, only talk in restaurants, bars, offices, and apartments. Manhattanites consider it their privilege to exist at a slight critical remove from the world. Apart from the brutal shock of the event itself, the destruction of the World Trade Center caused a lingering overtone of mild shock that such an eventful event could occur at all in the metropolis of talk and thought.

Of course, there was a Joe before I knew him, a Joe before this stopped—but not pitiable—version. By the time I came along, that Joe existed in dozens of boxes, a slightly obsessive auto-archive stacked on floor-to-ceiling metal shelves along the wall opposite the door. Inside were all sorts of treasures. A playful "target painting" collaboration with Jasper Johns, the brush they used glued onto it. A beautiful note of apology to Keith McDermott. A cherished pair of torn and embroidered bell bottoms—very '60s!—maybe from when Joe was begging on the streets. You're not supposed to go through other people's stuff, but as I told Joe, "You almost have the right when you're subletting—" I caught my breath in alarm, *"Not that I ever did that when I was here!"*

He chuckled.

Joe couldn't figure out why I was interested in him. "I would get it with John Ashbery or somebody. But I keep thinking, 'Why me?'"

Gentle as he was, everything had to be his way. With hesitant murmurs he ran everything according to his routines while I talked and talked, sometimes nervous flights of nonsense, sometimes scathing contempt for, for example, the unoriginality of Akita owners: what was going to happen to all those big wintry dogs?

We were often the only ones in the restaurant, because it was Joe's habit to eat at six-thirty.

"Boring," he allowed.

"No!" I said devotedly.

Every so often he became self-conscious of the sameness of our evenings and, very deliberately, decided he would teach me something or that we'd do something different. One night he taught me how to fry bread in butter, the only thing he knew how to cook (besides peanut butter and jelly sandwiches). One afternoon we went out to buy the biggest TV possible. Once he decided he would come to visit me in Hudson—very surprising, since it was difficult to get him to travel. He loved the laundry that fluttered on lines zigzagging across backyards everywhere. The laundry made Hudson at that time look like a Hiroshige ukiyo-e of Edo on a festival day. Plum, gray, brick, pale yellow, and blue were the colors.

"Want to see something bad I did?" he asked back in New York. He showed me a German reprint of a '60s poem of his. "It's really awful. But sometimes you just have to publish whatever," he said meaningfully. "I don't know why these Germans like it, but they do. Here, I'll show you something I think is good…" He opened an art magazine and sat me down, completely unlike himself.

Though everyone loved him, he was solitary. Like a tightrope bicyclist he balanced two particular loves on a long beam: Kenward, the rich older one, and Keith, the beautiful young one. Both of them saw other people, but you had a feeling maybe they pined for Joe. Joe always lived alone. He ran into a friend of mine in a bookstore, and though they hardly knew each other, Joe kissed him hello and goodbye—Joe was a big kisser. My friend later told me with a grin, "Him kissing me was so—I mean, he's really the only person like that: he lives alone, but you don't feel at all sorry for him." (Like art for me, my friend's agonizing fixation was love. In Joe he thought he recognized someone free of the rules.)

I read *Sentimental Education* while I was staying at Joe's, and its willfully intense bleakness made me throw myself on Joe's bed, crying. What was the point in going on? I wasn't at all happy in those days. That whole summer I wrote Joe endless letters and lived for his unpretentious responses, "Why me?" always between the lines. But there was a limit to the consolation Joe gave, if only because there's a limit to the consolation possible in life, especially when it comes to the vast and painful unhappiness of someone young. As a matter of fact, Joe's limits gleamed very bright and you felt as if his clockwork and the clockwork of the universe, of the possible, were identical: "I don't think I feel like it," he'd Bartlebyze as easily as he said "Hello."

Any Tulsa-boy luxury Joe indulged in, the Armani suit or the cashmere blanket or the TV, would stand out like a sore thumb in that barren, undecorated loft. Each thing was its own complete idea, and he had no need of the well-knit, false background of a "lifestyle."

"Where do you get your money, Joe? Everybody says Kenward gave you millions of dollars or something."

He laughed, "No. I just sell pictures. You gotta live, right?"

"So you think of yourself more as a painter than a writer?"

"Oh, yeah."

As I mentioned, recognizing Joe as an artist was a kid thing, a feeling. It now occurs to me—and my remembering all this is surprisingly uncertain, finely layered with strange old emotion—that I also felt like he recognized me, even though, no matter what I may have wanted to call myself, I wasn't really an artist yet in that I hadn't done much. Maybe either stopping or starting caused me an identical horror. Art's eternity and my childish, idle, personal sense of eternity must have seemed the same thing, too precious to disturb. As if I knew that from the moment I chose to do something I couldn't enjoy being aware of it anymore. As if I knew you can't live forever at a critical remove. As if when you start to live, you die.

Joe didn't think less of me for being a rich kid, possibly spoiled. He also never scolded me for my sweeping judgments about everything or for my mirthful bitterness. Rather, he seemed to enjoy the wit of a good insult, though he was incapable of any himself. You would never have noticed how snarky I was—I seemed meek, coltish, obsequious. I made Joe write a letter of introduction to an author I longed to meet, and he summed me up as follows: "He's goofy. You'll like him."

In the same way Joe was tolerant of rich people, he also enjoyed the absurd culture of gay people, which surrounded him without swamping him in "lifestyle." He loved dumb gay cards and gay magazines, and gay parades—especially if someone reached out to stroke his furry chest. He also liked a restaurant called Christopher's on Christopher Street. This was probably the only "gay restaurant" at the time, and it harked back to an era long before the age of Akitas. Joe even felt the need to warn me that it was "really gay." No windows and a heavy portière gave the place an air of '50s secrecy and subversion. And the way the almost all-male clientele looked with dainty, yet subtly leering, expressions of ennui when we entered had a carnivalesque note of 1920s or eighteenth-century depravity. I'd certainly never seen anything like it. At the time I liked to pretend that everything gay was already the oldest of old hat and had nothing to do with me, but Christopher's was so exotic I really did feel completely alien, though I imagine the place wasn't that different from the awful gay restaurants on Eighth Avenue today.

Christopher's, as I remember it, was all black with small black tables. Pencil-thin spotlights shone down on tiny glass vases holding a single flower. There was probably a large black and white art photograph of a Calla lily on the wall. The nearly sexually dimorphic but same-sex couples and the queeny waiters drawling, "Joooe! Jooooe, you darling man! Still not answering your phone because you don't feel like it?" and the background of tittering and exclamation caused me a frisson of snobbery. WASPy politesse or love for Joe was enough for me to tough it out, though. I remember I was pretty frosty with the waiter that first time, which earned me a series of special, amused leers. My lofty manners must have looked immensely "gay," a perfect fit for the place.

On that occasion, endless chatter abandoned me and we fell into one of the relaxed silences that Joe believed were the true sign of companionability. He claimed he rarely spoke with Kenward all summer long in Vermont. Did I mind if he ate salad with his fingers? Of course not. Delicately, he ate a leaf of butter lettuce like a French fry. He wiped his fingers and, after a polite physical stutter, pulled my hand into the three- or four-inch wide pool of light. He placed his hand next to mine for comparison. I asked, "What do you see?" With the usual laughing half-murmur of hesitation, he said, "It's so interesting. You're hand is obviously really young. Mine isn't." As if drawing attention to a section of a painting he moved his index finger over the ridges of tendons on the back of his hand. "See, this part is actually covered with tiny lines, though you don't really notice them." He studied our hands for a long time, and it was wonderful to watch him look, really look, at something. He didn't like it so much the other way around, though. He almost got cross one morning when I stood next to him and announced I was going to watch him shave, because everybody did it in a different way and made strange, comical expressions. "No, don't. I don't really like that."

Ordinarily it was hard to get him to say he didn't like things or people. He didn't know how to hate. I considered this a challenge and asked him to think as hard as he could and tell me the name of someone he hated.

"Well, I don't like Van Gogh very much."

"No, come on! A real person."

He finally came up with a name, but cautioned me, "It's not that I actually hate him. But everybody says he lies all the time, and I guess I don't really like that."

He did start to work a bit. He hired some models and drew. For a long time, at a big oaken block of a desk, he practiced painting with a Japanese brush and ink. He shrugged that he didn't have that much ambition but said it felt great to work. I'd moved to Paris where I was just as unhappy as ever. When I visited New York I stayed with Joe. I got out of bed in the middle of the night and lay on the floorboards in a wash of streetlight. The place smelled of Joe, which was comforting, but I was feeling tragic because you can never get as close to people as you want. He would've hated me watching him in his sleep. Disliked. Before arriving I'd spoken to a friend on the phone. He said, "I talked about you with Joe last night. I got the feeling all you'd have to do is say the word and you could be with him." Looking at Joe in his sleep, I realized this could never happen and was probably not true anyway. That friend was speaking for himself and didn't know it: the two of us were a little bit in love but clueless about it or at a slight critical remove from the fact.

One painful thing was that no one knew Joe and I were friends. Joe operated like that. You got put in one of his autobiographical boxes. After he died I wrote a rather pathetic note to Kenward saying I wanted to talk about Joe. I'd never really met Kenward except to say hello a few times. But I felt like every link to Joe had snapped. So I mentioned the odd minutiae that Kenward's sister was married to the obstetrician who'd delivered me in Cleveland and had been friends with my Aunt Mary. It was a desperate, fly-casting sort of connection and Kenward never wrote me back, which was disappointing, though he was probably upset at the time. Luckily, I later became friends with Keith.

One of the last things I remember Joe saying to me was, "I'm not really here." On a summer day I was walking along Bleecker Street near Hudson and ran into Joe. It didn't occur to me how strange it was that he wasn't in Vermont. He knew it. He was acting guilty. Maybe his soft, panting laughter lasted a little longer than usual. He said, "I'm not really here." He sat me on one of the park benches by 11th Street and we talked. It was all very strange. Not routine. He said "a business thing" had brought him into the city. I told him everything was fine with me but I must have looked a little forlorn, because at some point he warned, "You know, it can always get worse." He made that gloomy thought sound friendly and gentle.

I realize I've made this essay a kind of butterfly. I'm still not sure why, but I haven't dared more that touch lightly here and there on flowers of the past. I do remember that when Joe's ink paintings were published along with some of Kenward's poems, I was immensely proud of the copy Joe gave me, though Joe was always giving little gifts. I usually never cared for the memorabilia of art, but in this case, the token from Joe—his work—meant the world to me. I even asked him to sign it, though ordinarily I find the fetish of the signed copy meaningless. He took the book and a pen and stalled, "I never know what to say in these things."

"Well," I said, "You could try, 'For David. I think you're a great guy and I love you. Joe.'"

Joe happily printed my dictation in his block hand. I couldn't help feeling a ghost of real disappointment, which I tried to make comical by pouting, "But now I'll never know if you really meant it. You would've just written whatever I said."

"Not whatever," he answered mysteriously. His lingering smile made fond fun of me, but also somehow acknowledged the notion that I had a real worry, because, of course, you can't ever really know what people mean.

A BITE OF
THE BIG APPLE

VAL McDERMID

1979

AMONG THE QUESTIONS I HAD to answer when I applied for my U.S. visa was whether I was homosexual. I didn't want to lie but I did desperately want to visit America, so I ticked the box that denied who I was. Somewhere in Nebraska there is probably a repository that contains the visa application where I lied. These days, I wouldn't be refused entry for being gay. But at the back of my mind, there still lurks the anxiety that I might be refused for having had the temerity to lie to the U.S. Government.

I was twenty-four years old and I'd never found much in the

way of community. There seemed to be plenty of social possibilities for gay men, but not for women. There were one or two places in London where you could meet a reasonably wide range of interesting lesbians, but outside the capital, it was much harder to make contact. And I was determined not to settle for a relationship with someone just because she was the only other out lesbian in a fifty-mile radius.

Back then I was a fledgling journalist in Glasgow. It wasn't the easiest place to be out but it was too late for me to re-enter the closet, even if I'd wanted to. There wasn't much of a lesbian scene in Scotland. There certainly weren't any lesbian bars. Every time I'd gone somewhere mentioned in *Gay News*, I'd been the only woman in the place. On the rare occasions I found myself in the company of fellow travelers, they generally freaked out when I admitted to working for the leading Scottish tabloid newspaper. I was tainted by association, suspect because of where I worked. It never seemed to cross their minds that, if they were right to be afraid of my employers, I was the one taking the real chances.

I wanted to find somewhere I could genuinely be out and proud. So I took advantage of the cheap flights offered by Freddie Laker's Skytrain and headed off for New York with two goals in mind—getting my hands on as many American crime novels as I could stuff into the empty holdall I'd packed in my suitcase, and experiencing an authentic lesbian bar.

What I wasn't expecting was love at first sight. New York was everything I dreamed it would be. Manhattan was like the movies, only more so. Vibrant, glamorous, crammed with must-see, must-do, must-have moments. And a bit scuffed round the edges, a sense of possible danger always snuggling suggestively against the allure. I suspected she might be very bad for me, but I couldn't resist her.

I'd bought a gay guide to the U.S., which concentrated on the male scene, but did include some lesbian listings. I was staying with a college friend and her American husband, so there were a couple of evenings of social catch-up to be done before I could venture out into the city alone. Finally, I left the Upper West Side behind me and headed south on a smelly, rattling subway train. My destination: a bar full of lesbians.

Emerging from the subway at Christopher Street and Sheridan Square, I had the distinct sensation of having shifted into a different dimension. Everywhere I looked, my eye was caught by moments of unexpectedness. Men in leather with peaked caps. Men in tight denim with big moustaches and swagger. Two women arm-in-arm waiting to cross at the lights. All apparently no big deal here in New York.

In Glasgow, they'd have earned a kicking. Even in London, they wouldn't have walked the streets with the same insouciance. But in Greenwich Village they'd rioted at the Stonewall Bar for the right to be themselves, and here they were, ten years on, exercising it right before my eyes.

I checked the street signs and tried to breathe normally as I waited for the light to change. When it did, I didn't move. I stood on the corner through another three cycles of Walk, Don't Walk before I crossed over. What I feared was that it would be another disappointment. Another depressing dive full of gay men, another gauntlet of hostile stares.

I walked along the edge of the sidewalk, flicking my eyes sideways to check out storefronts and bars and apartment entrances. I spotted it right away. The Duchess, there on Grove Street where the guide had said it would be. Impossible to see inside, though. I kept going, all the way round the block, cursing myself for my cowardice. "How bad can it be? It can't be seedier than the back bar of that terrible hotel in Plymouth. It can't be scarier than that dive you walked into in Glasgow, where the barman literally growled at you," I told myself. It was New York; nobody looked twice at a madwoman stalking the street, talking to herself.

This time, when I rounded the corner, I pushed the door open and walked in.

My first impression was that it wasn't so different from other bars. Cigarette smoke and stale beer hung in the air; there was the mutter of conversation with music as a counterpoint; and several heads turned to check out the newcomer as I walked in. But almost instantly it dawned on me that this was unlike any bar I'd ever been in because everyone in here was a woman.

I looked around, drinking in the scenery. There were women in jeans and plaid shirts, women in chinos and tight T-shirts, women in dresses, women in suits, women in overalls. There were women in work boots and sneakers and high heels. Women with cropped hair, women with long hair, women with sharp stylish cuts and women with, frankly, bad hair.

With my Levis and sweatshirt, my black Le Coq Sportif shoes and my footballer's perm, I fit right in. No, really, I did. Well, I must have done because nobody gave me a second look. Apparently I belonged. I was a tourist only in the sense of being from out of town.

I made my way to the bar and slid on to a vacant stool. I waited for the bartender to finish serving a customer, reveling in the easy banter between them. Clearly they knew each other well; this was a place that had regulars who actually spoke to each other, unlike the gay bars I'd experienced in London, where the volume of the music made conversation impossible.

When she turned to me, the bartender smiled like she was pleased to see me, completing my sense of having been transported into another dimension. In 1979 in Glasgow, bar staff tended not to smile at lone female customers. It wasn't that long since women had only been welcome in pubs if they were in the company of a man. My local West End pub didn't even have a women's bathroom. If I needed to pee, I'd have to go to the Safari Lounge next door. (I'm not making this up, you know...)

I asked for a beer. I'd had time to scan the fridge and I knew enough about what I liked to ask for a Michelob by name. Trying to blend in with the local color is second nature to a journalist. But I couldn't quite hide the accent. The two women on my left leaned forward and gave me curious, appraising stares.

"Are you British?" I had already learned this was the inevitable question whenever I opened my mouth in New York.

"Scottish," I said. My standard answer. I'd discovered it opened up the conversation better than a simple, "Yes."

And we were off.

I revisited The Duchess a couple more times during the week I spent in New York. Every time, women talked to me, relaxed and friendly, curious about where I came from and what life was like there. Women even flirted with me, and that was fun, too. I wasn't looking for a sexual adventure, but it felt good to know that had been a possibility.

What I was looking for, what I found, was confirmation that what I believed should be possible could actually exist. In New York in 1979, I discovered that in at least one corner of one city, gay men and lesbians had started to achieve what I'd always dreamed of—an environment where we could live our lives as if we were normal. We could walk down the street hand-in-hand, drink in bars where nobody raised an eyebrow if a woman kissed a woman, and eat in restaurants where nobody blinked at the leather men and the drag queens.

It gave me hope. It sent me back to a city repressed evenhand-edly by Calvinism and Catholicism with a conviction that the possibility of change was worth fighting for. It gave me the strength to be myself. It gave me pride.

1987

MY LIFE WAS AT A turning point. I'd just emerged from a six-year relationship, bloodied but unbowed. My first book was about to be published, a crime novel introducing Britain's first lesbian detective. I was on the point of being promoted to Northern Bureau Chief of the national newspaper I worked for. It was time, I reckoned, to treat myself to a summer holiday back in New York.

By now, I was living in the North of England. I'd moved from Glasgow to Manchester at the perfect time. The capital of the North was just establishing itself as the capital of Gay UK with the development of the Gay Village, a section of town that was trying to graduate from sleazy red light district to stylish pink pound territory. In spite of a police chief whose response to the AIDS epidemic was to describe gays as "swirling around in a cesspit of their own making," we were trying very hard to be out and proud on Canal Street.

We even had a couple of lesbian venues. But Friday night upstairs at the Thompson Arms—a.k.a. Sappho's—was still a much grimmer and cagier proposition than my memories of The Duchess. I wanted to remind myself of the easy camaraderie I'd found in the other Village.

The friends I'd stayed with on my previous visit were out of town for the summer and were happy for me to borrow their apartment for as long as I wanted it. It was, by New York standards, pretty glamorous—the penthouse of an apartment block on West End Avenue, with its own roof terrace. In my naïveté, I thought this was how most people lived in Manhattan. I know better now.

When I emerged from the subway at Sheridan Square this time,

I was instantly struck by how much more visibly gay the area was. It wasn't just the people on the streets. Newsstands displayed gay publications, boutique windows displayed outfits that seemed to epitomize camp, other stores promised S/M equipment and sex toys. And there was one place that advertised body piercing, "With or without pain. Your choice." The streets bustled, the bars were busy, the whole area was buzzing with life.

This time, I crossed the street on a high, eager to see what changes time had brought to The Duchess.

I almost walked past it. Mostly because it wasn't The Duchess anymore, it was The Grove. I felt a momentary twinge of anxiety. Not all change is for the better, after all.

I pushed the door open and walked in. It was dimmer than I remembered, the music more insistent, the feel a little more sophisticated than the old neighborhood bar that occupied such a prominent slot in my nostalgic memory. But the air was still thick with smoke and beer, and there still wasn't a man in sight. I relaxed and made for the bar.

Nursing my Michelob, I looked around. It still seemed to be home to a wide range of women who liked to talk. When a stool came free, I hitched myself on to it and smiled at the woman who half-turned to check out who had moved in next to her. She smiled back and the woman on her other side spoke to me.

"Hi, you're new here, aren't you?"

So, still a neighborhood bar in its own way. "I'm just visiting," I said. And of course, the accent worked its usual magic. Before long, the three of us were swapping stories, trading tales and sharing jokes. Naturally, because I was bursting with pride about *Report for Murder*, I had to drag the conversation around to my upcoming debut novel.

"Really? That's great." The woman next to me said, her face

lighting up in genuine appreciation. "I've got a book in the works. too. It's not a mystery, though. It's about a lesbian vampire."

Yes. It's true. Of all the bar stools in all the world, I'd ended up sitting next to Jewelle Gomez, the inimitable creator of *The Gilda Stories*. It would be a few years before Firebrand published her groundbreaking book of lesbian vampire stories, but that night in 1987, I heard about the adventures of Gilda for the first time. Jewelle gave me her business card; I still have it in a box of mementos from that U.S. trip. These days, we'd have swapped email addresses and kept in touch via Facebook or Twitter. We didn't have that ease of contact back then; now, we just grin when we run into each other, remembering that night all those years ago when Lindsay Gordon and Gilda first bumped fists.

Really, that would have been enough of a good memory for one trip. And a certain kind of memoir would leave it there, the meeting of two lesbian writers preserved in a snapshot. But my memories of New York in 1987 are so intimately bound up with Sandie Reilly, it would be dishonest to rub her out of the picture.

I can't remember who introduced us, but it was definitely that first evening in The Grove. Sandie Reilly in a business suit, long legs crossed on a bar stool, a high-heeled shoe dangling from the foot that beat almost imperceptible time to the music. Red hair, sparkling blue eyes screwed up against her cigarette smoke, a half-smile never far from her face. I didn't know the expression "lipstick lesbian" then, but it wouldn't have made any difference. I've never been one for putting people into boxes. What I remember most is her firecracker sense of humor and the way she would put her hand on my arm when she wanted to make sure I was paying attention. I couldn't believe she was single. More than that, I couldn't believe she was interested in me.

We shared a few beers, then she announced she had to go. I was disappointed; I'd dared to hope for a more spectacular end to the evening. But it wasn't the end of the story. "I really do have to go," she said. "I have an early meeting. But we could meet tomorrow, if you like?"

Of course I liked. She disappeared in a cloud of Camel smoke, leaving behind a promise to meet me next evening in The Grove.

I don't remember what I did the next day except that I went shopping for breakfast and tidied the vast bed, so much bigger than the ones we had back in the UK then. Showered and changed, I walked into The Grove twenty minutes early. And she was there already, Sandie Reilly in a different business suit but just as gorgeous as she'd been in my mind's eye. She greeted me with a kiss then rubbed her lipstick from my mouth with the side of her thumb in a surprisingly intimate gesture.

We drank a beer and she smoked a couple of cigarettes then she suggested a bar in nearby Christopher Street where there would be singers from musical theatre on their off-nights standing round the piano, a free performance for anyone who happened by. I've always loved singing, especially the impromptu kind, so I was happy to be led by the hand to a crowded bar where we squeezed into a corner that imposed its own intimacy on us.

It was after eleven when we emerged from the bar, hoarse from singing along with show tunes and torch songs, and we both knew we were heading back to the Upper West Side. I made for the subway station but she pulled me back firmly. "Are you crazy? At this time of night? It's easy to see you're a tourist," she scolded me as she hailed a cab.

All I am prepared to say is that I'm very glad Sandie didn't have an early meeting in the morning. Or the morning after that. Or the whole weekend when the sun shone on our penthouse terrace and we only got dressed to answer the door to the food delivery boys.

It was the kind of adventure everyone should have at least once in their life—an interlude that makes no demands beyond itself, that is its own reward and needs nothing more. For me, it was the perfect stepping stone between the end of a relationship and the launch of my new life as a published writer.

After the weekend, we unglued ourselves from each other and Sandie went back to her ordinary life on Wall Street. I was headed out of town for a few days, visiting my hosts in upstate New York. But I'd be back by the end of the week, and we made plans for the following weekend. Dinner, the opera and, of course, a return visit to The Grove.

Meanwhile, I had to plug myself back into my normal life. My friend Antonia and her husband have a house on the shores of Lake Champlain, that long finger of water that forms part of the border between Vermont and New York State. Antonia and I became friends at Oxford, in spite of the difference in our backgrounds. She was a diplomat's daughter, educated at private schools, born to privilege and position. And it didn't matter a damn that I was a working class coal miner's granddaughter because we were equals in the things that mattered.

They'd just had twin daughters, and although the girls were the new center around which their lives revolved, that didn't mean an end to adult pleasures. That week, I felt I'd finally landed in the life I'd always wanted. My first book was due to be published in a week's time; I was traveling the world young, free, and single, able to dive headlong into adventures like Sandie Reilly; I had an interesting job and a beautiful house in one of the most dramatic landscapes in England. And I was staying in a glamorous house in a stunning setting, eating and drinking like a king, sailing and swimming to the manner born.

I had no premonition that anything existed that could destroy that feeling of contentment.

I was swimming in the chilly dark waters of Lake Champlain when it happened, though I was oblivious to it at the time. We came out of the water and ran up to the house, our only thought how soon we could get dried off and settled in front of the log fire with a glass of good malt whisky.

It was the middle of the night before I found out my life had changed irrevocably. I drifted out of sleep, woken by a distant phone ringing. I turned over and set my compass for unconsciousness but before I could make it, Antonia was standing in front of me, her face crumpled and distressed. "The phone…it's for you."

It made no sense, but I rolled out of bed and went through to the phone anyway. Her husband held the receiver out to me. "I thought it was Antonia's mother. She always gets the time difference wrong," he said inconsequentially.

The voice on the other end was familiar. My former English teacher, who was also a friend of my parents. It made no sense to me. "We've been trying to get hold of you," he said, his voice hesitant. "I had to phone your work, they gave me this number for you. It's your dad. I'm so sorry. He was playing bowls. He walked out on the green to play the final of the tournament. And he just dropped down dead." His voice kept going, but I couldn't make out the words.

Later that day, I was walking in the rain in Central Park. Antonia had organized everything; a flight from Burlington to New York, then a night flight back to Scotland via Paris. I'd been back to the apartment to pack my bags, but I still had four hours to kill. So I bought my first packet of cigarettes in years and walked. Smoke and rain, good excuses for a wet face and red eyes. The dye in my passport ran as I got soaked to the skin; for years, I couldn't escape remembrance of that day every time I traveled abroad.

Days later, I remembered my date to meet Sandie Reilly at The Grove. It felt like an arrangement made by someone else, someone whose charmed life had nothing to do with mine. Still, I left a message on her answering machine. I hope she got it. I wouldn't like her to think I'd stood her up for anything less than a funeral.

2011

THE LANDING GEAR ENGAGES WITH the usual whine and clunk as we make our final approach to JFK. I switch off my e-reader at the request of the cabin steward and return my seat to the landing position. The first time I flew into this airport, I was crammed in the rear of a budget airline, the ashtray in my seat arm equally crammed with cigarette ends. These days, I'm one of the lucky ones. This time, I'm in business class and the world I move in has largely been cleansed of tobacco. It's more comfortable and I definitely smell better.

One of the many other things that's different these days is that sometimes I have to do crazy things like drop my kid off at school in the morning then fly into New York for two nights and three days of business meetings and an awards ceremony. I know there are people who jet back and forth across the Atlantic on a weekly basis, but I don't envy them. I feel sorry for them.

But I don't feel sorry for myself. I could live without the travel, it's true, yet this trip is like a Christmas stocking, filled to the brim with good things. For one, I'm in New York, one of the few cities that still feel as magical as it did the first time I walked its streets. I'm going to drink cocktails and listen to writers and revel in the backdrop I've come to know so well over the past twenty-some years.

For another, I'm going to see my wife, Kelly, the lesbian publisher, who has been in her native U.S. on a business trip for the past three weeks. She's been sweet-talking her authors instead of me, cozying up to her distributors instead of me, spending her evenings with the Detroit Tigers instead of me. But for two nights, we get to enjoy each other's company, a brief reminder of all the reasons why this is the best of times for both of us. Meeting her in New York always makes me smile; although she's the American, I'm the one on familiar turf. It's me who knows her way around, me who has the map of this grid stamped on the inside of my eyelids, me who understands where we need our hotel room to be.

For a third, I'm going to be weighing up a troupe of publishers who are vying to publish my next book. It's a wonderful feeling, to be sought after. Believe me, I know how very, very lucky I am in these times when so many writers are being cut adrift.

But the real reason I'm excited, the peg from which all the other goodness hangs, is that I'm being honored by the Lambda Literary Foundation. The news that I was being given the Pioneer Award was imparted by Katherine V. Forrest, one of my earliest heroines in the genre of lesbian mystery; to hear it from her was an honor in itself. And then to discover that the other 2011 recipient was to be Edward Albee felt like piling on even more glory.

It's hard to say this without sounding boastful, but I've won a lot of prizes in my career. I've published twenty-five novels now, so although I'm still only in my mid-fifties, I've started to get the kind of "lifetime achievement" awards that come your way if you stick around long enough—the Crime Writers' Association Diamond Dagger for outstanding contribution to the genre, an Honorary Fellowship from my Oxford college, the Stonewall Writer of the Year Award. It's gratifying, but it also makes me uneasy, because I'm a writer who is still ambitious for her work. I think I still have it in me to pull down the pillars of the temple and I'm not about to stop trying.

The Pioneer Award felt different because it felt like it was about *more* than me and my work. When I started out, lesbian writers were published in a dark corner of the literary world. In the UK, we didn't even get reviewed because we tended to be published in paperback originals by small presses, and the review columns only paid attention to hardbacks.

But gradually, a handful of us started to carve out a space for ourselves in a wider consciousness. Jeanette Winterson made a huge impact with *Oranges Are Not the Only Fruit*, and that opened the door a little further. In the last twenty years, we've kicked that door wide open and now in the UK writers who happen to be lesbians are a major component of our literary world—Poet Laureate Carol Ann Duffy, Sarah Waters, Ali Smith, Jackie Kay, Stella Duffy, Charlotte Mendelson, and MC Scott, just for starters.

We don't all write lesbian lives all the time, but we all write fictional universes where lesbians reside. When I started out—reading Katherine V. Forrest and Barbara Wilson and Sandra Scoppettone and Mary Wings—I wanted to believe that was a possible future for us, though it felt like a pretty remote dream. But it has happened, and within my working lifetime. It doesn't mean there aren't still battles to fight and doors to kick in, but it gives me heart.

Receiving the Pioneer Award symbolizes much more than my own achievement. It shouts to the world that we have come a long way. We're not stuck in the corner any more. We're in the middle of the room, part of the conversation, and not just in literary terms.

I sit in a taxi that smells of hot dust and oil, closing in on the impressive Manhattan skyline. It's not me who should be picking up this award tonight. It's New York City. This is the place I came to all those years ago in search of the possibility of community. What I found here gave me the courage to be myself, to not be silent, and to live in the light.

IRRESPECTIVE OF THE STORM

MARK AMEEN

I WAS RENDERED SPEECHLESS BY the beautiful men.

In 1978, I entered a sweltering New York City from Lowell, Massachusetts, to spend sophomore summer vacation with my gay cousin George. The crowds, dizzying, disturbing; the heat rising from the sidewalk in sheets; the infernal noise of eternal traffic; the subterranean rumblings of the motor that is Manhattan. And dear god, the beautiful men. I was nineteen.

The first thing I needed was a job. Two weeks into my stay, I was hired by a Brew Burger on Fashion Avenue. A giant victory: I'd serve inexpensive lunches to impossibly rude people. Cousin George took me to Christopher Street to celebrate.

The Cock Ring, a dance bar set all the way west where Christopher met the highway and the Hudson, was small and soiled, and sufficiently cramped that one could study from the sidelines the musculature of mid-floor revelers. Discos were becoming vast and impersonal, all about "losing yourself," but the Cock Ring remained a theater in which to be found. Cousin George, thankfully, had to work in the morning. He left the bar and I boogied on solo, mortified but drunk enough not to show it, until a bearded guy, wiry and energetic, decidedly not beautiful and for that reason irresistible, signaled me to join him. He seemed surprised when I complied. We carried on until four in the morning, when we ended up awkward on the sidewalk. He invited me home, and again seemed taken aback when I accepted. Obviously insecure. Or perfect.

His name was Barry. We were in bed for three days, in Kew Gardens, Queens, where I learned that spanking was a sexual act. For Barry. I loved his beard in my mouth and his rubbery lips, his fresh-ground coffee and minuscule hips. After a shower, he wrapped his thinning hair in a full-size bath towel and sashayed about. I wondered if he secretly desired to be a girl. I knew he'd never been beaten as a child. There was almost no ass there, he was just so skinny, but spank him I did. And gave him long, conscientious massages. I devoured all his "natural" peanut butter, on thick slices of toasted black pumpernickel.

Over the course of that summer, we returned many times to the Cock Ring, where, working up a sweat, almost athletic, I often outlasted Barry, leaving him exhausted on the sidelines, watching other men watching me. I made him proud, he said. I made myself delirious: I was sharing a stage with the players who left me weak-kneed on the street. I remained sadly speechless—shunning eye contact, fearful not to stare at their crotches—but they recognized me nonetheless. One, all in white, the hottest in the house, sporting Fu Manchu facial hair, bulging biceps, a significant basket in his bleached 501s, and an immaculately shaved head, reached inside my bubble, slowly dragged his fingers across denim and squeezed my butt. The audience, including Barry, applauded.

Barry was the vehicle, but I was married to Mr. Clean.

BY 1980 I WAS FINISHED with college and back in New York for good. The Upper East Side, thick with singles bars, poodle parlors, and manicure salons, was hardly the place for me—my half-naked, half-repressed, wholly gay longings—but it became my first Manhattan location. And it was there that I met Jim, my first Manhattan boyfriend, who lived in the same apartment one flight above. We made our acquaintance on our shared 73rd Street fire escape one hot summer night. Wild and romantic, I thought, a chance encounter, until he confessed he'd been watching me, my reflection in facing windows, as I did my nightly stretches, and had followed me outside to force a meeting. My ardor was only stoked by this reinforcement.

Jim was a string bean—sinewy, elongated—with soft hair everywhere and a bit of a lisp. He taught me what men could do in a bathtub. With one another, for one another, at one another, to one another. I ached for him with every inch of my body. His heat-emanating thighs, the puffy asshole like a magic flower, the rubbery, swollen helmet of his dick. Even when we were together, I was all ache. Maybe especially then. A forty-year-old office worker, Jim had cultivated a love of the opera, its brilliant passions, but no ambitions for himself short of psyching studs to their knees in his local back room. My mistake was to burn not solely for Jim, but for his past. Jim's mistake was to tell me, too many times, about that past. I tried to catch up, certain I'd never be his equal if I couldn't match his history. I shouldn't have moved in with him—my talent for cohabitation had never been tested, and his was worn thin—but when I lost my dirt-cheap sublet below, there seemed little choice. Amidst incrimination and STDs, our magic soon devolved into mania. I suffered cruelties at Jim's hands I was certain I would never transcend.

But it is, after all, the arching toward glory I remember; two blissed-out if stressful years during which I, madly, had become a poet, and Ronald Reagan, sadly, a president. (I remember standing in the corner Arab deli, fingering the front pages, appalled that America had become the laughing stock of the world.)

As the uptown relationship sputtered, I made frequent excursions south to the East Village. Anthony, my inaugural downtown hookup, led me from "The Bar" on East 4th Street to his Spartan digs on East 2nd Street. I knelt on his studio's parquet floor to suck a beautiful dick wrapped provocatively in a leather strap. He opened a closet door to view the scene pornographically in a full-length mirror—vain, proud, selfishly enthralled, I imagined, to watch his middle-aged centerpiece perish repeatedly in the mouth of a kid. I was thrilled, too, by the act if not the reflection. (He'd made me take off my eyeglasses, so I could see the dick before me but not the reproduction.) He referred to my asshole as a "pussy;" I feared he was trying to establish credentials as the only man in the room. (With Jim, by contrast, my uptown almost-ex, my asshole was my asshole and all things equal, each doing all things to each. Naively, perhaps, I considered that ideal: Did it not make sense to resist categorization when passion so easily toppled the pre-ordained? Jim, too, was ostensibly a "top," but I loved more than anything to mount him hungrily, his legs thrown over my shoulders, while huffing into his mouth, "You burn me up, your're so hot in there.")

I moved downtown, away from Jim and toward Anthony, to lower 2nd Avenue near East 12th Street, a "basement flat" that was more accurately an illegal box. One did not merely enter, one descended, passing the boiler room on the way to my front door.

"It's like a permanent room at the baths," extolled Jim during a visit, "minus the repetitive music and the towel-wrapped trolls." Recent abuses notwithstanding, we couldn't seem to completely sever our connection. I remember Jim between my legs on the foam rubber: "Baby, look at your fucking dick." In general, I feared my penis unsatisfactory, but there were nights, like that one, when it impressed even me. Inflated and inflamed, I was twenty-two and single. My room in the cellar, at once thrilling and humiliating, radiated sex and thus the potential for glory.

I JOINED AN EXPERIMENTAL THEATER company, improvising scenarios then scripting them for performance. I bought contact lenses. The awkward and ugly blossoms. The diffident child of New England tragedy goes onstage in New York to do comedy. My eyes were large, heavy-lidded, their lashes improbably thick after a decade behind protective shields. Moments of reinvention, particularly for young gay men, are hardly unusual; that doesn't make them any less seductive. My cruising apparatus now included rings of coal-black eyeliner carelessly applied.

Work, the paid kind, was part-time at night—waiting tables, slinging cappuccinos—but days were my own. If not writing or rehearsing, I'd buy biscuits at DeRoberti's Bakery, read the paper on my building's front stoop. New York's unceasing parade was an inspiration. I recall a spiky-haired blond. We made eye contact, he made a U-turn, and I invited him down. Smooth and arrogant, he had long vascular arms and big fingers. An angular face one couldn't help swooning to suck. I felt competitive but longed to lose. My cellar was magic. His dick, a god-given real estate, gave him the edge. I preferred his harsh beauty to a hunk of foam rubber, but he wanted me from behind. I was gritting my teeth, groaning, when he stopped on a dime. "I guess you like it rough," he said, and I felt pegged without consent to his hooligan continuum. Every encounter held grievous potential: it might offer up some clue regarding my core.

Anthony, a frustrated musician, stayed connected, seemingly charmed by all I was insecure about—my struggles to be a poet and an actor. He helped me out financially. He bought me my first Melitta coffee pot. But there were problems: Muscled arms pumped skyward in showy frustration, stock gesture of the urban Italian, Anthony was apt to sing out his prejudices, among them a racism that made me cringe. He performed chin-ups on city buses when inebriated. Ever uncertain if I was about to be embarrassed in public, I feared I was repeating my childhood. Anthony, for his part, dubbed me fundamentally unfit, mostly because I happily fucked black men and refused to deny it. We drifted.

I painted a wall blue in my cellar apartment, placed a massive oak desk, found on the street, before it, and clipped a lamp to the water pipe. My typewriter, semi-electric, was an Olivetti. After obsessing on a poem until midnight or beyond, I'd pour myself a cocktail. It made sense to tank up at home: Not only did you save money, but you were spared a sober entrance into a room full of gay men. I'd begin locally, then saunter west from The Bar, the sole establishment in my vicinity, with the chummy, artistic bent I secretly preferred, to the smorgasbord of anonymity on Christopher Street I felt pressured to embrace. That crosstown trek, an audition, was at least as much fun as the final destination—this or that watering hole with cruising codes of performance etiquette cracked just frequently enough to keep me coming back for more. The gregarious and friendly patrons it was advisable to ignore—neighborhood drunks, likely, with little to lose. The rest of us, unfriendly and feigning boredom, posed for animal crackers and failed to connect.

In the event of an inextricable deep freeze, panic approaching, I extended my quest, departing Greenwich Village via West Street.

On that urban highway, tall in my cowboy boots, free momentarily of false armor, I could taste, once again, liberation. The twenty-minute journey offered shadowed sightings of leather-clad couples, or a drag queen giving my ass the thumbs-up. Arriving at the bars of Chelsea, with their heightened sense of costume masculinity, I generally felt the better for my little stroll. The Spike was more serious than the Eagle's Nest, and slightly older. I especially appreciated Monday nights, when one didn't have to clear a path each time one moved. I'd position myself beneath an archway where I could view the main room while also enjoying the bar and toilet traffic.

WHEN HE ENTERED, TALL AND muscular, on long legs slightly bowed, everyone else seemed abruptly an amateur. Beard and mustache clipped, chest hard under a leather vest, forearms exquisite, he was probably late thirties, and wore chaps over his tight, faded Levis. As he strode to the bar, the tension in the joint quadrupled. He depleted every one of us of oxygen. Upon his return, bottle in hand, he stopped momentarily beside me. My brain begged my face to offer up something alluring. It didn't obey, and, as usual, it took too long: He moved on, gliding his leather-framed bulge to the more populated main room and leaned on a pool table.

The milieu was his, and yet he continued to include me, facing me if not actually looking at me. Short of dropping to my knees and crawling to that space where his leather met denim, however, I remained at a loss. Initiating was difficult. If I approached and faltered, found nothing to say, would he help me out or write me off as damaged and saunter away? I was myself the rankest amateur, greater-Boston hick, poet-naif adrift in a cannibal metropolis.

And a dilettante to boot. Leather had limited appeal beyond a vague threat of deeper-than-average debasement. A threat that seldom panned out, as the men in leather bars were often dilettantes themselves. In public, showing off, they'd twist your nipples, bark out a command; at home, suck and fuck like everyone else, with maybe some sloppy slapping to force a point. Or, as was often the case, often enough to have become an enduring cliché, the butchest biscuit in the bar wasted little time, privately, in getting his legs airborne. An ego-nullifying childhood had ill-prepared me for penetrating, yet two years with Jim had brought me up to speed sufficiently that I relished the opportunity. In fact, I loved to fuck men, and was willing to fight for it, adamant, when it seemed right. Topping, however, was seldom the motivation, the inner vision straightening my posture, when I dragged myself somewhere like The Spike. Nor was it being called up by the glorious specimen in chaps who was challenging me.

If he's so butch, why do I have to make the move? And why in the middle of the room?

I regarded the soft hair, rugged face, and resolved to cease fretting and give it a whirl: With a sip for fortification, I caught his attention, and, before he could look away, I turned my back on him. The about-face, dramatic in itself, was followed by a switch of the hips worthy of Mae West and a palm placed like punctuation against the doorframe. Much as his initial eye contact had extended a lifeline only to leave me hanging, I presented my backside like an Erté hood ornament and waited. When he appeared, grinning, beside me, a sweet sense of victory quickened my pulse. I had allowed myself to compete, and, this time, had come back a winner. "The name's Terrence," he drawled. "How's it going?"

We conversed easily, excitedly. Though it was clear in an instant that we'd be departing together, he bought us peppermint schnapps and we prolonged the delectable tension. Apart from the choice of nightcap, which I thought fey and affected, he seemed utterly himself. He'd grown up on a farm—excellent!—and now he was...well, a psychology professor. Whatever.

I chugged my liqueur.

He lived in Pennsylvania, so we were going to my place.

"Do you want me to keep my leather on?" He slipped out of his jeans then re-donned his chaps, while from a cloud, holding my dick, I looked on. His penis, as expected, was a soul-stirring challenge. Each time I pulled back, inhaled him in recline on my foam rubber mattress, the spirit piercing my chest reminded me of love.

I was an endless itch. His whiskers, like sandpaper, punished my ass. My ass was the main event: I had used it to corral him; now he fucked it with finesse. He was contained; I fell to pieces. Clawing at his buttocks, I tried to swallow his tongue, my throat delivering moans into his mouth. I held him within me for as long as possible, until he popped free and headed for the john. I couldn't speak; I followed and lay down in the tub. He obliged, while verbally reiterating the excavations so recently enjoyed. I showered him from my surface but left him inside.

He was waiting, chaps folded neatly upon my desk. Could he read, at a glance, the spin I was in? He held the covers open like it was his bed, not mine. I kissed his fingers, felt the weight of him, thought, my god, he's spending the night, then prayed that it wasn't just too late for him to drive back to Philly. The next day, to my "Good morning," Terence's smiling response was, "Suck my cock." I'd known myself to oppose even a hand on the back of my head when the individual applying the pressure hadn't earned it, but Terry had only to speak. I was thrilled. When he fucked me again, it hurt; I glared into his eyes until he came.

He had his shower. I did my best to annihilate the blues, lest the torrent overwhelm him and he float away. I let him speak. Here was his address and long-distance number. I could phone anytime; I could visit Pennsylvania. Like the handyman, the ranch hand, or the responsive father who'd never existed, he'd happily fill a need, but each and every time I'd have to ask. I wasn't sure I could do that. He failed to remember where he'd parked, so together we scanned the neighborhood, kissed and said goodbye on the street.

I stopped for morning biscuits. All I had to show for the preceding eight hours would be gone as soon as I sat on the toilet. I stuck fast to a tamped-down, roiling sadness. He probably has a boyfriend. Or several. If I get involved, there'll be three-ways, which I can't abide. And most certainly endless jealousies, which I won't survive. Allowing only the grief, I convinced myself never to call. A few days later, I went to a subway bathroom, had sex in a stall.

I thought about Terrence for years, pondering the what-ifs. I screwed scores of men. I moved from "basement flat" to wobbly fifth-floor walkup at East 4th Street and Avenue B.

I MET ERIC IN STUYVESANT Park, a cruising ground on lower 2nd Avenue, all overgrown brush and nonstop activity. Rather than do it in the park, to which he seemed utterly resistant, we went to my place. Eric was handsome—with an upper body highly developed, toned and beautifully muscular—yet not quite the "A Gay" I initially imagined, that mythical type about which I knew precious little and in the presence of whom I remain to this day utterly speechless. He had the gift of gab, even while tricking, which set him apart and put me at ease. Our time in the sack, even so, was grating, an irritation—a struggle of sorts ensued, in which both tried to take over, willing to fight for it, and neither took pleasure, each secretly seeking the same thing, namely Terrence my Philadelphia college professor in chaps.

But we stayed in bed talking. He sensed I was an artist. I told him I wrote poetry. He knew someone who ran a small press; he'd speak to them about me. I considered this incredibly generous, especially since we hadn't really hit it off. But that's also what made it acceptable. He may have said he wrote prose, maybe even fiction, but didn't tell me he was Andrew Holleran, author of *Dancer from the Dance*, a terrific bestseller, one of the first gay novels to really fly. He did confess that he wrote under a pen name because he had never come out to his parents.

Though I never saw him again, Eric was as good as his word, and his word led to a manuscript submission and finally a contract. I was paid two hundred dollars for my first book of poetry and stories, and I had to fight even for that. Welcome to gay publishing, a vale of tears. Years of work, my soul on the page, and what I got for it was less than a single month's rent.

I WENT TO WORK AS a doctor's receptionist on West 57th Street. A few months in, the office was burglarized. I discovered the jimmied desk drawers on a Monday morning after opening up shop. An inside job, apparently, as the office doors themselves had not been damaged. When the good gay doctor, arriving for his shift, insinuated I was his prime suspect, I quit.

As if on cue, my wobbly apartment at last exhaled: Two ceilings collapsed and a radiator fell through the floor. I begged my landlord to complete the renovation kicked off by gravity and neglect. Much to my surprise, he consented. An animated crew of illegal Dominicans arrived in a flurry, knocked down the remaining surfaces, ripped out the tub—and disappeared. Anthony, who'd been my "sponsor," in a sense, when I'd moved into the neighborhood, and with whom I'd recently returned to civility after our extended run of bad blood, kindly offered the use of his shower. Anthony no longer drank, and was able to refrain from pointless arguments. Blessedly, his racism, too, was in remission. Grabbing our second chance, we became friends.

After my showers, we sang our mid-'80s blues on Anthony's bed: mine concerned my decimated apartment, the not-unreasonable fear that I might crumble into dust along with it; Anthony's, the final-stage dementia of his most beloved ex, Bruce, a dancer just thirty years old.

On the day Bruce finally passed, Anthony, stricken, asked me to assist Tom, another of Bruce's lovers, in the dispersal of the dead man's belongings. With the destruction of my own home weighing me down, the last thing I wanted was to upend somebody else's. "C'mon, Mark," Anthony urged. "There's lots of stuff that'll wind up on the street. I can't take it; Tom can't take it—the memories would make both of us crazy. You might find something for your place."

Tom, tall and bony, saucer-eyed, and benign, picked me up in a Porsche belonging to his boss, then briefed me on the chronology of Bruce. Tom came after Anthony but before Tim, a third lover meeting us at the scene. Tim, the third, had broken it off post-diagnosis, a betrayal Anthony deemed unforgivable but for which Tom was willing to extend the benefit of the doubt. "If Bruce even suspected that Tim was hanging on out of pity," said Tom, "or worse, a sense of duty, I'm sure he made their lives a living hell. There's only one reason Bruce was with Tim in the first place."

"And?" I asked. "What was that?"

"His dick."

"Oh," I said, my face tingling.

Tom laughed. "Looks like you might give him the benefit of the doubt, too."

One glimpsed, when Tom laughed, beneath the middle-aged, gay-blasé surface, the tormented eyes of a brutalized child. Being happy made him a bit crazy, set him on edge.

It was the second floor of a two-family fake Swiss, on a traditional Queens block of lookalike brick. Inside, I met Tim, gangly and excitable, and tried not to stare at his crotch. Tom laid claim to the record collection, Tim took a bit of shared property, and I accepted a sofa, a Parsons table, and a captain's bed. The remainder we deposited on the sidewalk.

Tom and I in the Porsche, Tim in a U-Haul, we headed for the stacks of Sheetrock I called home. Sealed by hanging blankets, my bedroom served as the oasis in a plaster-dust storm.

"When are they gonna put up the walls?" asked Tom.

"They said they'd start again Monday. They also said they'd be finished in a week, but it'll take these guys that long just to do the bathroom."

"Maybe you could clean some in the meantime," said Tim, pitching his voice to suggest a Betty Crocker helpfulness instead of an insult, but annoying me nonetheless, as men whose crotches I'm trying not to stare at invariably do. "Why do you stay here?" he continued, indicating my compromised abode. "You could get a great deal in Brooklyn, or something out in Queens near me."

"C'mon, Tim, I have a two bedroom in Manhattan for under three hundred."

"If you consider this Manhattan," he mumbled, forcing a grin lest I take offense.

"Well, I do," I replied. "I like it here."

"It's great," agreed Tom. "Just check out the height of those ceilings."

"There are no ceilings," said Tim.

"Picky, picky," said Tom.

"So you two work together?" I asked, changing the subject.

"We work together," said Tom, "but that doesn't make us peers." Tim didn't acknowledge the insult; he yawned.

"And where is it you work?" I persisted.

"It's called The Fifth Season."

I laughed at that. "Anthony filled me in some, but what is it, exactly?"

Tim stiffened at the mention of Anthony.

"It's an alternative health club," said Tom, grinning.

"A pussy parlor," said Tim, yawning.

"A whorehouse, right?" I asked.

"But we're not allowed to call it that."

"Why not?"

"Gladys doesn't like it."

"Is Gladys the owner of the Porsche?"

"That's her."

"Does she need anyone else?"

"Maybe part-time, at the lower desk. But it's a shitty job."

"That'd be ideal. I'm not into working."

"You'll love it," said Tim.

THE "PUSSY PARLOR" WAS LOCATED on a sub-floor of a high-rise, but before I could go there, I had to meet Gladys, removed from culpability in an office across the street. She was middle-aged, long-haired, and about four and a half feet tall. Her boots were maroon-colored, loose-fitting, and about three and a half feet tall. My impression was of an oversized head atop a mound of Gucci. Everything else was plastic. "I like my people to look inviting," she barked, tottering on her stilettos. "It's a party club; they come for a good time."

Is she suggesting I'm too homely for her whorehouse?

"Normally I wear contacts," I stammered. "But I dropped one into a pile of what used to be my ceiling. See, they're tearing down my place, and... Anyway, what I mean is..." I stripped off my eyeglasses. "This is what I look like. Normally, I mean, with my lenses in."

"They come for the girls," she said, "but it doesn't hurt to have good-looking guys around. Why don't you have a job?"

"Well...I was working for this doctor—nearby, actually—but he tried to scale back my hours with no warning so I—"

"Where are you from?" she growled, cutting me off.

Had she picked up on my accent? "You mean originally?"

"Jesus Christ, I know where you live now, don't I? You think I'm stupid?"

"Massachusetts," I croaked. "I'm from Massachusetts."

"Do you see your family?"

"I'm in touch with my sisters, but try not to bump into my parents."

The foundation cracked around her lips. "I like my people to like their families."

My god, I thought, the Reagan/Falwell/Meese epidemic of so-called "family values" is infecting entrepreneurs even of the sex industry. "Well," I offered meekly, "like I said, I'm fond of my sisters."

"That's good, honey," she cooed, utterly cheerful. I was beginning to think she was nuts.

"I've always employed gay men," she boasted. "Clean, not interested in the girls, and relaxed about sex, which is conducive to the atmosphere."

"That makes sense," I lied, having long since exploded for myself the comforting fantasy that having shitloads of sex could be interpreted to mean you were "relaxed" about it.

"We have nice clients," she said.

I tried to look interested.

"You don't do drugs, do you? I won't have drugs at The Fifth Season."

"No, I—"

"Okay, go on over. I've got work to do. Tom will show you the ropes. And don't forget 'em. Your contacts. Get a new pair."

THE FIFTH SEASON HAD A private entrance. No awning, no marker, just a buzzer by which one was electronically admitted to a darkened corridor, there to be greeted by the lower half of a plastic mannequin, artfully lit behind a Plexiglas window, feet stuck in the air like an invitation. One heard second generation disco hits beckoning. Around a funhouse corner, more plastic body parts, and then, through another security door, the front desk, where Tom was stationed with the requisite forms. Here, the member dropped his first payment: sixty-five nonrefundable dollars for thirty-minute use of a room. If Member desired the deluxe Hollywood Room or King's Room, and knew that up front, he'd cover that as well, an additional fifteen or twenty-five dollars. With bathtubs, multiple waterbeds, and wall-to-wall mirrors, these special order rooms could accommodate a crowd or a sense of grandiosity. How the latter might coexist with the act of paying for sex was, at the time, beyond my comprehension.

Member descended to club proper, by and large underground. I sat behind a cube at the foot of the stairs, desk lamp halo of fluorescence cutting me into relief from the polyurethane ambience, like a bookie in an old-time gangster flick. I didn't deal directly with clients, merely detailed the sales slips sent down by Tom, adding name and prepaid accommodation. And I took phone calls, snapping up incomings with a crisp and professional, "Good evening, Health Club."

Nearby, in shadow on the orange sofa, sat Jack, the club manager. White-haired, pot-bellied, and every inch the Boston Irish cop he'd once been, he was a jolly enough presence, greeting members and guests, indulging whoremeister small talk, swilling scotch. But if trouble arose, he swung into action, which impressed me, for I knew he was a drunk. He kept a handgun inside his jacket.

Member was assigned one of four hostesses, each of whom wore the same spongy outfit as the whores, but none of whom pulled the material into her crack like a G-string nor rolled the front straps away to become topless. On the hostess, the cheesy one-piece appeared modest. Chatting amicably, Hostess led Member to a locker-lined changing room where Tim, he of the legendary dick and Betty Crocker demeanor, offered a towel and a key-on-a-bracelet. Disrobing, as nonnegotiable as at a gay bathhouse, here served a purpose more practical than erotic: Straight men—even, or particularly, inebriated ones—were less likely to cause trouble when naked.

Towel-wrapped Member was accompanied by swimsuited Hostess to the pool, which, like the steam room, was seldom utilized except by employees. A deejay/lifeguard spun records from an elevated booth. The Fifth Season had no liquor license, so the men brought their own, and a bar was set up to one side. While Hostess mixed, Member mingled.

When a selection was made, Hostess hustled out to my desk. I pulled the requisition slip, penciled in the female's stage name and a room number, then duplicated the info on my At-A-Glance blotter. Hostess carried slip back to Whore, couple trotted off to their room, and, when the plywood door closed behind them, a small red light bulb in the center of a mirrored circle buzzed into life beside me on the wall. Not counting the King's Room, the entrance to which was directly behind me, obviating the need for electrical signal, there were seven rooms, seven red lights, seven mirrored circles. I jotted the time of illumination and, in thirty minutes, if that bulb continued to pulse, Tim or I would go knock on the door. Whore then brought Member to the mountain, or, better yet, rebooked him, doubling not only his sixty-five dollar room fee but her own mandatory "tip."

The latter had to be at least seventy dollars; gentlemen never tipped below a hundred. The cash was sealed in an envelope and handed not to the Whore but to the Hostess, who passed it to me.

Once Member was safely departed, Working Girl, wet from the shower and more or less nude, rushed me and opened her prize. Sometimes, a smile of contentment; sometimes, a shout to the effect of "that cheap, ugly, motherfucking pig."

"HEY, MARK, MY LOCKER'S STUCK," said Tara. The girls all had stage names like Tara or Samantha, Roxy, or Chevon. "Can you give me a hand?"

"Go ahead," said Jack, my boss, the drunken cop. "I'll cover the phone."

We cut through the King's Room to the women's toilet. Tara pulled out a tiny brown bottle. "We have to take care of you," she said, feeding heaping miniature spoonfuls into my nostrils. "We know that witch ain't paying you shit to push them papers around." A loud flushing sound, and Vanessa, half naked, emerged from a stall. "And not only that, baby, you cute as a button. I only wish I could say the same for them creepy-crawlies out there on the floor."

"Isn't that always the case?" I asked.

"Shit, no," they sighed in unison, laughing at their unexpected synchronization.

"No way, baby," said Vanessa. "Those young dudes from the record companies, I'd do those pricks for free." Tara shot her a look. "Okay," Vanessa corrected, "let's just say I wouldn't do it at all if it was like this every night." Tara agreed at last, nodding as she capped her bottle.

"And you blush, too, baby," said Tara. "Here, now, take another toot."

I looked in the mirror, glassy-eyed and startled between two sets of jiggling breasts.

EVEN FOR CHEAP, UGLY, MOTHERFUCKING pigs, a visit to The Fifth Season—entry fee, tip, hand-offs to hostess and locker room attendant—ran a guy two hundred dollars. Why were they willing to pay, some of them, two or three times a week? I wanted to understand, but, numbed by overexposure, bored and often stoned, I failed to arrive at empathy. I think I was depressed, cloaking myself in cocaine-spun sadness and stupidity.

When the joint was jumping, Hostesses ran to and fro with bookings, Working Girls begged for the next available room, the place started smelling like what it was, and Jack, the manager, was drunker than anyone who considers himself on duty ought to be. Riveted to the clock and my bank of red lights, I stuck to a first-come, first-served system, unswayed by the earnest appeals of regulars, including a father/son combo whose fetish required consecutive use of the same woman. It would occur to me all at once what I was doing, neither meaningless nor quaint: I was helping "entrepreneurs" of every stripe, many of them "family men," relieve themselves in clandestine fashion; and I was doing it for the hourly wage of a McDonald's employee. And I didn't even get to suck any cock. Well, other than Tim's once in a while.

At shift's end, Working Girl stopped by my desk, paid her cut to the house. When tipped a respectable hundred, her take from a two hundred-plus visit remained a mere seventy-five.

A HOT AUGUST NIGHT; THE club's air conditioners struggled to accommodate. Tom and I drank gin from the Hostesses' booze stash. Jack, our drunken boss, entered from the King's Room behind us. His grin made me wonder if he'd just had a blowjob. "Go see Tara," he said. "She claims you're the only one who can fix her locker. What're you, screwing her?"

He was laughing, and so was Tom, as I slid from my desk chair into the darkened orgy parlor and spotted a flame burning in the center of the room. With a cry of "Surprise!" the lights were jerked up. Surrounding the fat candle stuck awkwardly atop a tiny cake, the ladies were striking poses: Vanessa, nude, splashing in the circular tub; Toni and Tanya rolling on the waterbed; Lily, bent over, slapping her ass; and Tara, my favorite, jiggling her breasts. My red-faced reaction got lots of laughs, and, as they sang "Happy Birthday," I was close to losing it.

Tara said, "Blow out the candle, 'cause if you don't it'll crush that little cake to smithereens. By the way, it would be bigger, that cake, if there was a snowball's chance in hell you were gonna be hungry." She handed me a small brown bottle of my own. Jack made a show of glancing elsewhere. Along with the powder, they gave me a fifth of scotch and a card that read, "I always wash my pussy with scented soap." Inside, someone had scribbled, "Don't you?" Somehow, I was not offended. Tom stood behind, hand on my shoulder. I was twenty-seven.

ON THE WEEKENDS, TOM IMPROVED on the renovations within my apartment. He tore a closet from an abandoned flat across the hall then reconstructed it piece by piece in one of my bedrooms. He forced shelving units into obscure corners, using planes and levels and other tools I hadn't laid eyes on since childhood. His masterwork, however, was the transformation of a loft bed into a lacquered bookcase that towered above my desk and gave me goose bumps. When he was through, I had an attractive apartment and very nearly a serious cocaine habit. And I had Tom. He attended my poetry readings, offering support and encouragement, companionship and more cocaine. On Sunday nights we watched *Masterpiece Theatre* and hooted at the inevitable gay characters. We were friends, we were stoned, we were going to bars together. In the midst of our carousing, I'd catch him eyeing me the way a puppy regards his leash. He wanted to love me, but I couldn't allow it—not like that.

A few years later, he'd be dead. His sister discovered him naked on the floor of his place, incoherent and incontinent, staring at the ceiling. She carted him home to rural New Jersey and then to her local hospital. They wouldn't take him. Hoping to force an admission through the ER, she called an ambulance service; they, too, turned her down. Those were the days. Luckily, she'd once been a nurse. She set up a guest room, finagled a morphine prescription, kept him drugged, gave him life, loved him until he left. Pity the gay man without sisters.

NOT LONG AFTER I QUIT the whorehouse, in 1985, *A Circle of Sirens* was finally published. I took a copy, with its self-designed cover, into the bathtub, where I found myself for once able to cry, then called my sisters, June and Margo, to share the news.

I thought about Terrence for years. I wrote him a sonnet ending with the words, "I'll never shit again." When it was about to be printed, I decided to reach out. If nothing else, he'd get a kick out of the poem. Deep down I was hoping for more: Maybe I was mature enough now to handle perfection, and Terrence, by now, less than perfect. It took several weeks for the reply: "I liked your poem. Terry would, too. I'm the boyfriend. Terry's dead."

AT A WASHINGTON DEMONSTRATION AS the decade neared its close, I spotted Bob, who long ago had been the first lover to Jim, the man with whom I'd spent two years on the Upper East Side, the man with the flowering anus, the spongy helmet, the man who made me ache at twenty-two.

Bob smiled and worked his way over. "How's it going?"

We had never gotten along, but time had healed the wounds no one could see.

"Not bad," I said. "Same as always. Are you still a chef?"

"Yeah. Still bitching about it, too, like why couldn't I be the movie star God intended?"

"Tell me about it," I said. "How's Jim?"

Did I not know better than to ask that question?

Bob said nothing, merely lowered his gaze, smiling gently, shaking his head. My first Manhattan boyfriend, who taught me what men could do in a bathtub, was dead.

Amidst chants to the converted, I found a solitary spot for a memorial moment with Jim, whom I hadn't seen in years and hadn't known was sick, who may have fallen from my life but who was waiting, patiently, when I closed my eyes. Irrespective of the storm, the soul struck by lightning time and again, throughout the abominable '80s there they were: compact, beautiful men spreading the cheeks of their asses on beds of gently rushing water.

MY LAST BIG ADDICTION

MARTIN HYATT

SOMETIMES I STILL EXPECT IT to happen. I think I'm going to wake up in a house trailer in the middle of Manhattan. And part of me wants that. Sometimes I feel like I don't belong here. That I've never belonged here. And other times, I feel like it's the only place for me. But I stay, because I am hooked. New York City is my last big addiction. And I am okay with that. I always knew that I would end up here.

After all, there are some things that you just know about your future. You can picture those things so clearly that they simply have to happen. Living in New York was one of those things for me. From the pages of *Creem* magazine, I saw my radio heroes all strung out and glorious in their destruction. While other kids were outside playing baseball, I was inside listening to Blondie and The Ramones, knowing that someday I would live in New York City. And that I would also be a drug addict.

These days, when I walk the streets of New York, it's a different world from when I arrived. When I look at the pavement I used to pass out on, I wonder how I survived. I am not unique. Many people before me have tried to destroy themselves, only to fail and come out on the other side. But because it is my story, it feels unique.

My New York story is not beautiful and clear. I could start by telling you how I arrived on West 8th Street on a hectic, hot August day in 1994. I could start by telling you about how I was scared to death. I could tell you about how I had come here after two years at Goddard College in Vermont to finish up my work at Eugene Lang College in the Village. Instead, I will tell you about how I came here to find myself, but ended up losing myself. Then found myself again. Just as my father had gone to Chicago with dreams of being a musician or something other than a depressed carpenter, I came to New York City to become someone. Someone different than the skinny kid from the Ozone neighborhood, different from the burnt-out bikers and convicts who surrounded me. I wanted to be different from the prom kings and queens who never became as spectacular in adulthood as they had been in their teens. I wanted to go to New York to walk alongside the ghosts of Edna St. Vincent Millay and Jack Kerouac on the streets of Greenwich Village. I wanted to go to the place where Montgomery Clift and Laura Nyro lived their last days. I wanted to grow up to be a writer in NYC.

My New York City story can be divided into two parts. The time before I almost died, and the time after.

THE AUGUST I ARRIVED, I didn't have much but a partial scholarship, a student loan agreement, and thirty dollars. I had a lot of heart. And dreams. And fear that I would get lost somewhere in the city. I feared that couldn't be a hick and a New Yorker at the same time. That I would lose the part of me that loved dirt roads as much as seedy punk rock bars. I was afraid that everyone could see through me, and could see my fear and my dreams. I was afraid that I would be sent home. I thought that my dreams would die, and that, like my father, I would end up back in Louisiana.

That first year in New York, I learned to navigate around the Village. In classes, we would sit around tables and talk about each other's writing. I did well in those rooms. I learned to talk about writing in ways that I didn't know was possible. During that time, I also learned how to drink. A lot. I worked in restaurants and learned how to stretch one shift drink into ten. I would spend my days in school searching for my writing voice, and my nights in the East Village searching for everything else. Bars and street corners were the only places I felt safe.

I had never known of rock-and-roll fag bars like the ones I found in New York. A place named The Bar on West 4th Street and 2nd Avenue became my second home. The jukebox had Richard Hell and Sonic Youth and everybody who meant something to me at that time. I would drink with models, musicians, poets, and other people filled with hope. I thought I had found my place in the world. I thought that I really belonged. Drinking can do that for you. It can make you think that you are at home, even though you are actually never at home when wasted.

I don't remember the first time I scored cocaine in NYC. I don't remember the first time I did heroin. I don't remember the first time I blacked out and woke up completely unaware of how I had gotten home or into the bed of a stranger. I don't remember the first time I hurt my boyfriend with lies about what I did late into the night. I don't remember how many times I would just disappear into the apartment of a drug dealer, and stay there for days, thinking that the world inside those walls was the entire universe. In fact, I cannot remember much from my twenties. It's all dark, blurry images. It is amazing and terrifying to have an entire decade of your life become a blur. When I think back, even at its most clear, it is still like looking through a windshield during a rainstorm. I can't really see it.

West 4th Street seemed to stretch for miles into the night during those years. And I would go the edges of it, scoring medicine to make the pain go away. I didn't know I was in pain back then, but I was. Nobody spends almost every night of a decade searching in the darkness for something to make them numb, to make them complete, unless there is truly something missing.

There was a hole in me. A giant wound that would sometimes take over and swallow up everything in its path: every drug, every drink, every man, every woman, every story, every poem, every song. On the streets of New York, I devoured everything in my path, and I was still starving. I have a disease. They say it's a disease of more. I want this and that and more of that and more this and more and more and more until there is nothing else to have.

Somehow, just as writing had helped me to survive in Louisiana, it helped me to survive during the '90s in New York. I snorted and drank my way out of Lang and into the New School MFA program. I had the privilege of studying with some of the most sought-after teachers in the city. They were glamorous and smart. Their reputations were big and their personas were even bigger. They were kind to me. I was too high to appreciate it.

In Abigail Thomas's class, I found my voice. I remember her calling me at home after reading an early draft of A Scarecrow's Bible, to say "Bravo." I remember Amy Hempel doing her best to help me with my work even though I was so high in her class that I couldn't sit next to anyone. I was so anxious from the drugs that I always made sure there was at least one empty desk between me and my classmates. And I remember when I lost twenty pounds one winter and had to drop out of a class with A.M. Homes. In her class one night, while I was on cocaine and Klonopin, during a writing exercise about a narrator trying to get something, I wrote about trying to get a bag of cocaine. The class was completely silent after that. Afterwards, I took a leave of absence for the rest of the semester.

I don't say any of this to glamorize my self-destruction or to show off. In fact, I don't know why I say it. I tend to tell on myself in my writing. Even in my fiction, I tell too much. Maybe I'm like my Southern aunts: I will tell you everything. Otherwise, I'll tell you nothing. For me, the alternative to telling all in writing is complete silence. This is the way I talk. Unless I write something down, it's like it never happened.

At that time, in those classes, I thought I was the ultimate New York writer. I thought I was being like those rock stars from *Creem* magazine. Like those poets from the Jazz Age. Like those ghosts of drunken Dylan Thomas and junked-up Burroughs. I thought that this was the way a southern boy becomes a writing man in New York.

I thought it was how I would not become my father. If I was going out, it would not be quietly. It would not be private. It would be in blaze of attempted poetic prose and drugs and drink. It would be noisy and people would notice. My destruction would be documented and witnessed.

I disappeared. From school, from my family, my boyfriend, myself. The streets became my teacher, my mentor, my faculty advisor, my family, my guru. Nothing mattered to me at that time. Not even the people who loved me. I didn't just get lost in the nights of that New York winter, I had become the night. I was the winter.

Looking back, I had almost everything when I was twenty-six. Great teachers, a brilliant, Italian physicist boyfriend, a family back home who loved me, an agent, a promising writing career. I had managed to become one of those poets and artists that I had dreamed of becoming. With pen in hand, I would stay up for days writing. And I felt that I had nothing. I had New York City, and I didn't know what to do with it. I would mostly find myself sickly underweight, shaking on street corners, nose bleeding in bars, and for the first time in my life, I was completely alone. It was just me and my drugs. The nights got longer until that year became one long night. There were times when I almost didn't wake up. Once on the couch in a Village apartment, while my boyfriend slept in the other room, once at the Chelsea Hotel with the phone ringing off the hook because a friend was desperate to find out if I was still alive.

On another night at the Chelsea Hotel, I was doing cocaine with a fashion designer friend of mine who was in love with me. She was so beautiful and poised, but we were both way too broken to really love. We had a disposable camera. And we took pictures of ourselves and of each other. We thought it would be fun and beautiful to take pictures of our night of going over the edge.

I never had those pictures developed. But I kept that camera for years. I liked to imagine that in those pictures, we looked like rock stars. That I looked like the son of Iggy and Bowie and Richard Hell. I liked so much to believe that. But now I know that's not what I looked like at all. In fact, I'll bet that if you looked at any of those pictures, my friend might come out nicely, looking beautiful and cool. She always photographed well. But at the table, in front of a pile of cocaine, with some yellow light coming in from outside, there would be a chair facing a faded wall. And you wouldn't be able to see me in that chair, even though that's where I was sitting. I wouldn't be in the photograph at all. At that time, in that hotel, in that room of my New York City childhood dreams, I could not have been visible. I had ceased to exist.

THERE WERE PLACES WHERE THEY sent young men like me in the summer.

When they closed the doors, and locked them, I knew I would be inside the hospital for a while. A lot of my time was spent waiting in line for medication so that I could stop feeling sick. So that the pain in my stomach would go away, so that the seizures wouldn't come every time I tried to sleep.

This is what my New York dream had become. Somewhere up in Midtown West, I was all locked up. I couldn't get to the streets, but I wanted to. They would put us in groups to talk and talk and talk. There was a lot of kindness in those places. People tried to help. So much. And in those rooms overlooking Manhattan, the city I had so wanted to conquer, to be part of, I wondered if there would ever be a way for me to walk the streets again.

They told me I was a "garbage head" addict, meaning that I would take everything and anything to numb the pain. I thought back to my aunts who had overdosed on pills and my uncles who had drunk themselves to death. I thought about my older, half-sister who had first given me crystal meth when I was thirteen. And who had first shot me up with cocaine a few years later. That was my heritage.

I thought about my brother. His cerebral palsy and autism had prevented him from ever coming to a place like New York to live out a dream. I thought about how his mental retardation had only allowed him to watch his big brother go away on trains and buses and airplanes. How he was left rocking back and forth on a sofa every time I would leave to go back to New York, unable to express what he was feeling. Unable to ever be the one to leave home.

I would find myself in those hospital rooms in those NYC drug wards awake at night rocking back and forth. In those detoxes and rehabs, I would think a lot about all those times I would bring home A's on my report card, while my brother would be struggling to speak. I thought about how he would watch me with my new racket, hitting a tennis ball against the back wall of the house, knowing that he would never be able to move like that. I thought about how he would watch Dick Clark every New Year's Eve and talk about Times Square like he would someday go there, too.

"You've lost the ability to take care of yourself," a nurse told me in one of the many detoxes I was in during that time.

Like James, I thought. Like my brother. I had spent my entire life trying to cripple myself. Trying to be like him. After all, if I was a cripple too, then that would make us even. Then we could really be equals, really be brothers.

I spent many Thanksgivings and birthdays in such places. I couldn't string together enough sober time to amount to much. I was still writing, but not really. I was on the verge of my first book deal, a book I had written while being completely wasted. In literary circles, my addiction was no secret. I had managed to live out what I had written about. And what I had written about was very tough to live down.

Sometimes, I would go far from the city, convinced that New York was the problem. Some of the places had pretty, tranquil names like Silver Hill and Palmetto. In rehab, I blamed everything on NYC. It was too hectic, too competitive, too sophisticated for me. After all, I was really a hick deep down. I should have been driving a truck or hunting or doing work on the farm. Or making a living off the shrimping boats like my Uncle Raymond had taught me. I should have been on a John Deere tractor or stocking the shelves at Piggly Wiggly. Then the pressure of being a writer in NYC would go away. I had messed up by trying to be something more than what I grew up around. I should have taken the lesson from my father. Cities don't work out for country boys like us. The city will always kick us in the heart. It will destroy us. Dreams die slowly for musicians and writers like me and my father. And when it doesn't die, we try to kill it.

There's nothing like wanting the desire to create to go away. There's nothing like going back home to a life less charmed than what you had dreamed of, to the life you were expected to live.

If my father hadn't been able to sing on the Grand Ole Opry, if my brother couldn't go to away to college, if so many gay men who had come before me had wasted away before they had achieved greatness, then why did I deserve what I wanted?

One night when I was having withdrawals, I found myself in a hospital room in the Village, at St. Vincent's. In the ER, I had overheard the doctor tell a nurse, "He did it to himself." She was right, of course.

I spent the night there, in that room, doped up, but aware that it was the very same hospital where so many other aspiring men had died. And I wondered why it hadn't happened to me. If I had been born a few years earlier, no doubt I would have found myself in one those same rooms, sick from another disease.

While the rehab stays and detoxes all blend together in my mind, I do remember that night at St. Vincent's. I remember it because I understood how so many people floated away from those rooms forever. I understood that I was doing everything in my power to make that very same thing happen to me. And for one of the first times in my life, I felt grateful. Maybe it was the ghosts in those hallways that made me appreciate being alive, struggling, but still here, alive in New York City.

MY NEW LIFE, AND MY new New York life, began when I was thirty-four. I started all over. Just like when I had first come to the city as a student, I returned with less than fifty dollars in my pocket, no job, and moved into a run-down room in an apartment in Washington Heights.

I had lost everything. And still the pull was back to Manhattan. I am not sure why. But I couldn't go anywhere else. I couldn't stay in Louisiana. I had often dreamed of Santa Monica, but New York was still the place I felt I needed to be. It felt right.

I was defeated when I took a nine-dollar-an-hour job rolling burritos in Chelsea. I was defeated when the idea of a good time was taking the bus all the way downtown from Washington Heights because it was cheap. I was defeated when the mice would play around my un-air-conditioned room on summer nights. This was a long way from professorships, book deals, and Greenwich Village life as the partner of a leading physicist. It was all sort of terrible, and yet it was one of the best times of my life.

I met other people like me, struggling with the same issues, the same demons. I kept going, kept rolling burritos, kept living. A friend said to me, "If you keep doing this, one day you won't have to do it anymore." I didn't know exactly what that meant at the time. I didn't believe him. In fact, people said a lot of simple things to me that year that I had trouble believing. But slowly I got it.

It was during those days, during that time, that I first started to really pay attention to the city, to see what it really looked like, to figure out how I really felt about it. At first, I was simply on autopilot, trying to survive, and then slowly the city began to open up for me.

Places that I had been to but had not really been present at began to figure into the landscape of my daily life. Lincoln Center was wonderfully grand, full of grace. Not the same as when I had passed out in the third row years before. Central Park was greener than I had ever known it was. Not a place that I was too sick to walk across. The buildings in the city came alive. They were no longer things to hide behind. The people looked varied and diverse, and they all seemed less scary than they had before. In this new New York, nothing was blurry. I could see it all.

There were still things I didn't like. The agitating subways and what I consider to be long winters became more pronounced when I got sober. But it was all balanced out by some wonders I had not appreciated before. When I would go to the end of Christopher Street, by the water, I began to feel I was part of something that was happening now, and something that happened before I was even born. A place where people before me had found their voices. When I looked in the window at the Julius bar on West 10th Street, I loved to see the older men watching *Miss Marple* and *As Time Goes By* on PBS. It was beautiful that they had lived through history, and that they were here to tell their stories.

During that time in Washington Heights, I began to dream again. This time, my dream was simply to make it through the day and then to make it through the next day. I worked hard, and moved on from the burrito place to the restaurant next door to a new teaching job. My first book came out. I began to get my life back. But it wasn't my old life. It was a brand new life. And I was there to see everything. To feel everything. The good stuff and the awful stuff. I hadn't known what it was like to feel so much.

My life is now a quiet one. I teach, I write, I am a partner, a son, a brother. My life is a far cry from my early days in NYC. I am usually in bed by ten. When I walk near my house, through Madison Square Park, I am aware when the seasons start to change. And how, if I lie on the grass and look up, the buildings sleep against the sky. And in those moments, it feels as tranquil to me as an open field in Louisiana. It feels safe. It is home.

I sometimes think about how different I was then. I didn't even know who I was for so long. When I walk alongside the ghosts of poets and writers who made up so much of my world when I was a kid, I think how it's okay to come from that. And when I listen to Merle Haggard on my headphones in the middle of the city, I remember my uncles on tractors and fishing boats, and I know that I come from that, too. And when I walk down Christopher Street, past the Stonewall, and think about all the men and women who have walked that street before me, also in search of themselves, I know that I come from that, too. It took me a long time to accept that I am all of these things. That I am a man. A writer. A New Yorker.

After seventeen years, it's true that I've been here a while, but I have really just arrived.

MY FAMILY TREE

AMOS MAC

I REVEL IN TRANSSEXUAL HISTORY. On my off days I can be found in used book and magazine shops searching for any piece of proof that shows me where my trans sisters, brothers, mothers and daddies came from—to somehow get a grasp on who I am, who I could've been if born in a different time or body, while linking the historical connections to my life today. On rare occasions I'll find an old transsexual magazine, or a book that was not written by an outsider looking in, but by a queer person who was there and lived it. Intrigued by the hardly documented transgender past of my forefathers, I consume everything I can to help me see where my cultural family tree began.

Exhausted by gay history, at this point I only crave knowledge about *trans* history. A history that is barely documented except in tiny corners of black-and-white photographs from the Stonewall rebellion, from scandalous yellowed newspaper clippings about a "man found to REALLY be a woman," or on death certificates and police reports from years past. The bits and pieces of stories I hear from my elder peers I take in absolutely, and I listen harder and truer than I ever listened in any history class. I feel linked to all of the people who came before me and consider them all my family. Currently, trans people are growing as a community and as a culture because we are living it and talking about it openly. Our experiences matter and are relevant and become stronger and more documented the more we share ourselves with the world.

I learn a lot about the queer culture I missed out on through documentary cinema and art books. I like to watch *Gay Sex in the 70s* and crave the freedom that the men in the film muse over, probably because it is not an option for me. I watch the men on the screen talk about AIDS and how all of their friends are dead, and narcissistically I wonder how I will look when I am their ages, as a man in my 60s, if I am even still alive at that time. I wonder what it would've been like for me as a "passing" transsexual man in the 1970s, hanging out by the Piers, the trucks, the baths. Would I have wanted to be a part of that world? Would they have let me? Would I have kept my pants on to hide the identity of my body, only getting on my knees to suck anonymous cock in the back of a dark truck in the West Village? Do you think Robert Mapplethorpe would've wanted to photograph me? Or would I have chosen to hide away, been stealthy, or craved a heteronormative life? As a queer trans man, where do I fit in with the history of gay New York City? How much of my current lifestyle is made up from the people who came before me that made me realize it's okay to be a faggot and a man with a pussy at the same time? Would I have felt an internalized pressure to conform with these men, gone a different route and gotten bottom surgery so my genitals matched theirs? Were there any men with vaginas that hung out in that scene? It isn't surprising that such a subject isn't mentioned in the documentary.

I think about the '80s a lot, too. When I pine for being a young queer in 1980s New York City I tend to forget that I am trans. In my dreams of being a young artist in the '80s in New York City I have a dick. I know I would've been friends with Keith Haring. Maybe even lovers. We would've met in art school, started a fake band together, gotten arrested together for destroying subway advertisements with paint pens. I would've listened to hip hop before anyone else. Worn Adidas sans laces. Probably would've scored some of Keith's throw-away art and looked back on it and been proud to say, "Yeah, we were friends, here's my collection of his napkin drawings, I don't show this to just *anyone*, you know." Basquiat too. I swear! I would've been all up in that world, coming up with ideas that Warhol would borrow. As for the '90s, I kick myself for not having the balls to run away and become a preteen drug addict with Michael Alig and his club kid cult after I saw them on a daytime TV talk show. The final days of worthy NYC culture, slipping away into a K-hole before I was even in high school. With so many years of "missing out" to think about, it's hard to remember that the act of simply existing and producing work as an "out" transsexual artist in this contemporary world is paving the way for the next crew of kids in a post-gay world. The fascination of linking my current self with queer culture of the past is in part about not feeling connected to any particular scene in the gay world or my blood family, mixed with the desire to carve out a space of my very own.

When I started to medically and socially transition from "female" to male in New York City in the 2000s, my New York City didn't look anything like the *Gay Sex in the 70s* New York City. By the time I hit New York, it was a glossed over, bland mall. I've only personally known the West Village as a place with high-end salons, where expensive salads are consumed on sidewalk patios under giant red umbrellas. The cobblestone remains, but no dark alley blowjobs are to be found. Believe me—I've looked. My bank account felt that I was much better suited to live in an old yarn factory in the Bushwick section of Brooklyn. Being a fan of dirt and grit and blooming creativity, Bushwick and I were a much better match. It was 2006, and I was only peripherally friends with other trans people. There was no one I was close to that I could ask questions or share my life with on a relatable level. I was working at cafe on West 14th Street where some regulars included RuPaul and John Cameron Mitchell, plus tons of Hollywood actors who preferred the quiet, overpriced neighborhood brownstones than what Los Angeles had to offer. Some days I'd think of the cafe as a living, breathing tabloid. I actually referred to it as that exactly in a text message to my mother from those days. Like something out of *US Weekly*'s "Stars: They're just like us!" section, I'd wait on Oscar-winning actors first thing in the morning who came in to get coffee with no make-up on, on their way to boxing classes or en route to dropping their screaming toddlers off at high-end day care. When I think about these days all I can remember is the feeling of my transition being on a stage. Despite that time so early in my transition being incredibly private, the fact that I had to leave the house at all made me feel a very public panic. Although my job as a barista wasn't exactly the same as performing in an amphitheater, making lattes for a hundred people a day felt public enough for me that it was a constant mental break down that I kept to myself.

When it comes to my life, I feel that I'm ten years behind. I like to say I was sixteen years old emotionally when I started to transition. At twenty-six, my self-esteem was below average and stunted. I had trouble making myself and my art visible in the world until I felt respected as a human being. I was an artist living in a shell.

My photography was all about hiding in the background and not being noticed. I wanted to document the culture and the world that I lived in, but I didn't want to have to actually take part in the *living*. My lack of self-esteem and self-worth exuded from my early work. I never wanted to have to speak to another person about photographing them, so I shied away from portraits. I dubbed myself a "street photographer," by default, and most of the images I took pretransition document various street scenes: broken glass and ironic graffiti, lots of images off of Knickerbocker Avenue in pre-gentrified Bushwick, images of people in the East Village from afar, usually with their backs turned to my lens. All of my self-portraits consisted of separate body parts up close and personal, and in a few you see my hand and fingers holding a flaming middle school portrait— quite literally flaming, since I had set it on fire. The school portraits from my preteen years, the years when my body was changing and you could classify me as the most miserable—I wanted that part of my history to disappear, but at the same time I wanted to show the viewer that I was making it fade away. I find the images that I shot then to be beautiful, but at the same time, they are sad to revisit.

I was given my first prescription of testosterone in Chelsea at Callen Lorde Community Health Center in March of 2007. I went outside and took a photograph of only a mittened hand outstretched, holding the scrip above the dirty snow-covered sidewalk on West 18th Street so I'd never forget the day. I remember how quickly I was able to get prescribed testosterone—just an initial intake meeting with the doctor, and then a one-time required meeting with their psychologist to deem me mentally fit enough to make this decision. After a month on hormones, my thin teenaged-looking "dirt stache"—the only thing I originally had to help me blend in as male pre-T—grew into a full-blown moustache, framing my new, much more angular jawline. My voice quickly deepened, forcing me to come out about my transition to my closest family members because I couldn't hide such an obvious change. Before I realized it, I was "passing"—no longer being seen as in-between, only being noticed as a young boy.

The change in my photographic work could be seen as soon as I started to socially transition. I used my art as a vehicle to meet other trans people and connect with those I felt I could relate to. I began documenting trans guys in Brooklyn and Manhattan that were accessible and around my age. I reached out to other human beings, and not only that, I would talk to them during the entire shoot, hoping to make the experience a personable one, where they didn't feel like I was an outsider prying into their experience, but rather as a peer and as someone who understood them and was using these photographic images for positive documentation of a world most people had no idea about. All of these images are the beginning of what would turn into a series I started working on that eventually turned into *Original Plumbing*—the trans male quarterly magazine I launched out of my bedroom with my friend Rocco.

The subway became my biggest battleground. I was harassed by all kinds of males, from teenage boys to adult men. They saw my demeanor and body language as a sort of quiet, flamboyant threat. I was chased after with a bucket of water (that was eventually thrown on me) in Bushwick for mincing down the street in a neon green polo shirt. I was screamed at and called a faggot for smiling in the general direction of a young father and his child sharing a bicycle. One afternoon I dared to look a man's shoes for longer than two seconds and he noticed and got offended, telling me I'd better not stare at his shoes if I wanted to live. I remember riding the L train with a Yoko Ono T-shirt on, fitted baseball cap on my head, and blue jeans. A group of five boys sat across from me on the long subway bench talking about me as if I wasn't there.

"What is it, do you think? Is that a guy? I can't tell."

"If we punch it in the face, I'm sure we'll find out."

The only thing I would do in situations like these was to stare back at the people, as if their words didn't affect me at all. Not the fighting type, I fought back with a silent, false sense of confidence.

Some people find it odd that I chose to leave San Francisco before I went through the motions of having a "sex change" in New York City. I guess I couldn't get past the feeling that if everyone else was doing it, should I? In 2001, when I first moved to San Francisco on a Greyhound bus, I immersed myself in the queer scene, and for the first time I actually witnessed people my own age starting their physical transitions with the use of hormones and surgeries. I was overwhelmed with my own gender panic and identity, and after a few years, while dating a straight woman, I chose to completely remove myself from the queerest city on earth and relocate to a city where I could feel the most anonymous—to be able to revisit who I was and see where I felt my gender was situated and if I was actually happy.

I got the word "Bushwick," a dead bee, a few noodles, a lucky rabbit's foot and Pee-Wee Herman's red bowtie tattooed on my arms. I vomited all over the sidewalk of St. Marks Place, the Upper West Side, the West Village. I broke up with a straight girl and fell in love with two queer girls while revisiting my attraction to gay men and falling for trans women while realizing my sexuality could no longer be categorized. While on a day trip to Coney Island with some San Francisco travelers I was reminded that a queer community existed somewhere. We inhaled poppers as the Cyclone slowly made its way to the top of the first rickety hump, then held our hands up and laughed and choked on the sea air above and below us. That year at the Wreck Room bar on Flushing Avenue I dressed as the California wildfire for Halloween. Red jeans, red suspenders, red baseball hat and a white T-shirt with a gold spray-painted cutout of California on my tightly bound chest, I held one lit match. Something about California was calling me back. I felt the strongest pull I had ever felt to rejoin the queer Mecca as a transitioning human being. I reached one year of hormone replacement therapy in 2008 and decided to move to San Francisco, this time as a second-time transplant. I moved there for my photography, for the muse I had met on the roller coaster, and to find my place as an artist. I got an apartment in Noe Valley, I got sober, I became close friends with two trans men who were my age, yet at very different stages of their transition, and realized I could have male friends who understood me more than anyone ever had. For the first time in my life I was connected with a group of people among whom I felt we truly completed each other. We were living in a new world as transsexuals during a time when we could create a different kind of history—a history that has the room to focus on the beauty of it all rather than the struggle.

And now I am experiencing the life of a person who was doesn't exactly feel—or strive to be—a man in the conventional sense. While I never truly identified or felt female, I transitioned to feel more comfortable in my body, which in turn made it a more male-appearing body, all the while never really wanting to become a man. I look at my peers, fellow artists who are transgender, transsexual, genderqueers and cisgender people, and I see a beautiful display of masculine and feminine and neither, and I realize the space we have created for ourselves by pushing ourselves to be who we feel we are inside, regardless of what history has told us.

At age thirty-one, I work for myself. At one point I wanted ano-nymity, but I got anything but that. My artistic career path led me to a place where a lot of the work I do involves the trans community and where I am an extremely out and visible artist in various areas of the world. Now when I walk down the street I no longer shy away or feel afraid of what people will think of me, or what they may assume about my sexuality or gender.

My sense of self is deeply affected by the gay New York City culture that has past, yet I rarely feel connected to what is happening in the gay present. I'm so inspired by digging up trans artifacts and feeling that I missed out on something huge in old gay New York that sometimes I forget I am creating my own history every time I snap a new photograph, write another article, or publish another magazine.

It is of the utmost importance for trans people to accept, recognize, and, most importantly, to honor the people who came before us. It is what has kept me going forward, to create a larger space than the one that was made for us by the people who have fought for every bit of visibility we have today. It is just as crucial for us to create a broader, more documented history of our world for the trans and gender variant people who will follow us long after we're gone. It's up to us to continue this family tree and realize that by living it, we are making it grow. I'd like to think that by sharing my story with you at this second in time, I've created one more leaf.

THE OPERA SINGER'S PANTS, AND HOW I GOT IN THEM

JUSTINE SARACEN

For most people, New York City has a sound track. Friends tell me it's traffic noise, ambulance sirens, and jazz. For me, it's opera.

The Manhattan-is-music meme was begun, no doubt, by my first great love. I had just returned to New York from grad school in California when she strode into my Upper West Side apartment and played a Chopin nocturne on the piano. Honest to God. That did it; I was hers. During the nearly ten-year relationship that followed, the house was filled with classical music and our preferred entertainment was attending a concert.

But finally, fate, in the form of a job change, ended both the New York City residency and the grand passion.

So there I was, moping around in the hinterlands, teaching in a hinterland college, and getting my musical fixes from recordings, radio, and television. After life in Manhattan, I was in purgatory.

Then one evening, while I ate my lonely dinner and channel-surfed the television, I came upon a puzzling scene. A gorgeous woman, in a cuirass and buskins, was singing a passionate love song to another woman. My forkful of spaghetti grew cold as I held it, rapt, before my open mouth. I remember the moment exactly. It was Mozart's *Idomeneo*, and Frederica von Stade was singing the role of the prince in love with the daughter of his father's enemy. An early Mozart work in the Baroque style, but somehow it had previously escaped me that in Baroque operas women dressed as men sang love songs to women. The tiniest bit of research revealed there were many more such travesties.

Quelle révélation! Not only Von Stade's handsome Idamante, but Cherubino, Annio, Romeo, Siebel, Sesto, Xerxes, Hansel, Nicklausse, Orfeo, Prince Orlovsky, even Julius Caesar himself, were all sung by mezzo-sopranos in pants (or armor and buskins). I had stumbled into a lesbian fantasy world.

What made these operas all so titillating was that the mezzo-in-pants was usually paired romantically at least once with the lead soprano. This visual titillation—and some stage directors carried it quite far—fueled by the soar of opera music, was like drugs to the brain. My library of opera videos grew exponentially.

My biggest "rush" however, came from Strauss' *Der Rosenkavalier* which, more than all the others, seemed calculated to shock. The opera opened with the orchestra musically mimicking the sexual act. An ever-accelerating *bumpa-dumpa-dumpa* culminated exquisitely in not one but two orgasms, followed by a sweet afterglow in the flutes and violins. When the curtain went up, there were two women in bed, singing about how fantastic their sex was. If this wasn't enough of a tease, as the inevitable operatic conflict unfolded, with betrayals, conspiracies, and duels, I discovered—ohmygod!—the third person in the love triangle was another beautiful woman.

The opera climaxed, thematically and musically, with an incandescent trio that gave me shivers of pleasure, and at the end, Octavian did yet another lip-lock, this time with soprano number two.

Think Xena and Gabrielle's first kiss, with full live orchestra.

How could I not become a trouser opera queen? I spent the next year flying into Manhattan for performances at the Met, learning the history of opera and the names of all the great divas, their roles and voice types. I corresponded with singers, shook hands with them after performances, bought all their recordings.

Exile will do that to you.

But like all drug users, I eventually craved a bigger fix. Opera on television was no longer enough. I wanted in.

Singing seemed to not be in the cards for me. I was prepared to sell my soul for that ability, but alas, the devil never returned my calls. Surely there was another way into the opera life. And what *was* the opera life, anyhow? Did divas live like the rest of us? Did they ever catch cold? What happened at rehearsals? How did it *feel* to sing melodrama in front of four thousand people? They were not questions you could ask in a fan letter or during a quick handshake after a performance. I stared at my stereo, brooding on how I could manage a long face-to-face chat with an opera star.

Then fate—perhaps to compensate me for demolishing the first great love of my life—came to my aid. Lo and behold, *Der Rosenkavalier* was scheduled at the Met, and a well-known German mezzo-soprano (whom I shall not name so she can't sue me) was to sing the role of Octavian. And there was icing on this cake: rumor had it the mezzo was gay.

I knew the Met, and I knew how to get backstage to meet the singers after a performance. Most of the time, you could have a little one-minute chitchat with them before the next person in line elbowed you out. The real challenge was scoring an actual sit-down conversation with her. How could I contrive such a thing?

My inner demon whispered shocking temptation. *Trick her. Tell her you're a reporter and get her to talk.* My inner angel was horrified. *You're barking mad and besides, it would be THIS close to stalking.* (She held up an angelic thumb and forefinger.) My inner demon, however, had the closing remarks. *Go for it, you fool, or wallow here in the boondocks clutching your pathetic opera videos.*

I went for it. Nothing to lose, after all, but my self-respect. First, I wrote a letter to the diva via her agent telling her I was writing an article for a German newspaper. It was only a little lie. I was not a reporter, I was not writing an article, and I had no connections with any newspaper, German or otherwise. Okay, so it was a big, brilliant, audacious lie. But I'd covered that ground already in my head. I would get the interview and offer it to a newspaper later. Or not.

Fate aided and abetted me further, for that season the above unnamed mezzo was also singing in *Die Walküre* at the Met, so I flew to New York to attend. With its breathtaking mythical staging, the performance alone was worth the trip, but I left the auditorium during the curtain calls. I was not there for Wagner; I was a woman on a mission.

There were surprisingly few people backstage to greet my mezzo, so I did not have to wait long before she appeared, dressed in street clothes, in the public corridor. I paid all the usual compliments and introduced myself in German as the person who had written the request for an interview. Her manager stood by her side, as well as another young German woman whose role I could not determine. She was attentive to the singer in the way a personal friend would be, but I had no time to study her. In my most professional manner, I handed over the carefully crafted questions for the singer's scrutiny. She glanced toward the manager, whose expression registered disdain, and I knew I was busted. He must have heard the "interview" ruse before, though he said nothing. The singer was gracious but vague and, realizing I was out of my depth, I retreated.

An early morning flight brought me back to my wilderness life, and in the weeks that followed, the lack of a reply convinced me that my reporter story really *was* over the top, and that no one in her right mind would buy it. Somebody must have checked with the local German language papers and discovered they'd never heard of me. I imagined the three of them, the singer, the manager, and the "Other German Woman," backstage at the Met, having a good laugh. It was humiliating, but I deserved it.

Then the postcard arrived. A simple one-liner. "Meet me in my dressing room right after the Thursday performance and we can talk."

Meet me in my dressing room. The sexiest words ever written. I fanned the air over my blushing face.

Not that there was anything sexual in the air. I was beyond such fan illusions. My desire at this point was not to intrude on my mezzo's person, but on her magical world. Besides, there was that Other German Woman.

Thursday finally came, and, after teaching my last class, I caught a 4:00 p.m. flight. New York City was never more enchanting than it was that evening when I got off the plane at La Guardia. Unlike the other concert trips, this time I was not just a fan. I was "with the band." And the artist knew my name. Sheer anticipation brought a kind of euphoria. The skyline seemed part of the stage setting; everyone I passed was an "extra." I hummed the Final Trio as I walked.

The performance of *Der Rosenkavalier* itself was an extraordinary experience. I was not so much transported as fully engaged. Not only could I mentally hum along with the now-familiar music and beam, watching the all-woman love triangle unfold, but I half-imagined the spectacle from inside the performance itself. I felt my mezzo's purposeful stride in boots and britches, my wrist twitched during her choreographed fencing with the villain, I sensed her glee in the double cross-dressing scene, and my lips moved along with hers as she sang the famous Trio. I even shared her obvious relief in the curtain call when the high notes were over. And then it was time.

If "Meet me in my dressing room" were the sexiest words I'd ever read, then an Octavian in full costume standing in a doorway inviting me inside was the sexiest image I'd ever beheld. She had taken off her wig, but was still in her third act outfit, a hunter green riding suit. As I came in the room behind her, she took off the handsome frock coat and hung it on a hanger. I glanced at it in passing. Brass buttons from collar to hem. Eight inch cuffs ornamented with vertical black velvet slashes, each one ending with an engraved brass button. I desperately wanted a coat just like that. Hanging next to it was the slender Act II sword with its jeweled pommel. I ached to have a saber, too.

Even without the dashing coat, in her gray green breeches tucked into knee-high suede boots my mezzo was a swashbuckling sight. She waved me toward an upholstered bench and then swaggered over to a stool where she perched, the high heel of one boot hooked into the cross bar. Her white shirt was rumpled from three hours of singing under hot lights, but only the sleeves were visible emerging from the brocade vest that ended at mid-thigh.

Freed from the third act wig, which was perched on a wooden dummy nearby, her dark hair was short and pixie-like. I sat down, enraptured by the half-fantastical person in front of me. The shepherd children must have felt that way beholding the Lady of Fatima.

Just over her shoulder I could see on a hanger the suit from the second act's "Presentation of the Rose" duet: Octavian's white satin breeches and waistcoat studded with silver and pearls. The dazzling fairy suit, the falling-in-love-suit, the suit that was in all my dreams.

There was a knock at the door and I cringed. Had the singer's manager traced my steps and was now rushing in to free her from my fraudulent clutches? But no. It was the Other German Woman, the one who had been in attendance during the Wagner opera. Were they lovers? Either way, she was collecting a suitcase and I wondered what was in it.

My mezzo twisted sideways to speak to the intruder and I took advantage of the moment to study her enchanting ambiguity. It was not the somewhat sexless androgyny of the blue-jean-and-sweatshirt butches I knew from Greenwich Village, but a subtler and enticing gender play of an attractive woman in the guise of a count. She was still half Octavian and had just been in bed with a princess. If Queerdom needed a noble icon, at that moment, she would have done nicely.

The dressing room door closed and we were alone again, so I began. I asked her boilerplate opera interview questions, when she had started singing, what roles she had performed, how she liked the New York audiences, etc. Her answers were candid and thorough, and she spoke lovely German with a warm contralto voice. I was glad the recorder caught it all because I could not have taken my eyes off her to scribble notes.

I focused on what she was saying, but as I began to visually separate the woman from the costume, the needle on my gaydar went way over into the purple. It wasn't just the pixie hair and the musketeer pose, either. There was also the growing certainty of the Other German Woman. My feverish imagination pictured her unpacking the suitcase in their love nest in some elegant New York hotel.

Gradually, my questions veered toward the one subject that obsessed me. How does it feel to be Octavian? Realizing the question was too vague, I added, "Are you conscious of the costume and props?"

I still have all her answers in a transcription of the interview and I read with a certain nostalgia her description of the rehearsals where she could practice the rapid costumes changes between and within the scenes. *Rosenkavalier* is all about costumes and—literally—transvestism. That was all the fun, she pointed out, changing from gentleman's hunting habit to silken ceremonial pants to female "disguise" and back to the britches of Act I. She loved the burlesque, the grappling and dueling, and the opportunity to act. "Though you do work up a sweat," she amended.

Octavian sweating into her costume was not an image I wanted to dwell on, so I pressed forward. What went through her mind during the famous Final Trio? I had sensed that evening how everyone in the audience had fallen silent just before the Trio began, but I wondered how she felt on stage.

My mezzo thought for a moment and then gave me the serious answer I was hoping for. The interview was over twenty years ago, but my notes show that I remembered it correctly, almost word for word:

"Then you are not aware of the public, or even the
desire to perform for them. At that moment, your own
honesty comes to the fore, and your own heart lies exposed.
You are carried completely by the music and you no longer
think. You are simply there on the stage, in a trance, and
the music carries you away to another place."

She paused for a moment and then added, "Those are the moments that make the whole profession worthwhile."

I didn't dare speak. In a conversation of nearly an hour, she had told me what I came for—but I wanted to hear more. I wanted to stay with her, inside her memory, reliving the ecstatic moments. Most of all I longed to know what it was like to kiss the other two women on stage. Did either one of them stir her lust, just a little, if not with lips or bosom, then with her voice?

But those were questions I could never ask.

The spell was broken by a second knock at the door. It was the Other German Woman again. "The wardrobe mistress is waiting for the costumes, and we've got to get going," she said looking pointedly at me, perhaps forgetting I could understand German.

"Tell her I'll have them for her in just a moment," my mezzo said, and I knew the interview was over. I switched off the tape recorder and made some vague remarks about sending notice to her in Germany whenever the article appeared in print. She seemed content and, mercifully, didn't press for details.

We shook hands and, in a daze, I let myself out. In the corridor, I passed the Other German Woman. Having deposited the suitcase some place or other, she was headed again toward the magical dressing room where she would witness the dis-enchantment—Octavian slowly disappearing with each discarded article of costume, and the woman emerging as herself. I shook off that sobering image and made my way down the long hallway to the stage entrance of the Met.

They were probably lovers, I decided, as I meandered out onto the now quiet Lincoln Center Plaza. I imagined them going out for a late supper at some quiet uptown restaurant and then retiring to their expensive hotel room and their bed. That's how it went. But whatever jealousy I might have felt for their love, if that's what it was, was beginning to fade before a more complicated sensation.

Lincoln Center was almost deserted now, and I glanced back at the arches of the majestic Metropolitan Opera, with its five-story glass archways and the high Chagall murals flanking the entryways. I was certainly not the first to think of the Met as a secular cathedral. A place to be transported and beguiled by singers, instrumentalists, stage directors, set designers, lighting experts, costume makers, and makeup artists. Half of them were gay, I knew, and all of them were adept in the conjuring of spirits.

I turned away from the Met façade toward the fountain at the center of the plaza, spotlights illuminating its exuberant shower. It gurgled and hissed comfortingly as I stared into the spurts of light-filled water, trying to make sense of my emotions. I almost laughed when I finally grasped the obvious.

Like the fountain, the opera was artifice, a joyous fake. Hugely elaborate, complicated, expensive, and intoxicating, but in the end, only a show. I was smitten with a fiction that a poet had invented and a thousand magicians had brought to life. My mezzo was one of the conjurers, of course, and though I would have welcomed a chance to know the woman inside the pants, it was the *pants them-selves* I wanted to get into.

I all but slapped my forehead. As much as I wanted Octavian, I also wanted to *be* Octavian, and play the charade. I longed to embrace the two sopranos wearing the hunter green riding suit with the dashing frock coat and riding boots. I swooned to imagine myself in the sparkly-pearly white-and-silver waistcoat and breeches with the glittering saber. I wanted to sing the Rose Duet, then ferociously dash from one adoring woman to the other, fighting a duel in between. On the Viennese Rococo set of *Rosenkavalier*.

Then my epiphany had an epiphany. I *could*.

I could get into Octavian's pants, and into everyone else's. I could swagger in them, sing in them, sweep across the stage in them, and I would always be able to hit the high notes. I simply had to write a novel.

In the following months, while my mezzo went off to sing in other opera houses, perhaps inspiring other lesbians, I sketched out my own *Rosenkavalier* tale. The plot evolved in desultory fashion over the next several years, then stalled. The interview never saw light in any newspaper and I never contacted my mezzo-soprano, so I silently begged her forgiveness for the fraud. But for all that, she achieved a different kind of acclaim after all, and one day I will seize the courage to tell her about it.

Twenty-three years later, *Mephisto Aria* was published by Bold Strokes Books, with features of my mezzo distributed over the two main characters.

Thank you, my mezzo-soprano, for giving me the loveliest and most chaste hour of my lesbian life, and for inspiring me, in my own way, to wear the opera singer's pants.

"Wie du warst! Wie du bist!
Das weiss niemand, das ahnt keiner."

THE SUM OF
OUR PARTS

JEWELLE GOMEZ

WHEN I ARRIVED IN NEW York City in 1971, John Lennon was still alive and Louis "Satchmo" Armstrong had just died. A lot of people voted for Mayor John Lindsay because they thought he was good looking. Frank Serpico risked his life to testify against police corruption; then his story became a major motion picture. That same year, two days before my twenty-third birthday, the prisoners in Attica took over that "correctional facility" and demanded better food and living conditions. When the State Police took back control, more than thirty people were dead, mostly prisoners. Stevie Wonder's song, "Living for the City," played in my head continually, sometimes a celebration, sometimes a dirge.

The great-grandmother who'd raised me back in Boston died that year, putting my world on tilt, which is why I spent so much of that first year afterward on drugs and at the movies. My favorite films were *Sweet Sweetback's Baadasssss Song, Klute, Play Misty for Me, Harold and Maude, Johnny Got His Gun,* and *The Andromeda Strain.*

I knew more about the Native American takeover of Alcatraz than I did about the Stonewall riots, and nothing about the Compton Cafeteria riot that preceded them both. I still had a hangover from the sit-ins, demonstrations, and final exams of my college years in the 1960s, so I gorged myself on gritty realism, political surreality, and mind-altering substances, figuring that somewhere in there I'd find the meaning of life in general or of mine in particular. I was too far away from family, away from my first and only lesbian lover and from my neighborhood. I was adrift and everything around me was strange in both a good and a bad way. I needed connection desperately and the mythology of the gay community of New York City held out that promise.

But the promise would have to wait while I started my NYC career working in television—the pilot shows of *The Electric Company* at Children's Television Workshop. They were designed to teach kids to read—something that schools seemed unable to do even back then.

I spent my first months in the city working at CTW's studios where I was in painfully over my head technically. My production assistant work at WGBH in Boston had not prepared me for the frantic pace of NYC studios. I was picked up by a company car at 7:00 a.m. and arrived back home at 7:00 p.m., if I was lucky. Since I never emerged from the studio during business hours I had to send my production assistant out to rent me an apartment. I felt like a character in a Hollywood movie made in New York.

I was so overwhelmed that I asked a (now *former*) friend to help me after hours to get up to speed. He knew the worldly ways of broadcasting outside of a small town. Unfortunately I'd still be waiting today on the darkened sound stage for him to show up and help me if the studio guard hadn't kicked me out three nights in a row. So much for brotherhood! Before I was fired I did get to see— up close—some of the best comedic talent in the business: Rita Moreno, Judy Graubart, Bill Cosby, Lee Chamberlin, and Morgan Freeman. That experience kind of set the scene for my early New York City years—comedy out of tragedy.

Once I was unemployed, I followed the path of many others who couldn't figure out what to do with their lives—I went to grad school. Of course I had to work at the same time so I taught theater and documentary filmmaking at The Loft Film & Theatre Center in Westchester, where I got to be the most radical out lesbian in the county. It wasn't that difficult an accomplishment since no one else seemed to be in the contest—maybe the one dyke printer I had an affair with in Yonkers.

I loved The Loft and the students but it was about as far from gayness, mythological or actual, as I could get. And the pastoral life of living over someone's garage in a small wealthy town that had proscriptions against selling real estate to blacks and Jews was a bit anxiety-provoking, not to mention galling. As time moved along I could tell everything I did was pulling me further away from the world of gay people (that word fit us all at the time).

The women I worked with at The Loft, Susan Ingals and Caitlin Roberts, were (gasp!) feminists so I was not alone in feeling like an outsider. They helped me put my life in a recognizable context. I came to understand why my "brother" had abandoned me to drown in my first attempt to make it in the big city. Once immersed in the politics of Flo Kennedy, Anais Nin, Gloria Steinem, and Molly Haskell, I understood why graduating from Columbia School of Journalism wasn't going to even get me an interview at CBS News.

One local station told me out loud they didn't hire females to work the night news desk! Nobody *wanted* to work the night news desk at a TV station, but the editorial staff would be damned if they'd even interview a girl even if she had the right degree and work history. So far, I was striking out with everything but my intellectual/political interior life.

It was 1974 before I found my way to the West Village, when Susie invited me to be her roommate on West 11th Street. I stopped working at The Loft and started to look for employment that might be within shouting distance of some other queer people. By then I'd not had an ongoing relationship with anyone since I parted from my high school sweetheart (and she got married to a guy) five years before. I did meet gay people when I worked in theater but everyone—especially the women—were so coy about it I didn't understand all the signals and I lived in fear of misreading someone. The obscure, underworld approach to lesbianism held no allure for me. Lesbianism isn't just a sexual practice—it's a political state of mind! I knew the lesbians were out there and as soon as I found a steady job I'd take the time to find them.

When I could, I wandered the streets of the Village hoping I'd bump into a critical mass of lesbians. I was on the hunt for the weekly meeting of Salsa Soul Sisters or at least reading Kate Millett to alleviate my sense of isolation. But my compass started to work with a couple of specific touchstones. First, I discovered the Oscar Wilde Memorial Bookshop; a bookstore is the place one can always find your people. Crowded, worn, bursting with energy and information; here was the portal through which I finally entered the world of gayness—through the doors of a book store that happened to be situated at the corner of Christopher and Gay Streets. Could it be more iconic! While I didn't yet venture down Christopher I'd at least made it to its beginnings, the place where its roots were planted; the gay bookstore that could be home to all of us…even those who, like me, were too shy to talk.

And I was morbidly shy. My first Gay Pride March, in 1975, I spent leaning out the window of my West Village flat listening to the marchers pass below. I still didn't know any out lesbians and was afraid of going downstairs to join what I saw as a predominantly white, male event. That's how it was presented on the news, in the tiny bit of coverage it received; that's what I saw when I looked down Christopher Street toward the Hudson River.

The mystery of the mythic Christopher Street remained in place for a long time and the sense of that street being out of bounds for me was real and not imagined. The clubs and other businesses catered predominantly to young white men who were at the height of their self-identification following Stonewall. The street was narrow, dense, seedy, noisy, crowded with men in tight jeans or short shorts—not a space that called out to most women except, perhaps, those older ones who fulfilled themselves living through the beauty of young gay men. That was definitely not me.

Then later, another discovery—the Duchess, which became my dyke bar—located where Christopher met 7th Avenue and Grove Streets. Again, seedy and suspect, but the bartenders, Pat King and Laurel, liked the women who came in, watched out for us, and as the theme song for *Cheers* testifies, we all want to go, "where everybody knows your name." I would walk from my job—by now I was gainfully employed—south from Union Square down to the 4th Street station of the IRT just to have an evening martini before I went home to Brooklyn. I could meet friends there before dinner, have a drink before a movie or just hang out. The community of women who sat along the bar was New York's Finest—municipal employees of all kinds, bankers, taxi cab drivers, postal workers, professors, writers, and maids. We talked romance, books and bands then rushed home to see the weekly episode of *Beauty and the Beast*. I held a reading for my first collection of poetry there, and it was so crowded I had to read from the steps of a ladder.

I was no longer freelancing as a stage manager, trying to break into broadcasting or university teaching; I had a "grownup" job at the New York State Council on the Arts. The director of my program, Gregory, invited me to a meeting with a group of guys who were angry enough to respond to the *New York Post*'s demonization of gay men because of the AIDS crisis. At first I was reluctant to add one more activity to my schedule—I was trying to write fiction. But I bumped into writer Vito Russo in the Village and he was that kind of insistent enthusiast that was hard to resist. I ended up at the meetings that resulted in the creation of the organization that became GLAAD. That work offered another opening in the lacey curtain that separated me from the world of gayness.

During that period I spent more time with gay men than I ever had before. We met after hours at my office and at the homes of different folks, including some who lived in the Village. I started to see gay men beyond the veneer of cockiness that lacquered Christopher Street, and I met lesbians who were willing to share their organizing skills to save lives. In meetings we focused on strategies for holding the media accountable for the hatred it plastered across its pages. It was when we were walking out for drinks or coffee afterward that the rage we felt gave way to reveal the hurt and fear of losing so many friends. I walked down Christopher regularly then; I knew the guy who had the smoke shop on the corner, I was recognized when I went into the bodega further down the street, and it was like going into some unique, protected universe. Even as the crowd of men that hung out on Christopher Street thinned, the myth of its life grew.

With the ease of entering what used to be foreign territory I realized that the mythological place I was venturing into was not that difficult to find. It had taken me a long time to realize that the path was through the people. The monolithic, white, male world of gayness was a construction that could be chipped away when I looked at it through individual faces. Not that the racial and gender segregation of the general population doesn't exist in the gay world; we do, after all, learn how to love at the knee of our often narrow-minded families. I still do value bonding within our own unique groups (gender, ethnicity, professions) without the "other" (whoever that may be); it's extremely comforting and crucial for building an emotional and political core and makes us more centered before we form bonds with other groups.

But what I discovered was that seeing individual people lifted the veil of mystery from a community in which I felt invisible. Whether it was Craig Rodwell at Oscar Wilde Bookshop helping me sell my first collection of poetry, Pat at the Duchess (who still sends me holiday cards), or Vito deliberately pulling me in to those early GLAAD meetings—one by one individual connections made it possible to see my way to a gay "neighborhood."

Sometimes the mythology of a community can overwhelm recognition of the individuals who make it a community. Life is daunting when one is faced with monoliths. Black (like any ethnic designation), female, white, male, transgender, queer, are all both the sum of their parts and more than the sum of their parts. Just as Christopher Street is made up of a bunch of really different houses, stores, and people, our movement is, too. A myth is not what we live in, a neighborhood or a house or a family is where we live. Finding my way in and learning to balance my fears and to thrive on all those differences is the way I change myself and change the world.

THE MYTHS
OF THIS PLACE

SHAUN LEVIN

I'D COME TO NEW YORK to visit my brother who'd been living there for a couple of years, more or less since I'd moved to London from South Africa via Tel Aviv, and although I was in my mid-thirties I still hadn't been to New York, but I'd read the books and seen the movies—I felt as if I knew the city—so when I got off the plane (I'd flown in from a cousin's wedding in LA) it was like walking into my own dream. I'd wanted to hail a cab, all bright and yellow, and tell the guy, "Hey, buddy, there's a hundred bucks in it for you if you get me to Brooklyn by noon. Step on it, pal." I did say something to that effect, but it definitely wasn't a hundred, and we'd driven into Brooklyn, me in the back of the cab feeling mildly silly, but exhilarated, the windows open and the hot air blowing into my face like I was in the desert.

There'd been a moment, driving into Brooklyn, when I'd thought: *This sure ain't London.* I thought: *Fuck London. Give me fucking New York City any day.* I didn't care if it was scorching hot and that my back was sticking to my shirt, the whole of me plastered to the leather seat! I just wanted to get to my brother's apartment and take the subway into Manhattan and walk through the Village, those streets that had been part of my psyche for years, from long before I ever thought I'd get here—the myths of this place, the poems and stories of Kerouac and Frank O'Hara and James Baldwin that have steered me through the years. It had always been enough to know that New York existed, a kind of promised land, more than San Francisco, more, of course, than London; England is more suited to my disposition—its melancholy, its unpredictability, its gloom, and to my tendency to deny myself the pleasures of the body, though that all changed in New York on that visit, with me landing up on my knees in Central Park around midnight, sucking dick.

It was May, but as warm as mid-summer, and I'd met Hilton downstairs at The Monster Bar, opposite The Stonewall Inn; later, we'd walked, mildly drunk, the long walk to Central Park and found a bench in a secluded spot and he'd sat down and unzipped his trousers and taken out his cock and I'd knelt before him, just like that, and sucked it. He'd recently got back from Afghanistan, or maybe it was Iraq, and all that evening he'd talked about the pain in his tooth, a throbbing ache at the back of his mouth, a wisdom tooth that was rotting and which he was going to have extracted the next day.

He liked to call me baby.

As in, "It's just me and you, baby," which is what he'd said when this old geezer came and stood behind us and started jerking off while I was on my knees on the grass. I'd never been called baby before, not by anyone, and I wanted to flee and I wanted to crumble. It was that kind of time, that time in my life, probably one of the worst. But New York was glorious. It was steaming hot, even at night, and me and Hilton were invincible. In pain, but invincible.

"Just keep sucking my pee-pee," he'd said.

"Your pee-pee?" I said, smiling up at him.

"Yes," he said, and put his hand gently on the back of my head.

"I want to go," I said. I wasn't ready for an audience.

We went to some bar after that, a place on 74th Street, down a couple of stairs from the sidewalk; I ordered a Corona and Hilton drank rum and Coke and we sat at the bar like regulars. There was a small rock behind the counter with the words fairies welcome chiseled into it and that made me happy, and Hilton knew the bartender, which, too, made me happy. Like I belonged. Like I was making connections, because after three years of scraping around in London and keeping the wolves from the door and various other clichés of the writer's struggle to survive, I'd come to realize that London was not a good place to be alone and penniless; nobody poor was doing anything interesting, not the kind of writing and art that inspired and sustained me and had kept me going for so many years. Like the writers in New York who'd been scribbling and sweating for the past forty-odd years, in Andrew Holleran's *Dancer from the Dance*, in Melvin Dixon's *Changing Rooms*, David Wojnarowicz's diaries, Jane DeLynn's *Don Juan in the Village*, and all the stories of love and sex and the Everard Baths and the Anvil, everything that had been handed down to me, branded like an ancient topography on my soul, transmitted through my DNA as if this is what my queer ancestors, my real ancestors, have been doing since long before I was born, and suddenly I'm here. I'm here to find out where I'm from—this is where I'm from!—here to discover my roots, in Brooklyn, in Manhattan, in Central Park, the dew of its grass still wet on my knees.

At the wedding in LA, I'd oscillated between feeling like an untouchable and imagining myself as some hipster, especially that night in Bar Marmont, beneath the hotel where John Belushi died, where my cousin and I had sat and ate and watched the maitre d' from our table, ogling the guy's thick eye shadow and the rouge on his cheeks, his false eyelashes, his Lycra trousers with that crazy snakeskin print, and his bright blue shirt open to mid-torso, his chest all pumped up and waxed.

I loved that dimly lit bar, its reds and golds—yes, it did feel like Paris—and we'd eaten oysters and shrimp tamales, dim sum, tuna steak, salmon in filo pastry with horseradish and salsa. We drank cosmopolitans and smoked—was it that long ago?—and at some point a young man, a boy of about twenty came up and asked for a cigarette, said his name was Mick, and stood with us, his arm brushing against mine. I remember staring at him, fascinated by the vast dimensions of American youth, its energy, which gradually sapped some of my own.

"So..." Mick said. "You guys live here, or you just visiting the fine city of LA?"

"He's from London," my cousin said.

"London?" the guy said. "Now, London is cool. London is cooler than this place."

And just the thought of home made me despair, to think about the moment I'd walk through the door, maneuvering my suitcase past the bicycle of the upstairs neighbor, lodged there in the entrance hall, everything feeling small and dingy, a dirty place to come back to: the stained carpet, the wallpaper oily with grime. I couldn't bear to be in that house any longer; I'd stretched my misery to its limit. I'd always lived my life like that, waiting for the point of no return, not trusting my desire until it was almost too late. For a long time I lived the almost-too-late life.

"YOU WANT ANOTHER DRINK?" HILTON said, smiling.

"Sure," I said.

"Kiss me, baby," he said.

"Sure," I said. And did.

The lights in that bar were dim, too; I was grateful then for those shadowy places, underground, hovels to escape to after dark, engulfing, so that when we came back out onto the street the brightness of the city was a surprise, especially that late at night. We walked toward the subway station, me catching glimpses of myself in shop windows, my reflection, as if a ghost was following us down Broadway, not Hilton, myself but not myself, me as unrecognizable. The ghost looked like my father, who by then had been dead for six months, but there I was, having crossed an ocean and a continent, encountering the ghost of man with hair darker than mine, almost as tall as me, as my father had been. I didn't say anything, not to Hilton, who was still focused on the sharp pain in his jaw, his rotting tooth, which he was about to have extracted the next day at the Veteran's Hospital, or maybe later in the week, I can't quite remember, but it all happened when I was there.

We stood together at the entrance to the subway, him about to get on the train to the Bronx, and me in the other direction, eventually to change to the F train that would get me to Brooklyn. He was beautiful, perfectly formed in that American way, every part of his flesh the right proportion, a body built for battle or porn, which sometimes amounts to the same thing. We were kissing by then, aware that what others would be seeing was a white man and a black man embracing, and I thought about *Another Country* and Wallace Thurman. Then it started to rain, a slight drizzle, an attempt at a respite from the heat; the tiny raindrops caught the light from the streetlamps so that it seemed like the air was streaked with glitter and I said, "See you tomorrow." And he said, "Yes, baby, yes, see you tomorrow."

On the subway I thought how everything that had happened that day was what I'd been hoping for. There'd been a eureka moment on the plane from LA, somewhere over the Rockies, me by the window eating Oreo cookies, and I'd decided, *I will enjoy New York, everything it has to offer; I will make the most of my time there.* Misery and discomfort had become my addiction, and like my father, or perhaps because of my father, I did not trust joy. My uncle had told me a story about sitting with my dad on the beach in Malibu one evening some years back. They'd been out hiking in the hills all day; the previous day they'd gone deep sea fishing and my father had said to my uncle, "There's something wrong with this country, Neville. Nothing can be so good. When you find out what it is, tell me." But my uncle said there was nothing to tell. *Things really were that good.*

I can tell you one thing that is wrong with New York: The waiters! They rush you when you've finished your meal, become proprietary, mark their territory, make it clear that they will be taken into account. You cannot ignore the waiters in New York. This is not Paris. In New York there is always the waiter to include in the equation. He is a witness; a servile lover; a bossy bottom. Those were the kinds of thoughts I'd been having that afternoon at Fanelli's on Prince Street, pretty much straight from the airport, while my brother was at work, before I'd met Hilton and we'd landed up in Central Park around midnight... or perhaps the whole waiter thing happened later during that visit, but I definitely went to Fanelli's. That much I do remember. Now, I always go to Fanelli's.

I remember it because that was the afternoon they played Van Morrison, and hearing his voice took me back to my father's hospital bed and my mother saying to me, "He was a best friend. We had fun. We did things together. We liked reading the same books and listening to the same music."

"But Van Morrison...," my mother said. "I could never understand how he liked him."

And since then, Van Morrison keeps appearing in unexpected places, like the week before New York in the shop at the Getty, Van Morrison was murmuring through the speakers, a whisper from my dad. I kept quiet about it, didn't say anything to my cousin; I've learned that sometimes sharing can dilute a moment; the essence evaporates when the conditions change. Purity is in the private experience of a moment.

BY MID-MORNING, TEMPERATURES HAD SHOT past thirty-five degrees Celsius—ninety-five degrees Fahrenheit, the TV news said; I felt trapped in my brother's apartment, housebound by the heat as if there was nowhere to escape to, not even to the coolness of Starbucks on 7th Avenue. I had to get out, to move, to create my own breeze. Walking toward Prospect Park, I began to notice that the city's intense heat created its own music and decay, television noises from open windows, the whirr of air conditioning units, the way some buildings seemed to crack like parched earth. No one sweated as much as I did! It was as if I couldn't keep my pores closed, as if I were opening up, leaking out, as if my entire insides were melting; everything could come gushing out at any moment. My Chinese-medicine doctor back in London had said I was the kind of person who couldn't hold onto good things, that I had to arrive at a place empty, to purge myself before I went in, to create the kind of vacuum that got filled with dread and guilt and self-doubt.

I considered going into the cinema on Prospect Park West to get out of the heat, but *Frequency*, *Gladiator* and *Keeping the Faith* were not movies I wanted to see. Instead, I took the train to Coney Island, expecting to find, as they'd promised in the inflight magazine, decayed grandeur, but what I found were people selling used car parts, faded CDs, clothing from the 60s, furry toys—everything bleached by too long in the sun. The game arcades were open but empty, loud music blaring from their doorways; and vast counters of hot dog vendors selling cheese dogs and onion rings, French fries and cheese fries. I'd stood in the queue at Nathan's Famous hot dogs, transfixed by the woman behind the counter, her twangy accent. I lost my patience and headed towards the beach, past more boarded up restaurants and hot dog stands, Mama's Italian Ices, the fun-fair rides, many of them brown from rust. I watched two Hasidic boys get into cars on the racing track; the guy on duty kept announcing over his megaphone, "Your gas is on the right, brakes on the left," over and over until I was too far away to hear, the sound of the waves against the shore drowning out all other noises.

I bought some onion rings and a corn on the cob from the Grill Bar on the boardwalk and went to sit on a bench by the sea. A couple was playing in the shallow water; others were lying in sleeping bags on the sand. The air was cooler. I could feel it on my feet, in the new sandals I'd bought from a wholesale shoe place near my brother's flat. "Crunchy granola lesbian sandals," he'd called them, and then he'd gone off to class (he was training to be an actor) and then to work, so I only saw him late at night, sometimes in the mornings. Since our father's death we seemed to appreciate each other's company more, as if me and him were fragments of our dad, ricochets, reminders of what we loved about him; just knowing my brother was in the same city was enough.

In Washington Square, later, waiting for Hilton, I'd watched three young men playing Hacky Sack; near them, a guy with a guitar was singing "No Woman, No Cry." And for a moment I was still again, paused in my lostness, my frantic wandering through streets. There, in Washington Square, I was surrounded by life, something bigger than me, and, like the sea, it calmed me, allowed me to disappear for a while. I kept my eyes on the singer, tall and slim, his skin brown, until he spotted me and smiled, quickly and easily, which is when Hilton turned up and sat down, nudged me, looked across to where I was looking and smiled at the guy and shrugged in a way that said, *He's mine*, and the guy nodded back, bowing out gracefully.

"How did it go?" I said, my heart about to explode.

"All gone," he said, and took his tooth out of his pocket, neatly wrapped in gauze. "For the tooth fairy," he said. "Extra cash for my birthday."

"When is it?" I said.

"Friday," he said.

"I'll be gone by then," I said.

"We'll celebrate tonight," he said, and produced two tickets from his back pocket, another gesture no one had ever done for me, surprised me with tickets to a concert. "Worth their weight in gold," he said.

A friend of his had to leave for a work trip and had offered Hilton the tickets: seats to the opening night of Keith Jarrett at Carnegie Hall.

"But I thought he was ill," I said, the tender notes of the Koln Concert already playing in my head, images of him hunched over the keys.

"Well," Hilton said. "He's back."

May has always been the month of birthdays, especially when I was growing up, a couple of twins at school, my father, my nanny, my cousin in LA, and then later Simon and Boris, both of them lovers, one killed by the virus, the other, for all I knew, still with his wife. May has brought many men I have loved into the world.

When we got to Carnegie Hall and discovered that the seats were so high up, Hilton went to one of the ushers and said that his boyfriend—his *boyfriend*!—suffered from vertigo and would it be possible to sit somewhere else. The guy led us away. "Thank you, gay mafia," Hilton whispered in my ear as we descended two flights and were offered the latecomer seats on the side, padded stand-alone seats where we sat and waited for Keith Jarrett to come onstage. And it was as if he'd returned from the dead; illness had silenced him, kept him in the underworld, but now he was back, walking onto the stage. The audience rose to its feet, and waited for him to reach his piano, just him and the piano onstage, and he sat down, and we sat down, and he began to play. His long fingers tapped the keys, touching but not touching, a kind of egoless playing, Zen-like, the first gentle notes of "It's All in the Game," the words to which I knew from an old Van Morrison cover. I mouthed them as he played, a song that began with *"Many a tear has to fall"* and I kept going, my hand in the hand of the man next to me, smiling at each other, following the lyrics in silence till their conclusion, till the final words that promised me that my heart would fly away.

BUT NO. THAT WAS NOT how it was, not the last scene, not the ending.

What really happened was that my mother bought my brother and me tickets to see Keith Jarrett. She wouldn't be traveling anywhere for the next few months, not till the year of mourning was over, so she wanted us to go; she knew my dad would have wanted us to be here. So we sat in those seats reserved for latecomers, my brother and I, and we smiled and we looked at each other as Keith Jarrett began to play and we knew we were thinking similar thoughts, something perhaps about my father's joy in the face of such beauty, the love of rhythm we'd inherited from him, how he'd taken us out of South Africa all those years ago and driven us across Europe in a VW Combi van, music blaring from the speakers—Stevie Wonder and Earth, Wind and Fire the soundtrack to our exodus. And now, after almost twenty years in the desert, we have dispersed again, each of us on a continent of his own, our bond a man who long ago disappeared, but keeps reappearing in mysterious ways.

THE VOICES

CHARLIE VÁZQUEZ

THE VOICES.

I'll admit that when I began writing this I was a bit circumspect about my limited experiences on Christopher Street. It was after talking to my brother-in-spirit, Charles Rice-González, about how I felt trepidation about being vague on such a momentous queer historical discussion, that I decided to take on a more direct and fearless approach. Perhaps it's the ghosts of that famed lane that I seek to pay homage to here.

Christopher Street was never the location of my (prolonged) queer life—this was pure circumstance. It more properly plays the role of historical anchor for me instead—Rue des les Stonewall Riots or something like that. In the midst of 1990s-era globalization I was able—even as a struggling musician and writer—to visit various gay ghettos around the United States, Mexico, and Canada with relative ease, supplementing my voracious appetite for history books with personal experience both brilliant and forgettable.

I can still see the pin as it was back then in 1986. Or perhaps it was 1987. I was with my best friend Edgar in the East Village and had just had my then-luscious hair hacked into a ridiculous style at Astor Place Hair. I then watched as the barber who sacrificed my hair did a number on Edgar's. From Astor Place we went shopping for trinkets—pins, posters, and cassettes (yes, cassettes) of the latest records to satisfy our punk rock wannabe hearts. I think of that era as my "true" hatchling phase—"me," as who I wanted to be, not "me," who I was expected to be.

The vintage store was on Broadway at around 8th Street. Passing through rows of pastel-hued tuxedo shirts and military camouflage fatigues I saw it on a countertop, like a miniature beacon in the distance. I went for the rotating pin display and started cackling at all the outrageous vulgar outbursts printed on them. Sex, sex, sex—everything was sexual or sounded that way. Sex, drugs, and rock-and-roll. And while we're at it, add homophobia to the mix.

"Don't pick up your change on Christopher Street?" I asked my best friend, holding the pin up for him to see. I didn't get it at all.

He rolled his eyes. "Christopher Street is where the maricones hang out. Now do you get it?"

Being the sweet human being Edgar has always been, there was no contempt or damnation in his voice when he spoke the word maricones; not in the way I was accustomed to hearing that most dreaded word and insult intoned. Maricón was something I associated with brutal death, heartless abandonment, and deep Catholic sin—the most abominable things possible; even being gay itself, that most certain purgatory for, by then, my secret world of naïve homoeroticism was like a little hell I kept surrounded by a fortress of perpetual fear.

I WAS BORN AND RAISED into a working-class Puerto Rican and Cuban family in the South Central Bronx, lived and went to school on all sides of the Bronx Zoo and Botanical Garden, and discovered all the countercultural treasures that would launch me into underground music and literary culture in the East Village when I was a teenager in the 1980s. I was too young and broke to go to nightclubs and most concerts, but I knew that amazing things were happening around me. I heard music I'd never heard, saw posters of people and things I never knew about, and wandered in awe through more book and record stores than I care to remember.

In those days, Rastafarians smoked joints along St. Marks Place while peddling dub reggae cassettes, throngs of junkie punks lounged like dozing lions along the steps of buildings, and there was always a dangerous, yet thrilling, vibe in the air—an ecstatic sense of adventure despite the ravages of crack cocaine, heroin, urban decay, city bankruptcy, Reaganomics, and the escalating AIDS crisis.

But that was the East Village.

It was in the East Village that I learned about Christopher Street and the West Village where *those people* hung out. This was almost always expressed with a hiss of disgust and dread, for the 1980s had ushered in the onslaught of AIDS. And gay men, especially in the metropolitan centers of New York, San Francisco, and Los Angeles, were its vilified scapegoats. We were spreading a nebulous plague and were being ruled by a president who refused to acknowledge its existence. The 1980s was a decade of profound darkness for many reasons.

And in those early days of AIDS in New York, Christopher Street was the indisputable center of gay Manhattan (although this has shifted to Chelsea over the years).

The first time I went to that most famed thoroughfare was alone and in paranoid secrecy, just a few weeks after I learned of its "unholy" existence (as any nice closet case Latino New Wave teen from the Bronx should, right?). The newspapers and media reported on gays and AIDS with such venomous contempt in those days that my homophobia nearly paralyzed me when I ascended from the Number 1 train at Christopher Street by Village Cigars, which immediately looked familiar to me.

I walked all the way to Hudson Street along the north side of Christopher Street and returned to Seventh Avenue on the south side. Not sure of what I was supposed to expect, I was pleasantly surprised to witness colorful variations of what the ultimate street rebel could be in those times—the rebellion of punk had by then charmed my heart and my eyes were always on alert for things avant-garde and ballsy.

Lies and garbage, girl, you WORK!

Out gay men. Fierce gay men. Masculine leather men. Feminine Asian queens. Sex toys, leather, and porn stores. People drinking beer on the sidewalks. Gay bars packed with men. White, black, Latino, Italian—a rainbow of skin shades and attitudes. Lesbians, even. Eyes taking in everything. Primal visual instinct at work. A landscape of silent communication, celebration, and often of skeletal men living their last days. A bar door swinging open to reveal its contents—the stench of liquor and Diana Ross's "Love Hangover."

The occasional waft of a burning joint dashing by...

It was not the horror movie I had expected at all—that is, in my fleeting and youthful perspective. If anything, my first recollection of Christopher Street was something like a party happening in several different rooms of a large house, each with its own aesthetic ideal of what it meant to be gay. And as I would learn, those divisions of music and fashion and aesthetics had become a global phenomenon I would experience in my own development years later.

The first time I ever went drinking on Christopher Street was in the mid-1990s, sometime after I came out in 1992 at age twenty-one. I was living in Portland in those days, but came home to visit as often as I could. I went to The Hangar and played pool and flirted—but truth be told, there are pockets of time that I cannot recollect with accurate detail (yes, I was a party boy). I do remember feeling refreshed to be in a laid-back bar with friendly people of color for a change, as that was not as common in über-white Oregon.

It was at The Hangar that I noticed a small and unassuming bar across the street, Ty's, which is now often relegated to "bear bar" status in gay bar lingo. I remember spending afternoons there upon my first few weeks back in New York City in 2006, as well as Sunday evenings. It was the polite, working-class vibe that I liked about Ty's. Most men weren't there to show off their gym bodies and/or bad Chelsea/West Hollywood fashion sensibility; they were there to chat up other men like themselves—perhaps men who enjoyed baseball or classic rock music or hiking in the mountains.

I did not see the days of Boots and Saddle's country-western glory, but do remember a fun afternoon spent at a beer bust at The Dugout (and a couple of random visits to Pieces after indulging in books at the Oscar Wilde Memorial Bookshop until it closed for the evening). None of these bars was my ideal, but what I did enjoy about strolling down Christopher Street when visiting from the West Coast was the easy and flirtatious mix of eager locals and excited tourists.

My favorite and most memorable night there was in 2005, on the last trip I made to New York before moving back for good. My friend Michael was also in the city (we were roommates in Portland then), and, as he had also grown up in New York, we made a New Year's Eve pilgrimage to the Stonewall Inn—the mothership—but were separated by the insanity of the night and didn't see one another again until arriving in Portland a few days later.

While dancing to a bangra (Indian/Middle Eastern-flavored, percussion-heavy dance music) mix, I had one of those experiences where my mind seemed to separate from my body, while in the trance of dancing (I had by then quit doing all drugs and had put down, like, two cocktails, just to be clear!). I danced for hours without stopping. I kissed handsome men and chatted with friendly women. The music continued escalating into a sweaty and ecstatic universe of skin until I stumbled out at two or three in the morning for the long subway ride back to the Bronx.

I completely missed the pier scene that my dear *compadre de palabras*, Emanuel Xavier, documents so vividly in his early work. That's something I wish I could've seen, but as I was living so far away in my twenties and early thirties (and was so intent on getting laid back in NYC), the opportunity to experience a deeper and greater understanding of this famous gay folklore was thwarted.

As a result of my age and early transplantation out west in the late 1980s, Christopher Street holds a place in my heart in terms of my native city's history, the LGBT struggle as absorbed through our literature, and photographic nostalgia—the foundation of my own identity. Upon my return I dove into colorful New York history books such as *City of Eros*, *Low Life*, *Five Points*, and *The Gay Metropolis* to learn that Christopher Street, among many things, is one of the oldest streets in the West Village. (A brief aside: New York's gay bar history, with its mafia connections and police department payoffs, is amazing to study if you haven't already.)

As a Bronx Puerto Rican I was influenced by the Afro-Caribbean salsa music my father played at home during my childhood, then a touch of disco in the 1970s (*Saturday Night Fever*, anyone?), the colorful rap music of the early 1980s, and eventually heavy metal, New Wave, punk, post-punk, and hard electronica on the West Coast in the 1980s and 1990s. As a young musician, I took music very seriously. Excepting disco and in few cases rock music, these sounds were rarely heard in gay/queer bars for the most part (though in my experience, this began to change in the later 1990s).

Christopher Street's gay ghetto archetypes became emblematic of the universal gay ghettos I would visit while living on the West Coast for seventeen years. I came out in Portland's version of Christopher Street—then known as "Vaseline Alley," although I suspect that "Vaseline Alley" is and was the general name for any gay ghetto. Portland's Vaseline Alley was located then, and partially now, on Southwest Stark Street between around 10th Street and 13th Street.

It was a small spread compared to Gotham, but in those days quite a comprehensive one for a small city's red light district—as immortalized in Gus Van Sant's *My Own Private Idaho*, which was filmed right by my apartment on 12th Street. I cannot even count how many angels I encountered in those days—those who helped me and those who needed help.

At 10th Street was the Panorama disco where I worked as a nightclub photographer for many years, and CC Slaughters, a country-western-themed gay bar with line dancing and all things cowboy. At 11th Street was the Brigg/Boxxes, back then a youthful pop music meat market complex that would eventually connect to the Panorama to form a mega-complex of gay nightlife that became overrun by bridge-and-tunnel straight people on the weekends.

Scandals, just across the street, attracted a variety of men, old and young, in a relaxing and homey environment. Moving up the street was the Three Sisters, which was a delightfully sleazy tavern that underwent a series of changes and shifts of clientele over the years—though my favorite was when the Latina queens took it over for a spell and brought much-needed Mexican drag surrealism to the very white strip of Stark Street.

Straddling diagonal corners of 13th Street were the two eternal enemies: the Silverado and the Eagle PDX. The Silverado was a smoky flesh market, haven for strippers (often homeless/transient males) to make quick money, drink cheap drinks, and pick up johns—in a very high-energy house music and R&B environment complete with middle-aged drag queens à la Mae West. The Silverado was the most popular gay bar in Portland at the time and the boys of the Eagle PDX, where I hung out, resented this and most refused to go there. Things were very polarized in those days!

The Eagle PDX was the undisputed leather bar and it was there that I learned how to use handcuffs properly and flog someone—things we did for fun on rainy days (the activities I saw there I'll omit here for purposes of focus). It was at the Eagle PDX that I learned about BDSM, which in those days was called S/M, and general kink culture—as the men of the Eagle PDX were often unwelcoming of anyone who only indulged in what was and is referred to as "vanilla sex."

This was during a time, the mid-1990s, when queer punks started trickling in and mixing with the aging leather daddies, giving the often white male power-obsessed culture some new life. Though we were kept at arm's length at first, we were eventually welcome, that is, in our quest for "masculine" men and loud rock music. As punk boys, we already wore jeans and boots and leather jackets—but *our* way.

As I traveled to San Francisco and throughout the West Coast heavily in the 1990s, I explored the brilliant Castro Street and SOMA districts, the Capitol Hill scene in Seattle, surreal Davie Street in Vancouver BC, and a brief yet unforgettable encounter with Santa Monica Boulevard in 1999. Many of these excursions inspired different chapters of my first novel, *Buzz and Israel*, which I set out to write in 1995, after surviving a one-year relationship with a rather sexy and brilliant heroin addict.

Each of those districts offered the same exact music and entertainment as the others with few exceptions, and it was not uncommon to run into friends from other cities while traveling from one to the next (*"You're in San Francisco, too? Cool! How are things in New York?"*). But the predictable adherence to limited musical and cultural formats was what eventually drove me out of the gay bar scene—to seek more inclusive/diverse queer and/or intellectual and performance-oriented stimulus elsewhere. AIDS had by then slaughtered a generation of artists and their absence was felt like a pain in the soul—I knew this well.

As gays move into "undesirable" neighborhoods and increase their property values, there are always vultures lurking nearby to snatch the prize when everyone's looking the other way. It breaks my heart to read about people moving to the midst of Christopher Street—New York City's most famous gay drinking alley—and complaining about the street noise and loud queer youth of color from the boroughs who travel there to be themselves without fear of retribution. I don't think either side is right here necessarily, but this very real tension is counterproductive.

So what is the future of Christopher Street and other gay ghettos?

As gay marriage in New York and other states has become a reality and people feel more acceptance toward "alternative lifestyles"—whatever that means—the wall that functioned to separate homo and hetero will crumble, but I don't think it will disappear altogether. It's been happening for some time already. My guess is that there will be gay/queer/LGBT spaces in the future, maybe fewer than in the past, where we'll mix with our own kind and with our adoring allies and families. These places already exist and I don't think they'll ever go away.

I'm grateful for everything that my queer martyr ancestors

did to help the rest of us live easier in our skins now, as much of the cruising culture moves to a global community interconnected through the Internet and social media. The needs and interests of a burgeoning generation are always going to conflict with those of the generation in power—or the one on its way out. I've seen this for myself in my own personal growth.

I will admit this: If everything gay were to disappear from Christopher Street for good, I would feel profoundly sad. I hope that we have the humanity in our hearts and the sensitivity in our souls to honor those who perished to pave our way, those who opened doors that never existed before they created them—doors that we now walk through without even giving them thought.

These are the things I think about while on Christopher Street, the few times a year I make that special pilgrimage to the West Village to hear their voices. Their voices, their whispers—their joy and anguish and loneliness. Their victories—their secrets and stories and fantasies. Their tragedies and triumphs. Their smoky, hoarse laughter.

AS I STOOD FRYING...

FAY JACOBS

IT WAS NINETY-THREE DEGREES OUT by noon as we stood at the police barricade at 5th Avenue and 22nd Street waiting for the front of the New York City Pride Parade to reach us.

In my sweaty hand was the *2005 Pride Guide*, a glossy magazine listing events, the parade route, Pride organizers, judges and grand marshals, and a page headed "Accolade." It described the awards ceremony, to be held in the fall, to honor those individuals and organizations that embody the diversity of pride throughout the year.

I stared at the page. Above the story, in a pretty italic typeface, was the quote: *"Pride parades were born of brave individuals having the courage to come out as gay in often hostile, unsafe environments."*

And it was attributed to "Fay Jacobs, *As I Lay Frying.*"

I couldn't believe my eyes. I had no idea who chose to put the quote there, when the decision was made, where they bought my first book, or what prompted Pride organizers to use those particular words. But it sure looked good.

A friend e-mailed us the previous week, saying there was a quote of mine in the New York *Pride Guide* and I was pleased and curious. I couldn't imagine what kind of quote (Schnauzers or Rehoboth Beach life didn't seem appropriate), but I figured it was probably a quote among many, although I couldn't figure out why.

But there were my words, all by themselves, heading the page, in the publication in the hands of thousands and thousands of people and on the window sills or stacked up, free for the taking, in hundreds of New York City stores, bars, and restaurants.

I was by parts astounded, honored, flattered, and incredulous. And proud, for I meant what I said in the quote and this was Pride 2005.

It made me think about how far I had come over the decades, from growing up in New York with confusion about myself, to fear, to a toe out of the closet, to building a life with wonderful friends and family, to Rehoboth Beach and life as a writer, to a 2003 Canadian same-sex wedding, and now to a sweltering New York street surrounded by thousands of people with their own complex coming out histories.

I showed the quote to my wife Bonnie and her face lit up. "Cool!" she said.

But it was far from cool as sweat trickled down our necks, and the sun beat down, as we strained our eyes uptown to see if the parade was approaching.

And then we heard it. The thundering sound of motorcycle engines revving their way toward us. Ah, the dykes on bikes, breasts flapping in the wind, leading the parade! They were followed by the New York Police Department marching band, then by a parade of floats, dancers, music, placards, whistles, shouts, and cheers. Along with the PFLAG marchers, floats from bars, churches, health organizations, gay sports teams, liquor companies, banks and more, there were lots of laughs and some somber moments.

That year's parade theme, "Equal Rights, No More, No Less," was never far from people's consciousness. And the true diversity of the New York community shone bright: Latino contingents (Ah, the costumes and good looking people from Brazil!), Harlem Pride floats, Asian groups (OUT, not take-out!), black, brown, white all together, it was a refreshing and joyous mix. Gay firefighters, police contingents, flight attendants (duh!), rugby teams, you name it. We loved D-Flag (women and their dogs), gay dads with a sign, "We love our straight son," the naughty sign, "Brotha Fuckahs," and so much more.

One of the most touching groups (a few marching, a few riding) were some Stonewall uprising veterans, one with a sign, "Class of '69." They got sustained cheers and thanks from the crowd.

A contingent of walkers distributing "Honk If You're Queer" bumper stickers. The gay cable network Logo had a float, as did the Gay and Lesbian Task Force.

And of course politics had its day. New York Mayor Bloomberg led the way, with prospective mayoral candidates battling for applause behind him. A huge whoop of joy and cheers went up for political superstar Hillary Clinton, clad in her ubiquitous black suit and waving to crowd shouts of "Sister Hillary!"

As bystanders right against the rail, we were handed dozens and dozens of stickers, hand-outs, postcards advertising events, and a lifetime supply of condoms, which we passed back to some boys behind us.

By 3:00 p.m. we were parched, sweaty, and risking third-degree sunburn as the parade showed no signs of abating. A friend was volunteering at a party in the building behind us, at the *In The Life* offices. If you are not familiar with the show, it's a PBS gay news-magazine and I'm a big fan. Good luck finding it on your TV schedule, though. Each market hides it where they deem appropriate and mostly it comes on at 3:00 a.m. to outsmart sleeping bigots.

So we took refuge from the oppressive heat at the air-conditioned party, toasting Pride with a Mimosa and still having an awesome view of the parade from the *In the Life* office windows.

As I watched the spectacle below, my New York history flooded back. I was in high school in the mid-1960s, feeling different, an outsider, a geeky klutz among beautiful, feminine, straight-haired, and as it turned out, straight girls at my midtown Manhattan high school. My friends and I ran around downtown, sneaking into music clubs, ordering our bourbons and Cokes, woefully underage and unaware of why we felt so different, but so at home in the Village.

While my high school peers experimented with sex and drugs, my boyfriend and I talked incessantly about Broadway musicals; one of my drama club friends was rumored to be a lesbian, and while I was oddly scared of her, I was also oddly attracted; we heard about plays like *The Killing of Sister George* and *The Children's Hour* and didn't know what to make of them. We didn't know what to make of us.

As I watched the parade below, I had to laugh. After almost half a century since high school, the first years filled with angst, then evolution, what went around came around. I found my high school boyfriend—a charming gay theater buff and philanthropist who owns The Chelsea Pines Inn, one of the most awesome B&Bs in New York.

He came back into my life via the Internet when I went looking to book a gay B&B in the Big Apple. At the time, I knew two women who trolled Classmates.com and wound up leaving their husbands to run off with their high school sweeties. Apparently, the

Internet really is a great way to reach out and eventually get to touch someone.

I was incredulous the first time I heard a story like that, taken aback by the second one, and left wondering who'll be next. That both of my friends who linked up (no pun intended) with their former beaus were straight probably gave me a false sense of vicariousness to this phenomenon.

Then, one day, I found the Chelsea Pines Inn website on the Internet. I could not believe my eyes. The following is our e-mail exchange:

Hello—

I checked out your website and got a surprise because I recognized the innkeeper's name (*he who shall remain nameless*).

Are you the same (*first name*) who was my senior prom date in 1965? Rhodes School, Waldorf Astoria and then a post-prom ride to Bear Mountain State Park????

If so, we should have known we were both gay. Nobody else hates camping and likes Broadway THAT much.

I live in Rehoboth Beach (Gayberry RFD) with my partner of umpty-ump years (Bonnie) and will definitely have to check out your place when we head for New York!

Cheers,

Fay (Rubenstein) Jacobs

Dear Fay:

Okay, I'm stunned (and my office staff is driving me crazy, insisting that you became a lesbian after you dated me!) and here's what I remember:

We met when you were at the Rhodes School. You starred in the drama club play *Outward Bound* (you were pretty good, but what a bad play!), and we used to make out furiously in your parents' living room while they were out (Robert Goulet and Carol Lawrence lived in your W. 54th St. building, and so did the drunken Elaine Stritch, talk about your lesbian) and I hoped you'd never want to go further (which you didn't for a while), and we went to the Top of the Sixes for your prom, and you had a Corvette which you were still too young to drive, and our trip to Bear Mountain, and your visit to my home in Brooklyn (and making out in my parents' bed, which really freaked me out) and I still have photos of us dressed for your prom tucked away. And it's been 36 years since we last spoke!! And how cool to hear from you; It would be great if you and your lover would come to NYC and stay here; tell me how you got here from there over the last 35 (!!!) years.

Love, *(name withheld to protect the guilty)*

Dear *(he who shall remain in witness protection)*
Oy! Where to start!!!!!

First off, every man I ever dated (except the man I married, which is a whole other embarrassing story) turned out to be gay, so it had to be me that was the culprit, okay?

As for Drama Club (my pal Bob Smith calls it Gay Head Start), you were right about *Outward Bound* being a perfectly awful play. However, you were being too polite about my performance, as I'm a dreadful actress which is why I became a director. I foolishly tried to make my living that way for a while, but I have come to my senses.

Now to some appalling ancient miscommunication:

Yes, we used to make out in my parents' living room, where Goulet & Lawrence lived next door and Elaine Stritch dieseled to and fro. But, silly boy, it was I who prayed we'd never go farther than kissing; I was petrified and bizarrely disinterested. We sure could have saved ourselves years of angst if we'd just discussed it then. I've totally repressed the Brooklyn make-out session in your parents' bed (gawwwd!!!) and, contrary to your tragic misinterpretation, all I wanted to do was go to more Broadway shows with you.

What have I been up to? In college I majored in theater, watched all my friends get married, figured it was mandatory, married a freakin' professional accordion player (stop laughing), got divorced six endless years later, met my partner Bonnie in '82 and eventually chucked everything to move to Rehoboth Beach. By the way, that old Corvette croaked in 1973. I now drive the official lesbian car, the Subaru Outback.

We'd love to come to NYC and stay at your place. Thanks so much for writing, even with those seriously skewed memories. With all the stories you hear about people reconnecting through the Internet and running off with their high school sweethearts, we can both rest assured it won't happen here.

Cheers,

Fay

Suffice it to say that eventually, when I did stay at his B&B, I entered the room to find enlarged, grainy, frightening Xerox copies of my 1965 prom pictures, yearbook photo with me in the pointy white glasses, and other assorted artifacts adorning the walls. It was freaky!

As for my lesbian drama club pal, we, too, met up again, quite by accident at a book conference, and I'm pleased to report that she is now a happily transgendered male. Life is good. Life is weird. Go figure!!

As for me, here I was, happily in the life at the studios of *In the Life*, watching the parade below. I had been at these same studios several months before to be interviewed for the PBS show. Good thing DVRs were invented to record the 3:00 a.m. stealth showings of *In the Life* so when the producer called, I didn't say, "Hey, what?" like a nincompoop from the provinces.

The producer had read *As I Lay Frying* and wanted to include me in a series of interviews about coming out. "Can you come up to New York on Friday, if that's not too much trouble?" A tax-deductible trip to the Big Apple is my kind of trouble.

The producer ushered me into the studio, wired me for sound and leapt right into it.

"How did you tell you parents you were gay? How did they react? Set the scene for us. Do you remember how that made you feel?"

Did I ever. Like it was yesterday, not more than a quarter of a century ago. I remember phoning my father to tell him that Bonnie and I were buying a house together. He begged me not to buy a place "with another girl," insisting, "You'll never find a husband that way. What do you want to go and do that for?"

Sweat dripped down my forehead as Bonnie stood across the room, flailing her arms and mouthing, "Tell him, dammit, just tell him."

Finally I blurted, "I'm buying the house with Bonnie because, um, we want to spend the rest of our lives together…um, as a couple, uh, if you know what I, um, mean." It wasn't my glibbest moment.

"I…think…I…do," said Dad.

"Well, how do you feel about this news?" I asked, not really wanting to know and wondering why I asked.

His answer, in total, was the phrase, "Well…(deep breath) this *is* 1982."

Then he hollered to my stepmother, "Joan, can you get me a Scotch?" and we continued the conversation.

The producer probed. "How did you and Bonnie meet? What's life like in Rehoboth? Are you proud of your life as a lesbian?" And she didn't want just the facts, ma'am. She wanted to know how all of it *felt* and what it *meant* to me. For a person used to coughing up words, I got mush-mouthed as she said "delve, delve" like a submarine captain yells "dive, dive." So I bared my soul for forty-five minutes.

And when it was over, Bonnie and I headed to Christopher Street, stopped for a drink at the Stonewall Inn and prepared for a night of wine, women, then song, with show tunes at the legendary Marie's Crisis piano bar. Naturally, we also had plans to meet up with my high school sweetie. All in all, one of my gayest twenty-four hours ever. So now, I was once again at the *In the Life* offices. After several Mimosas, with the parade still chugging along below, Bonnie said, "Look in the *Pride Guide* and check what's happening in the Village where the parade winds up."

"Oh, you mean the *Pride Guide* with my quote in it," I said, my head swollen as Bonnie just rolled her eyes at me.

Can you blame me? We were consulting the same booklet about another million people were looking at. It was a very heady feeling being a part of the publication and the celebration. I admit, I was enjoying it.

So we fought our way through the throngs lining 5th Avenue all the way down to Christopher Street to the food and souvenir vendors. The streets were packed as far as the queer eye could see.

We met friends at Julius, had burgers and beer, bought the requisite Pride T-shirt with the Keith Haring design on it, and then realized just how far we had walked and how far it would be back to our car on 25th Street. It seemed physically impossible.

"We'll never get a taxi down here," Bonnie whined as I spied a yellow cab with its vacancy light on. A mirage? But a group of muscular young guys signaled the cab just as we saw it and it stopped to pick them up. The guys looked at us, we looked at the guys, and they must have taken pity on the two old sunburned lesbians clutching *Pride Guides*, staggering unsteadily and looking like Stonewall survivors. They insisted we take the cab. To those anonymous guys, we will forever be indebted.

And as we slowly pulled away from Christopher Street, I could see the streets still teeming with people, the gutters littered a foot deep in empty and crushed plastic water bottles, and the corner trash can overflowing with, among drippy pizza boxes, sticky Coke cans, and tons of other compost-ready mess, hundreds and hundreds of discarded *Pride Guides*.

Fame is so fleeting.

BORDERS, RIVERS AND TIME: GAY GOTHAM REVISITED

SHAWN SYMS

THE BIG GAY APPLE HOLDS its international neighbors to the north in an influential orbit. As a Canadian son of a border town, born less than a year after the Stonewall Riots filled the Christopher Street air with projectiles and cries of rage, I knew from an early age that New York City was one historic homosexual epicenter I had to discover for myself.

From my first visit as an impressionable teen from Niagara Falls, to my most recent return twenty-five years later, mere months after Governor Andrew Cuomo signed New York's Marriage Equality Act into law, the city has served as a queer cultural touchstone for me—a critical cynosure whose sway has influenced my development as a queer person and an intellectual and sexual being.

Over those decades—from early queer riots to angry AIDS

activism to a renewed exuberance of sexual culture—gay New York has been a potent symbol of rebellion, creativity, and freedom. But over the march of recent queer history, much has changed. On one happy hand, the racial and gender diversity of queer and trans New Yorkers speaking out, taking up space, creating art, and living proud lives is more multifarious and astonishing now than ever.

As communities evolve, their social context shifts. Over time, it has come to feel as if the unique possibilities for erotic identity and liberation that once helped define queer NYC—everything from naked sunbathing on the Christopher Street Pier to the resurgence of explicitly sexual milieus like the leather bar The L.U.R.E. in the Meatpacking District in the 1990s—are on the wane, swapped in the civic imagination with a desexualized and socially acceptable replacement.

I eventually fled my hometown on the border between Canada and New York State for my country's own largest gay Mecca—Toronto—but over the years I've returned to New York in every season.

During many a sweltering, odoriferous Manhattan summer, for instance, I've communed with friends at the Folsom Street East public fetish fair. And fifteen years ago I met and fell in love with an American, my husband, and we came together during one of the coldest winters on record for his admissions interview at the Canadian Consulate office on the Upper West Side.

I've cruised The Ramble in Central Park, and met men at West Village phone booths and East Village backrooms. I fisted a compadre in Park Slope, smacked around a greedy young pup in an 8th Avenue basement, and got to know a husky Italian from the South Bronx in a by-the-hour motel room. I caught a sexually transmitted infection in an NYC gay bar—luckily, it was treatable! I've been offered cocaine in the men's room of a Christopher Street bar, and courted by a queer junkie on 14th Street who wanted help filling an opiate prescription.

Each of these encounters was an instance of both personal development and, in its own way, community building. They also enriched my development as a writer, from my earliest experience as a journalist for a 1980s gay-activist press to my more recent efforts writing queer literary fiction. But as gay Manhattan increasingly gentrifies, I ponder the future of that rich queer tapestry.

Yes, gay marriage came to New York State last year—but the very same night an NYC gay bar, where sex-on-premises has been known to happen, was raided by the cops. A few months later, I returned to New York to revisit some once-gritty streets where I learned spirited sensual lessons about queerness, and found myself surrounded by fashion outlets, luxury brands, snapshot-grabbing tourists, and the perpetual presence of city street-sweepers. Yes, some rights and freedoms are being gained. But aren't valuable things, too, being lost?

GROWING UP ALONG THE CANADA / U.S. border, us Canuck kids developed pretty strong prejudices against New Yorkers—and Americans more generally. Niagara Falls, long internationally touted as the "honeymoon capital of the world," was a strange place to come of age. It's a hybrid—two cities with the same name spanning an international divide: think of how the two Kansas Citys hug the borders of Missouri and Kansas, except in this case, you need a passport to travel from one to the other. There's no place like home.

Immortalized by queer-favored diva Marilyn Monroe in 1953's *Niagara*, my hometown gets millions of visitors a year, perhaps a majority from neighboring New York. As a small child, I remember many a big car hauling up my one-block street with NY plates, the driver's side window rolling down to a release a deep-voiced bellow,

"How do I get to the Giant Wheel?" (This was an enormous Ferris wheel, a Niagara claim to fame in the 1980s, which stood twice as tall as Coney Island's Thunderbolt roller coaster.) After I'd point, smile, and shyly provide directions, the gas-guzzler would zoom off without so much as a thank you. Bronx cheer, indeed.

Eventually, I learned that what seemed like brusque rudeness from our Yank visitors was usually just a tendency to be forthright and frank, a directness that, when it came from guys in particular, came to feel refreshingly masculine. So even at that young age, the charms of American men began to make an impression. And as I came into an outsider sense of myself as queer in my early teens, performers and creators who wrote from or about New York City also started to capture my attention with their expressions of intelligence coupled with alienation from the mainstream. I became a twelve-year-old disciple of SoHo sensation Laurie Anderson, constantly quoting her offbeat monologues to the annoyance of my middle school teachers.

Fascinated by gay avant-garde composer John Cage, I made trips to the post office to send money orders to outfits like Lovely Music, then on Spring Street right near the Holland Tunnel to purchase vinyl recordings of his works—unearthly moans and operatic vocal swoops accompanied by the percussive plunks of random instrumentation. It felt like the future of sound, of art, of thinking itself—was emanating from New York City. I wanted to escape, to be a part of this strange symphony of difference. This desire was fueled by my estrangement from the mean, bullying kids who surrounded me as an awkward, chubby kid in our ersatz tourist attraction of a city. Maybe I could even live in New York one day. Home, I was sure, was elsewhere.

As puberty intensified, I discovered—and devoured—the work of queer writer John Rechy, whose 1979 novel *Rushes* recounted one night in a sexual underground based on NYC's piers, warehouses, trucks and Little West 12th Street's renowned S/M sex club, The Mineshaft. I became devoted to the overtly carnal work of "No Wave" performance artist and Lower East Side denizen Lydia Lunch, whose oeuvre focuses on drugs, violence, and sex.

I eventually got my hands on a landmark book by two New Yorkers, *The Joy of Gay Sex* by psychologist Charles Silverstein and queer man of letters Edmund White. For a lonely and curious gay teen, it was certainly eye-opening. The graphically illustrated book actually started my coming-out process with my parents—I "accidentally" left it somewhere around the house where they could find it.

As an adult, I had the opportunity to meet the good-looking coauthor of the revised edition, a New York legend himself, author Felice Picano. And last time I was in New York, I cruised Edmund White on the Silver Daddies hookup website, but didn't get very far!

Consuming these books and records alone in my adolescent bedroom, still having never seen another man's penis in the flesh, I knew there was a world—a dangerous, scary, erotic, and empowering one—beyond my insular local city limits.

The very first time I made it to New York City was a weekend road trip with my father and brother when I was fifteen. The day-long trek in Dad's rusted chocolate brown Lincoln allowed for two full renditions of Billy Joel's double cassette *Greatest Hits*, including, of course, "New York State of Mind."

To my risk-averse father, who'd heard of the alleged dangers of "places like Harlem," the best modus operandi was a cautious approach from a distance. He rented a tidy motel room in suburban Nyack as our home base. From there, we crossed the Tappan Zee Bridge over the Hudson River and descended into Manhattan two days in a row before heading for home.

On our way to and from the city that weekend, we kept passing the same abandoned car in a highway underpass. My little brother

Christopher marveled how there was never anyone anywhere near it, but each time we saw the vehicle, it was missing more and more parts. As for my dad, he began to show some frustration as I dragged him and Chris to yet another used vinyl emporium, like Second Coming Records on Sullivan Street (today the site of a taquería).

I was thrilled by my find there, a copy of the Leonard Cohen album, *New Skin for the Old Ceremony*, whose cover featured a 16th-century woodcut of two naked, crowned angels simultaneously flying and fucking. It would be years before I laid eyes on the much-storied Chelsea Hotel that Cohen sang about on that record.

As we departed Manhattan, a more earthly but still transcendent scene caught my eye. We passed through Times Square and outside an XXX video arcade stood a handsome man in a cowboy hat, enormous walrus moustache and a pair of skin-tight Levi's. The enormous bulge of his crotch was clearly delineated, its faded outline even more pronounced than the rest of his well-worn jeans. I watched him enter the storefront, and wondered what went on inside.

THE NEXT TIME I RETURNED to queer New York, it was a city deep in crisis. As an early teen visiting for the first time, I knew about HIV/AIDS, but it had yet to touch me directly. Still a virgin then, I already learned from my local newspaper that as part of the "homosexual high-risk group," I was forbidden to donate blood. But after high school I moved to Toronto and became an AIDS activist. The loneliness and small-town isolation I'd felt convinced me that direct action was necessary to change the lot of queer folks, and I wanted to be a part of it.

So at eighteen, I dived into gay politics—which at the time necessarily included AIDS activism. Toronto's AIDS activist group, AIDS Action NOW!—AAN—was directly inspired by the emergence in New York City of the AIDS Coalition to Unleash Power—ACT UP.

In fact, one of the group's founders was a transplanted American named Michael Lynch, an HIV-positive activist who divided his time between Toronto and New York.

I joined AAN's public-action committee, organizing pickets and protests along with my then-boyfriend who was eleven years my senior. In keeping with our radical gay ethos, it was an open relationship—in fact, he had two other boyfriends. When I got the chance to return to New York with Patrick and one of his other lovers, Rob, I took it. Forget about the bars—we were going to attend ACT UP meetings. In high school, I had seen Larry Kramer's play, *The Normal Heart*—maybe I'd get to meet the man in person!

ACT UP was a major inspiration to us in Toronto. In fact, NYC gay activism more generally had a strong impact on us in the Great White North. I was a volunteer reporter and editor at *Rites*, a left-of-center LGBT newspaper—and we were highly influenced by the US gay press—particularly Boston's *Gay Community News* and New York's spunky, controversial *OutWeek*. One of our tourist stops included the Oscar Wilde Memorial Bookshop at the intersection of Christopher and Gay Streets—and of course we posed for photos underneath the street sign.

Still a teenager, and a somewhat timid one at that, I didn't actually meet Larry Kramer personally, though I did hear his voice ring out across the auditorium when we three gay Canadians found ourselves in the middle of a rowdy, crowded assemblage inside the Lesbian and Gay Community Center. I was too shy to approach any of the people I recognized, from lesbian feminist icon Maxine Wolfe to handsome literary wisecracker David Feinberg. I did manage to partake in a bit of flirtation with Jon-David Nalley, a fellow queer advocacy journalist with whose work I was familiar from the socialist weekly *The Guardian*.

As one hour of the meeting stretched into the next, I was

exposed to what democracy in action looked like, as almost anyone on the floor who wanted to speak got a chance. The life-and-death urgency in the room was passionate and inspiring. Toronto's AAN was composed primarily of white gay men—and that night in the West Village we got a primer on an activist response that strove to be multicultural and feminist, and took into account issues like drug use and homelessness.

I left that night with a political button for my jacket that read "MEN: Use condoms or beat it!"—and an invigorated commitment to act up, fight back, and fight AIDS. Later that year I was one of the members of AIDS Action Now who joined forced with ACT UP and Quebec AIDS advocates to protest at the 5th International AIDS Conference in Montreal, marking the first time activists crashed the conference to demand that grassroots voices influence the scientific response to HIV.

The New York trip was not without intensity on the personal front too. My boyfriend's other partner had hoped the weekend might bring the three of us closer together intimately, something for which I wasn't quite prepared. After some tumultuous arguments, we headed back to LaGuardia and shakily homeward. I came out of the visit politically moved, but determined that future NYC sojourns would feature more emotional autonomy and sexual independence.

THE SEEDY TIMES SQUARE THAT tantalized me as a fifteen year old had an expiration date. When I visited a friend in nearby Hell's Kitchen in the 1990s, the location had lost its edge. But New York return visits over the early part of that decade gave me plenty of opportunities to reacquaint myself with the assertive New York maleness that first caught my attention as a young boy in a tourist-hometown.

I come from humble working-class stock with few savings to

draw on, so New York by bus, train, or plane was my idea of an affordable adventure. I returned about every year or so for decades, on my own or with friends or a partner.

On solo excursions, years before the advent of smart phones equipped with GPS and gay hookup apps, I learned how easy it was to meet men in the Village. At home I may have felt overweight and socially anxious—especially before the life-changing emergence of the bear movement—but on Hudson Street I could conjure up enough of a smile to attract the attention of randy, outgoing New Yorkers.

This wasn't only about mere carnal relief. New York men and their friendly admiration for my burly bod did a lot to prop up my sagging self-confidence. I remember meeting Michael, a good-looking Italian, passing the gay guesthouse where I was staying. I had just come out the front door, and together we went right back inside.

I was impressed not just with his oral prowess, but that he suggested we go to a movie together afterward, *Bullets Over Broadway*. Michael was an oncology nurse who'd conquered an addiction, and we became friends and fuck buddies, seeing each other on several subsequent visits before he moved to Florida to pursue a career change: he wanted to become a writer.

Other New York liaisons were more fast and furious. I visited Manhattan with two close friends for the weekend once, and left our perch at the Hangar Bar's front window facing Ty's to find a phone booth. I was cruised by a lean man in a suit as I put my coins in the slot to call my lover back in Toronto.

"Come over," he said as I hung up. I hesitated. "Just come," he said. "I live one block away. People do this in New York all the time."

Within five minutes he was bent in front of me in his living room, as I aimed for the speediest performance in my life. My friends were annoyed when I bounced back into the bar with a barely concealed grin.

By the time I discovered NYC, gone were the days of erotic abandon catalogued in Joseph Lovett's documentary *Gay Sex in the 70s*. But in the words of queer theorist Cindy Patton, "the erotic is intransigent"—and male lust resists social dictates about public and private space. In the 1990s, I remember naked, crowded, late nights at the safer-sex club J's Hangout in the basement of a flatiron-style building at the edge of the Meatpacking District, and randy afternoon make-out sessions at the raucous, bear-friendly Dugout where Christopher Street broached the Hudson River.

Most fun of all was the S/M bar, The L.U.R.E.—established by the owner of the Mineshaft almost a decade after that venue was closed by public health officials during the height of the initial AIDS onset. The acronym stood for Leather, Uniforms, Rubber, Etc.— and the bar was a cavernous rough-and-tumble leather playground unlike anything I'd seen at home. I've initiated a few friendships in dark corners of that place that I maintain to this day. And I had some momentary fun with guys I've never seen again. I vividly remember how one ardent fetishist had taped a paper note to the toilet tank that read in black Sharpie "Don't flush for piss." The statement read like a metaphor—an ecstatic call to action to celebrate all male bodily functions to excess. Sadly, all of these places are no more.

I DREAMED OF MOVING TO New York City as a teen—and my wish briefly came true in the summer of 2008 when I was accepted into the Summer Writers Colony fiction program at the New School. I was excited to spend a month on campus honing my literary craft— after all, the New School was where my boyhood hero John Cage had studied music exactly seventy-five years earlier.

At that point I had had been visiting New York for over twenty years and witnessed plenty of change—in the life of the city and in my own. For instance, the social climate may be more aggressively unsupportive of queer uses of public space—from protest to plea-sure—than ever. The Meatpacking District, where trans sex work-ers used to stand guard for each other and for tenants, now hosts designer boutiques rather than edgy queer bars. Sex-positive venues like the Eagle leather bar and Folsom Street East fair, both on West 28th Street, seem poised to be edged out by conservative interests in the form of a new neighbor—a construction of a massive 700-unit luxury condo whose owners will peer down onto the Eagle's frisky rooftop deck. But on nights off from my New School classes, I didn't have to travel too far to find old-school public pleasures, by taking a walk over to an East Village ursine haunt.

And while some of our political focus may have shifted toward marriage advocacy since the days ACT UP NY stormed St. Patrick's Cathedral and disrupted a mass to protest the Catholic Church's stance on condoms and AIDS education, that's not the whole story. New York is still home to an outspoken LGBT activist community working on a wide range of issues, from the radical anti-poverty efforts of Queers for Economic Justice to vocal queer participation in the Middle East advocacy group Siege Busters. HIV isn't over—and it appears the mantle for direct-action protests has been taken up eagerly by the agency Housing Works—which was borne of ACT UP in the first place.

The last time I sat on the Christopher Street Pier—rebuilt in 2008 and now neatly manicured compared to my earlier visits, decades ago—I looked out onto the choppy waters of the Hudson River and my mind wandered homeward to a sculpture adorning a bridge in my adopted hometown, Canada's largest and queerest city, Toronto. In the work by artist Eldon Garnet, enormous stainless let-ters read "This River I Step In Is Not The River I Stand In."

That inscription echoes the words of the ancient Greek phi-losopher Heraclitus. Capturing the essence of change in our lives through the dynamic interplay of people and our environments, he noted, "No man ever steps in the same river twice—for it's not the same river, and he's not the same man." Thinking all at once about that bridge in Toronto where I live, the famous Niagara waterfall where I grew up, and decades of meaningful New York experiences that have helped make me who I am—I fought the urge to take off all my clothes, walk right up to the Hudson River, and dive in as deeply as I possibly could.

WHITE ANGEL/ PALE BLUE EYES

NICKY PARAISO

"I hold this to be the highest task of a bond between two people: that each should stand guard over the solitude of the other."
—Rainer Maria Rilke

1981. SATURDAY, A HALLOWEEN NIGHT. It was a packed night at The Bar. The Bar was on the southeast corner of 2nd Avenue and East 4th Street, and at that time used to be the one-and-only gay bar in the East Village (this was way before the Tunnel Bar, the Crowbar, the first incarnation of the Wonder Bar, and Dick's Bar appeared on the scene). Men were bellying up three-to-four deep. I was there with my roommate, my dear friend and mentor, Bill Hart, who had recently moved in to my studio apartment on East 7th Street. It was a balmy fall evening and we were out for the night. I was happy, I was young.

I had just turned thirty. I had just joined Meredith Monk's interdisciplinary company The House, rehearsing for a piece that would open at The Public Theater in December, *Specimen Days*, which Meredith based on Walt Whitman's essay about the American Civil War. I was also rehearsing a cabaret theater piece called *Kierkegaard* with two actresses, Laura Mirsky and Catherine Tambini, both of whom I knew from New York University's Theatre Program; it would be directed by one of our teachers, Omar Shapli, and opening in November at the Westbeth Theater Center. I had also recently been performing with the great renegade actor/playwright Jeff Weiss in a play called *And That's How The Rent Gets Paid Part 3*, which we had first performed at La MaMa, and which was subsequently done at the Performing Garage and at the University of Pittsburgh's Stephen Foster Theater.

Like I said, I was happy at this particular time. I was lucky enough to be working with great artists who were also well respected and innovative. And the mood in the crowd at The Bar that Halloween night was kind of happy too, giddy and expectant. Anything was possible: it was 1981, and even though Reagan was in the White House, we—meaning we the sexual outlaws, queers, gays, homosexuals— could live our lives relatively carefree, doing what we wanted to do, behaving the way we wanted to behave, sleeping with whomever we wanted to sleep and have sex with.

Bill and I were standing at one of the corral-type counters at The Bar, drinking vodka tonics and watching the game at the pool table. That wooden pool table, with the green felt top, was the attention-getting center of The Bar any and every night of the week. Boys and men would be competing in a friendly game of pool continuously throughout the evening. Although I wasn't a pool player, I admired how the personalities of each player would become clear over the course of a few games. It was quite a sight, a theatrical arena, supremely sexy in its own right.

There were no cell phones, no one was texting, and everyone's attention was on each other. There was an implicit camaraderie of the kind Bill liked to call "the tribe"—a tribe of men and boys who came to drink and talk and be with each other and practice the art of cruising. *Cruising.* There were various ways to cruise. I never really got the hang of it. I suppose each individual had his own way of signaling and attracting the other guy standing over there, in front of you, to the side of you, or in back of you.

I was shy, I was scared shitless. It felt good to have Bill around as a buffer, to ease the anxiety I felt as a young gay man who was sexually available and hungry for sex, horny for the next available, attractive man who came my way. Now who could that be, you might ask, as I continually asked myself in those days, and continue to do, even today.

Well, I didn't have to wait long for the answer that Halloween night—that night of possibility, that night of expectations, except that anything could, might, and would inevitably happen to a young, horny gay boy waiting to jump off that cliff and go off into the night with whomever came his way and presented himself.

There was a young white guy playing pool that night who won every game, who just wouldn't lose. He was incredibly attractive and handsome. Handsome, that was the only word that described this young man perfectly. He looked like he was either in his late twenties, or in his very early thirties. I was standing next to Bill at that corral fence with our drinks on the counter, my face and body language probably giving myself away totally. I became fascinated, attracted to, obsessed with this young, handsome, beautiful man, who was on a roll playing pool and who was winning every single game. Yeah, kind of a pool shark, maybe, I thought to myself.

I turned to Bill, and I said, "See that guy?" Bill nodded in agreement, and made some astute comments on the beautiful young man's attractiveness and self-possession at the pool table. By this time, I didn't know who else was playing; I only saw the beautiful young man with the sandy-blond hair who was winning every game.

At one point, I looked away from the game for just a moment and when I turned back he was standing in front of me, smiling at me with those perfect pearly whites. Smiling at me. *What?* I thought. *This can't be possible.* And the first thing he said to me was, "Hi, my name is David. And yes, I want to sleep with you tonight," smiling the whole while. Whoa, that was totally a new one for me. No one had ever said that to me before. No one before, and no one since.

The noise in The Bar was deafening, all-encompassing. The place was packed. Like any other night, the jukebox was playing something funky like "Good Times" and then Chaka Khan wailing, "Tell me something good, tell me that you love me," alternating with Billie Holiday slyly insinuating, "Until the Real Thing Comes Along," and a few minutes later, the ever-classy and elegant Dinah Washington declaring, "I Wanna Be Loved." And, like so many nights I spent at The Bar, the playwright Edward Albee was drinking alone, somewhere in the corner. Edmund White might be in another spot with some friends, or engaged in an enthusiastic conversation with a smart young man who had probably just read *Nocturnes for the King of Naples* or *States of Desire*. Robert Mapplethorpe would stop in for a few minutes in total leather regalia and say a few words to one of the Black boys at the bar. René Ricard, Gary Indiana, Peter Hujar, and David Wojnarowicz—or sometimes it was Keith Haring and the musician Richard Sohl, Ron Vawter of the Wooster Group, pianist Evan Lurie and his then-partner playwright Harvey Perr—would be engaged in serious art world conversation in another corner, which could morph suddenly into sexual commentary about the latest hot-tie who just walked through the door. The great actor/playwright

Jeff Weiss might make an unheralded appearance, here and then quickly gone, fleeting. The painter/performer Bill Rice would be holding court and sipping a bottle of Bud at his special place near the corner of the bar. Right behind Bill would be the La MaMa contingent, scenic artist David Adams in conversation with the young, effortlessly sexy Mark Tambella.

That night, some people were in Halloween costumes, there were a couple of drag queens standing around dishing, but mostly it was guys in jeans, wearing sneakers or work boots, yeah, flannel shirts and T-shirts, relaxed and informal. No one had those huge muscles yet, and they weren't really skinny either, just sleek and healthy-looking, probably a few were smoking joints or had little vials of cocaine and/or bottles of amyl nitrate in their pockets. No indication that anything was wrong, that disaster and illness and death were around the corner for many of these men. But I digress.

"HI MY NAME IS DAVID. And yes, I want to sleep with you tonight."

And a whole world opened up to me. It wasn't just the sex, although it was one of the most memorable first nights of sex with anyone that I can remember, or care to remember.

David was charismatic, masculine, boyish with a *je ne sais quoi* softness, smart as a whip, and well-read—he loved books of all kinds, especially contemporary Latin novelists and poets like Marquez and Neruda, as politically left as possible. He was also an unapologetic alcoholic and addicted to heroin and cocaine. A mass of contradictions: he was both self-centered and self-involved, yet also totally selfless; generous to a fault and completely infuriating; as enigmatic as he was direct; completely loyal to those he professed to love, and yet as indiscreet and territorial as an alley cat.

The youngest of four brothers, David was from a middle-class

WASP family in upstate New York. He loved Asian boys, dark men, Black boys, anything culturally, ethnically "other" than what he had grown up with. His family was not from *money*, but could still send him to Andover where he played soccer, and then to Hampshire College, from which he dropped out fairly early on.

David's three brothers, James, Thom, and Kai Underwood were all straight guys who eventually married and had children. David was the black sheep boy of the family, in more ways than one, including being outspokenly gay. Although he never finished college, he was the intellect, the social and political activist, the lifestyle pioneer of his provincial WASP/Scandinavian family. When David fell in love, he fell hard. He could be in love with more than one man at a time, which added to the confusion and frustration surrounding his relationships. But it was not confusing for David.

Of course this was a time, almost immediately post-Stonewall, when multiple sexual and romantic relationships and affairs were the rule, not the exception. Or perhaps there was one main, relatively stable partner who ultimately suffered when the boyfriend with the roving eye was sleeping out three or four or more times a week, usually returning in the wee hours of the morning or the next day.

For David, it was all the same, and part of the complexity of life and being an out gay man in the anything goes, swinging '70s. He carried on and made love like there were no tomorrows. He was part of a network, particularly of young Asian men who all knew each other and considered each other as part of an extended family of men far away from home—home being Thailand or the Philippines, or in my case, Queens. The first time I heard the term "rice queen" was when I first met David.

Rice queen: a white gay man who is attracted to men of Asian heritage, such as Chinese, Japanese, Filipino, or Thai, for the most part. And what were we Asian boys called who were attracted to

white men? *Potato queens?!!!* I still cringe at the archaic, racist con-
notations of these categorizations, although I can see how the term
rice queen, as a descriptive term from a particular era, seemed to
ring true and was quite useful back in the day, though problematic
and "politically incorrect" nonetheless.

For David the term rice queen was a badge, entirely appropriate,
and an apt description, which succinctly defined his attraction to
Asian men. As gay men living through those days and nights, rice
queen (and its other variations describing other ethnic groups)
became part of the social patois for those who fell under that rubric,
racist as it was, and still is. As an Asian-American gay man of Filipino
heritage, I had, and still have, ambivalent feelings about such appel-
lations and descriptions. I was never one for political correctness
although I sometimes found myself the victim/object of racial dis-
crimination and verbal expletives, most of the time just silence and
stares, or rather, heads and gazes turning away. Gay men can be just
as racist as the next person. I am certainly not absolving myself of
that unacceptable, though human, flaw.

SOON AFTER I MET DAVID, I moved in with him. There was no
question. I kept my own apartment where Bill stayed and looked
after things. David was an irresistible magnet, a force to be reckoned with. I was under the spell of an inconsumable desire and
lust—the angel of love had come to get me. And he wasn't letting
go. David and I spent a tumultuous, tempestuous, unforgettable
year and a half together in his studio apartment on East 9th Street.
The one with the bathtub in the kitchen and the toilet we shared
with the neighbor in the apartment next door. When you were with
David, his love was unconditional. His loyalty and devotion were all
encompassing. The outside world didn't exist beyond his cocoon of
love, his cave of lust.

When David shot heroin, I couldn't look. I'd wince and look away. He was like a scientist doing an experiment, methodical and unemotional. It would take a few minutes for the drug to take its full effect; it was like counting backwards from a hundred. For David it was like going clear. Clear into infinite space. It was like hitting rock bottom, down to the depths of a limitless, infinite, bottomless ocean. "Down for you is up," went the words of Lou Reed's song "Pale Blue Eyes." *L'éminence grise.* Just like David's hero, William Burroughs, the grey eminence who articulated the history and archeology of centuries deep into the past and simultaneously could see the future with prophetic crystalline clarity.

I remember the night David trashed his apartment when he couldn't find where he had hidden his latest stash of heroin. It was quite a sight and I'll never forget the single-minded desperation with which he searched for the very thing that kept him high, the very thing that made him forget his loneliness, his solitude.

When you were with David you read books and you listened to music. David had the most amazing classic rock-and-roll and jazz LP record collection I'd ever seen and heard. We bathed in the glow and rocked to the flow of all the beautiful music that so easily and conveniently defined our relationship for as long as it lasted. We listened to seeming endless revolutions of Dylan's *Blood on the Tracks, The Basement Tapes, Planet Waves*; we listened to Van Morrison's *Astral Weeks* and *Moondance* and, later, *Beautiful Vision*; Joni Mitchell's *Blue, For the Roses* and *Court and Spark*; Patti Smith's *Horses, Radio Ethiopia,* and *Easter*; Leonard Cohen's *Songs of Love and Hate*; Richard & Linda Thompson's *Shoot Out the Lights*; Neil Young's classic *After the Gold Rush, Tonight's the Night,* even the gentle lyricism of *Comes a Time*; and any album by Aretha, Al Green, or Stevie Wonder from the '70s. We woke up many mornings to Kate and Anna McGarrigle singing, "Call me when you're coming to town. Just as soon as your plane puts down," the rollicking opener to their beloved first album; and we both loved rocking out to Springsteen's *Born to Run*, although both David and I shared a soft spot for the earlier *The Wild, the Innocent & the E Street Shuffle*. There was always time, once again, to hear the majestic chords of Tom Verlaine and Richard Lloyd's guitars opening the great, lamented CBGB house band Television's seminal album *Marquee Moon*, with the bracing power chords of *The Ramones* not far behind. David loved Charlie Parker, John Coltrane, Ornette Coleman, Miles Davis, and Sonny Rollins, too. I remember we went to see a Sonny Rollins solo sax concert at The Bottom Line, which was amazing, incredible, unforgettable. We listened to and became unadulterated fans of world music like Nusrat Fateh Ali Khan's vocal flights of ecstatic spirituality, King Sunny Adé's sunny and constant grooves, Fela Anikulapo Kuti's activism and joyful, sexy Afrobeat, Youssou N'Dour's infectious rhythms and glorious melodies, and the essential, bare-bones beauty of Abdullah Ibrahim's spare, gorgeous piano playing. And I never listened to so much Steely Dan as when I was in David's company—*Can't Buy a Thrill, Countdown to Ecstasy, Pretzel Logic, Katy Lied*. Donald Fagen and Walter Becker's world-weary cynicism and humor, and their surprising—catchy, though deceptively sunny—melodies, captured David's own personal, misanthropic view of the world perfectly. Certainly The Clash, The Sex Pistols, Joy Division; the downtown minimalism of Philip Glass, Steve Reich, and Meredith Monk, took turns spinning on the turntable, too. And the list goes on and on.

Listening to all that essential music, staying home evenings eating a good rare steak, baked potato, and salad that David cooked, relaxing and drinking red wine—and why not?—a few martinis (David's choice of alcohol was the classic gin martini), were some of the most joyous times I spent in David's company. And David and I would talk endlessly, philosophizing, analyzing, and railing against the conservative, political tenor of the times. It was a kind of personalized, homegrown postgraduate seminar I had stumbled into and couldn't help but learn from, in wonder and amazement, laughter and tears, completely inebriated and helpless. "Helpless, helpless, helpless. . . " as Neil Young would say.

If ever I had any doubts and needed a reality check about how David appeared to my small, rarefied world of friends and colleagues from theater, dance and the visual art worlds, David would always end up winning the Mr. Popularity contest. He was a big hit with all of my closest pals and confidantes. David's natural charm, intelligence, wit, humor and ability to hold forth in lively conversations would always come to the fore, even though he was already high as a kite when he walked through the door and into the room. And even though romantic bliss was brief and ephemeral, David's steadfast loyalty and friendship was something I could always count on. Our relationship as friends would last even as our very different life paths diverged from each other's intimate caress, and other deep, serial crushes appeared on the scene to distract and seduce me and create romantic/sexual havoc and literally mess life up all over again. Such were our lives then, until AIDS changed everything.

I'LL NEVER FORGET THE TIME David, Bill Hart, and my friend Jean Gennis from Oberlin College days came to visit my Filipino immigrant parents, Nicasio and Agustina, for a home-cooked luncheon at my boyhood home in Flushing, Queens. My eternally homesick mother was always threatening to move back to the Philippines and I needed to have my closest and dearest meet both my folks while it was still possible. I remember David being the perfect gentleman, so kind and accommodating with my folks, as were both Bill and Jean, whereas I was the complete nervous wreck showing off my friends to my clueless Mom and Dad. I had never fully come out to my parents; we were not only generations apart but there was also an abyss between us culturally. *What was the point?* I angsted over and continued to ask myself. *To burden and literally shock my elderly parents with this extraneous information about my sexual identity?* David and my friends of course fell completely in love with both my parents, especially my doting, overly possessive mom, who put on her best behavior, cooked the most delicious Filipino meal, and only exhibited the unconditional love and pride she genuinely felt for me, her spoiled rotten, only begotten son. Even though I was not out to my parents, my mother intuitively understood the caring role that David and my extended family of friends had so generously taken in her son's life.

I WAS CERTAINLY NOT THE only sojourner there in David's cozy man-cave on East 9th Street. There was Burt, his other Filipino boyfriend, who worked for some multinational finance corporation in Saudi Arabia. I remember their long-distance phone calls in the middle of the night, which were encoded conversations wherein Burt would refer to David as his "girlfriend" and David would refer to me as the current live-in "mistress." I remember moving out of David's apartment when Burt came to stay there during one of his visits from Saudi Arabia, and David later asking me to move back in with him. I simply refused, and said "No," which I remember devastated David; he would always remind me of my refusal to move back in with him. My decision to remain apart but still continue as friends was incomprehensible to him. And then there was Piac, a Thai, the true love of David's life and the one who eventually nursed him through HIV/AIDS and took him on idyllic trips to what was to become their home-away-from-home island paradise, Kohsamet Island, off the southern coast of Thailand. For David, being HIV-positive was like a badge or talisman that he willingly took on and wore proudly within his physical body; living with the virus further identified him as a proud, out gay man, a man outside the straight society that branded him as "other"— alien, a perpetual pariah, outcast, an untouchable.

David passed away from AIDS on Memorial Day 1994, just as I was in the midst of rehearsing *Asian Boys*, my first full-length evening solo performance work, which premiered that June at Performance Space 122, part of a festival commemorating the twenty-fifth anniversary of Stonewall. David knew I was working on *Asian Boys* and encouraged and supported me to the bitter end of his all-too-brief life on this earth. This fleeting remembrance of the East Village of that particular time is for David, who taught me how to love for nights on end in his four-story tenement walk-up on East 9th Street, and whose gallant spirit passed on much too quickly. I don't think I've ever fully expressed—even now so many years later—the grief and unfathomable longing and loss I have felt at David's untimely passing; his spirit and the memory of the times we spent together will always be with me. I realize this story played out similarly for so many survivors of the AIDS years.

We held a memorial in the back room of McBell's, David's favorite West Village neighborhood restaurant/pub where I worked as a waiter in the mid-1990s. David asked that two favorite songs of his be sung at his memorial, Lou Reed's "Pale Blue Eyes" and Van Morrison's "Into the Mystic."

> *Hark, now hear the sailors cry*
> *Smell the sea and feel the sky*
> *Let your soul and spirit fly into the mystic.*
> —Van Morrison

MY GAY NEW YORK: A SYMPHONY IN FOUR ACTS

AARON HAMBURGER

ACT ONE: SEX IN THE CITY

Late spring, 1998. I'd been living in New York for six months, and everywhere I looked, on the sides of buses, in train stations, and in newspapers, I saw advertisements featuring a nude actress—critical parts hidden—posed in a martini glass. The ads were for a new TV show called *Sex and the City*, which I couldn't watch because I didn't subscribe to the cable channel on which it aired.

Still, on my way to work and back, I kept coming face-to-face with naked Sarah Jessica Parker, who taunted me with her stare, as if to say, "I'm getting mine. Why aren't you getting yours?

The reason I wasn't getting much sex in my new home was that I was holding out for love. I'd moved to New York to make it as a writer, but I was also hoping to find a husband. I already knew the type I was looking for: handsome, kind, intelligent, interested in the arts, sensitive, a complex thinker. And a Keanu Reeves look-alike. The two of us would run away together from the city's dirt and noise and settle down in a renovated farmhouse in Vermont, where we'd raise two dogs and sire children with a nearby lesbian couple.

The trouble was that few of the men I met in New York shared my enthusiasm for quiet, small-town life, nor did they have an interest in long, languorous dates filled with meaningful conversation. The other biggest obstacle to my New York dating life was my address: Jersey City. As soon as I mentioned those two magic words to some guy I was interested in, the light extinguished in his eyes.

Despite my lack of success, I remained hopeful, doggedly pursuing a variety of strategies in order to meet my dream man. Of course I went to bars, but I also tried speed dating, blind dating, attending a gay reading group and a social group for twenty-somethings at The Lesbian and Gay Community Center. I even filled out a profile at Drip, a coffeehouse for single people that kept binders of profiles for their clients' perusal.

I also attended the gay synagogue, where one night during Friday services, I met Alberto, an Argentine with dark hair, fair skin, and a light Spanish accent. My friends Daniel and Bill and I took turns flirting with him between the prayers.

At the conclusion of services, we all went out to dinner at our usual Chinese restaurant and Alberto agreed to come along. Over sesame tofu and egg rolls, we listened, enthralled, as he told us about the difficulties he'd had growing up as a Jew in Latin America.

When the fortune cookies arrived at the end of the night, I couldn't tell which one of us he liked best, even after he asked for my phone number. So I was pleasantly surprised when he called the next day to ask me out for Sunday night. The timing seemed odd, but I was eager to go out with him and said yes.

On Sunday, I made the trek, first by PATH train and then by New York subway, to Alberto's place on the Upper West Side. I stupidly did not bring a change of clothes.

Alberto shared a one-bedroom apartment with his best friend, who was busy typing on his computer when I arrived. A few minutes later, the friend said goodbye and left the apartment. "Where's he going?" I asked.

"HE MET SOMEONE ONLINE," ALBERTO said, sitting alarmingly close to me on the couch.

"Really?" I said, trying not to sound nervous. "When?"

"Five minutes ago."

I was blown away by this information. I'd never heard of meeting someone over a computer and then going to that stranger's house to have sex with him. "So, what do you want to do?" I asked.

"Actually, I was hoping to spend the evening here," said Alberto, taking my hand and kneading it between his fingers. He shuffled closer to me on the couch and looked hungrily into my eyes. "With you."

His fingers felt strong and warm, and he was a passionate kisser. But wasn't I supposed to take things more slowly, really getting to know the inner Alberto to see if he might possess the qualities I was looking for a husband? Wasn't this a distraction from my central New York mission? Oh, well, I thought. The mission hadn't been going too well lately, and it felt good to be desired by someone. Plus, I was so tired of sleeping alone. Not to mention, he was a good kisser.

The next morning, a bit groggy, I crawled out of Alberto's loft, splashed some water on my face, and went to work. My stomach felt a bit queasy, so I skipped breakfast. I wondered if that meant I was falling in love. Maybe you could meet Mr. Right by sleeping with him on the first date.

I called Daniel and Bill to spread the news as well as to gloat, which was how I found out why Alberto had wanted to see me on a Sunday night. Because on Friday night, he'd slept with Daniel, and on Saturday, he'd slept with Bill.

I FELT A LITTLE DISAPPOINTED, but much more, humiliated. And when Alberto had the nerve to ask me out again, my first instinct was to take the moral high ground and tell him to go to hell. But when I heard his voice, so deep and insinuating and tinged with his sexy Spanish accent, I hestitated…

I said to Alberto that before I could see him again I had to tell him that I'd found out about him and Daniel and Bill. I'd expected profuse apologies, but Alberto didn't seem the least bit ashamed to be found out. In fact, he was proud to tell me that after sleeping with all three of us, I was the only one he'd called for a second date.

So why did I say yes? Part of me hoped I could reform him, argue him into being more romantic and to fulfill his role in fulfilling my Mr. Right fantasy. Also, his voice sounded so warm through the phone.…

When I went back to Alberto's apartment, I quickly realized both how different our personalities were and how compatible we were sexually. I could never imagine sharing a bed with him for the rest of my life, and yet his body fit so neatly in my arms that evening.

Several months went by before I heard from Alberto again. I invited him over to my place this time, and after several moments of pleasant and polite conversation, we ended up having sex. Another interval of weeks passed, and then months. I'd hear from him unexpectedly, we'd spend a night together, or sometimes a weekend, and then nothing. I found him charming and irresistibly attractive, and yet I never missed him when he didn't call. It was nice to see him, and it was nice not to see him.

But by this time, I was learning that ours was the kind of relationship that happened frequently in Gay New York.

ACT TWO: SLEAZE IN THE CITY

After my first year in New York, my dreams of finding Mr. Right were taking a definite back seat to finding Mr. Right Now.

By this time, I had a Manhattan address as well as a Manhattan sense of self-confidence. It was much easier now to hook up, though just as hard as ever to get a second date. I tried sleeping with guys, not sleeping with guys, calling them after one day, two, three, and four. I played it cool, warm, and middling. Nothing made a difference. They were continually busy.

Looking back now, I realize that what these men were really busy with was pursuing their dreams, the ones they'd come to New York to realize. And I too was busy with my own dreams of becoming a writer. More and more, I slept with men for the brief thrill of it, just because I was curious or bored or horny. I failed to return phone calls and emails. I stalked bars by myself.

Beyond the sex part of it—or sometimes despite the sex part of it—going home with all these different guys was interesting, and for a writer, it was a fascinating lesson in the art of characterization. You'd get to see all different types of apartments, meet roommates from various walks of life, peek into strangers' medicine cabinets and refrigerators, study the art they hung on their walls as well as the books they kept on their shelves. I was also impressed by how available sex was everywhere when you were looking for it. An extra long stare across a locker room at the gym. Glances exchanged in a bookstore or while exiting the subway.

And then there was a bar in the East Village called The Cock.

I'd heard stories about The Cock from my friends, particularly about a notorious party held there called Foxy, when guys would get up on stage and do all manner of lewd things for prizes. I remember vividly one man who inserted three fingers into his anus, removed them, and then smeared his face with what someone told me was melted chocolate. At least, I hoped it was melted chocolate.

The Cock also had a back room, where I told myself I would not ever enter. At most, I would stand nearby and peek inside. Except for one time when I did go in with a friend, but just to watch what was going on, to stand apart from the wandering hands and unbuckling belts, and the men getting down on their knees. My friend smiled across the crowd at me as he got a blow job from some stranger.

One Halloween, I went to a costume party in the East Village with my friends Daniel and Todd, and afterward we stopped by The Cock. After getting our drinks, we all dared each other to go to the back room, so we did, each going in one at a time. When it was my turn, I told myself I was just going to look as usual, but almost immediately I caught eyes with a startlingly handsome blond man who came over and kissed me. We began making out, until he stopped suddenly.

"I can't do this standing up," he said. "Do you want to come back with me to my hotel?"

"Where is it?"

He said he was staying at the Royalton in Midtown, an expensive hotel that I'd never heard of. The name sounded to me like some kind of SRO with heroin addicts sprawled in the stairwells. I had visions of myself being murdered in some flophouse, so I said no, and he moved away. A few minutes later, I saw him leave the bar with another man.

Then I spotted Todd, standing alone. As his Halloween costume, he'd dressed up as Linus from Peanuts, which added to his usual cute hangdog expression. I'd nursed a crush on Todd for months, ever since Daniel had first introduced us. Once, we'd gone out to the movies together on what I'd hoped was a date, but at the end of the night we just hugged. Apparently, we were just going to be friends.

I moved through the men who were in various states of undress to get closer to Todd, and then suddenly, almost as if drawn to a magnet, I lunged for his lips and we began kissing and rubbing our bodies together. Finally, he pulled away and said, "We should find Daniel."

"I guess so," I said.

When the three of us left The Cock and walked home together, Todd and I didn't mention to Daniel what we had done. As it turned out, Daniel's apartment was closest, and so after we dropped him off, Todd and I were by ourselves.

"Look," he asked me, "do you want to come over?"

I said I did.

"The thing is, this has to be a one-time thing. I just don't want anything to get confused."

I had heard this type of line before, but it was weird hearing it from a friend.

"Okay."

We walked another twenty minutes to Todd's apartment in Chelsea. I'd been there before, but it took on a much different light sneaking in at three in the morning, trying not to wake the roommate. Todd took a long time getting ready for the night, carefully flossing, brushing his teeth, washing his face, removing his Linus costume and stripping down to a baggy T-shirt with holes and boxers printed with dolphins, or maybe they were sharks. I was starting to wonder if we would even have sex or just sleep next to each other. But then when we got into bed, he whispered, "Is there anything special you want to do?"

"Hold me," I said, "as tight as you can."

He had rather large muscles and it felt thrilling to be squeezed between them. We began to kiss, and then I felt his fingers hike down my underwear.

Sex with Todd was different from the sex I'd been having with strangers, or near-strangers. I'd forgotten how it felt to be intimate with someone I liked and knew something about, to express affection along with sexuality.

I fell asleep smiling.

The next morning, Todd woke me up early because he had to go to church. As I slowly got out of bed, he put on a button-down shirt and khakis, dark socks and good shoes. I felt like a suburban housewife watching her husband get ready to go to work. We had breakfast on his living room couch and read the Sunday paper, just like those couples you saw in TV commercials or romantic movies.

But then I remember at one point, my feet touched his legs and he stiffened. The reaction happened in a split second, but the meaning was unmistakable. "I hate to rush you," he said, "but I'll be late if I don't leave soon."

"Sure, no problem," I chirped, slowly sitting up.

Maybe I wasn't as okay with this arrangement as I had pretended.

Act Three: Couples Therapy in the City

Half a decade later, my boyfriend Anthony and I appeared to be on the verge of breaking off our four-year relationship. We squabbled over everything: what we wanted to watch on TV, the right way to stack the plates in the dishwasher, whether black shoes with buckles instead of laces were fashionable.

One night, I got so angry with him, I stormed out of our apartment and slammed the door behind me, which felt satisfying, like a grand, theatrical gesture.

But after five minutes of pouting in the hall, when I tried to come back in, he'd put the chain on the door. (Later, he told me he took off the chain eventually.)

Fine, I thought. He doesn't want me to come back? I won't come back. So I left the building and stopped at a pay phone—I was one of the last New Yorkers to get a cell—to call my friend Daniel and ask if I could sleep over at his place.

Wow, I thought as I hailed a cab. This is really happening.

Nothing in my relationship with Anthony had followed the usual script. We'd met at a bar through friends of friends. At the time, I was fretting because I'd just turned twenty-seven and I said I felt old.

"You're still cute," Anthony told me with a little grin.

That night, he struck me as another in a string of cute guys to take to bed, a scenario I was getting tired of repeating, and so I blew him off.

Four months later, I ran into Anthony at the same bar and said hello. This time he was much more standoffish, still feeling burned with how cool I'd been to him when we first met. But somehow we started talking, and it turned out both of us were in therapy, busy with the work of self-realization. As our conversation grew more serious and personal, I sensed a depth in Anthony that I hadn't noticed when we'd first met. I also felt strongly attracted to him, and we went home together that night.

Right from the start, I felt we were embarking on something more significant than a one-night stand. We went on a second date, to see a depressing Brazilian art film at MoMA, which we both thought was excellent, and then we saw each other again, and again. After a month passed, he told me he was falling in love with me.

I was too terrified to say it back. And then we had our first fight.

Even when I was ready to say I loved him and I did say it, the fights didn't stop. Usually they'd start in one of two ways. Unused to expressing my feelings candidly, I would take offense at something and shut myself up in a passive-aggressive stance, or else I'd blurt out an opinion in a clunky, angry fashion. Either way, Anthony would call me on it, and then I'd get mad at him for cornering me, he'd spin into a fury, and before you knew it…meltdown.

And yet, despite our bickering, our relationship had lasted for four years, we had even moved in together. I couldn't imagine living apart until that evening when I walked out of that apartment and he wouldn't let me back in.

I spent the morning sitting on the newly manicured pier in the West Village, where in the '70s and '80s, gay men would cruise for sex. Today it was home to a trim lawn of Kentucky bluegrass and aluminum chairs. I sat by the water and wondered what would happen to me and Anthony. Then I worked up the courage to go home and wait.

Anthony came home from work so livid with rage that he could scarcely look at me. "Who's going to get the apartment?" he asked.

"We should talk," I said.

"I have nothing to say to you."

"Anthony, come on," I said. "This is me here."

We went back and forth like this for a minute or two, and then suddenly he was crying and we were holding each other. "I thought you went to some bar, picked up a guy, and spent the night at his place," he sobbed. "I didn't know where you were. I was worried about you out there. I was so scared."

After we finished crying, I said I wanted to go to couples therapy. Anthony, who'd just finished seeing a therapist, was averse to the idea of going back.

"Won't you at least try it?" I asked. "Just go once, as a favor for me?"

He kissed me. "Okay, for you."

We started therapy with a straight-shooting Italian gay man with curly hair and a mustache, very New York in my opinion. What I liked best about him was that he didn't pull punches. If you asked,

"What do you think?" he gave his honest opinion instead of replying, "You know, that's a great question. What do you think?"

We originally planned to go for a few sessions, but we ended up going for a few years. To me, therapy was a thoroughly wonderful experience. Before it, I'd felt as if Anthony and I had been speaking different languages. Now we were learning how to understand each other. Sitting on the couch together, under our therapist's watchful eye, I felt safe finding my voice and expressing it instead of muffling it in cheerful Midwestern platitudes. Moreover, I learned how to hear Anthony's New York bluntness for what it was: honesty rather than an attack.

As for Anthony, he realized that I wasn't trying to avoid him, but rather to take care of him. And that his self-protective impulses to push away people who might hurt him were in danger of succeeding all too well, leaving him isolated and miserable.

I could have gone on with therapy for the rest of my life. But Anthony found the routine of once-a-week visits to our therapist's office wearying, especially after three years went by. At that point, Anthony thought we'd learned all we could, but I felt less sanguine about the fragile progress we'd made. What if when we were at home, I said something that led to a fight and I could no longer count on a visit to our therapist's office to clear up what our misunderstandings?

In the end, we decided to stop going to therapy, and to my surprise, we were just fine. We still had our conflicts, but over time they became fewer and less contentious. We learned to laugh at these petty disagreements instead of taking them so seriously, as well as not to hash out each one in laborious detail. Sometimes we'd just recognize that we'd hit on one of our sore spots, one of those moments of miscommunication that were better acknowledged than explored. Our choices were to probe the psychic roots of my inability to remember to take out the garbage or his mania for leaving the toilet seat down, or to just move forward.

So that was what we did.

ACT FOUR: SETTLING DOWN IN THE CITY

A few days after gay marriage became legal in New York State, I went on a visit to my friend Joshua's apartment. He and his partner had just had twin girls with a surrogate mother and I was coming to meet them for the first time.

Like many gay New Yorkers, for the past few weeks I had been following the ping-pong of news stories about the fate of gay marriage legislation, whose passage seemed assured or doomed depending on what hour I clicked on the *New York Times* website. The governor was for it, the Assembly was for it, and exactly half of the Senate was for it. All we needed was one more Republican to tip the balance.

While Anthony and I watched various politicians and celebrities announcing their public support for gay marriage, neither of us had stated our private position on the matter. For years when people asked us if we wanted to get married, we'd said that we couldn't get married, so there was no point in answering the question. Now that marriage was looking like a possibility, we still didn't talk about whether we might get married ourselves, as if we were afraid to jinx the legislation's success by counting on it.

Finally, late Friday night, June 24th, 2011, the Senate finally passed the gay marriage bill, which the governor immediately signed into law. Two days later, Anthony and I went to the gay pride parade, which was coincidentally that same weekend, and waved signs saying "Promise Kept!" and "Thank you, Governor Cuomo!" at Mr. Cuomo himself, who marched in the parade. Next to him was his girlfriend Sandra Lee, the cooking show host. Lee had a gay brother, and according to news reports she'd been encouraging the governor to press ahead with the fight for marriage equality.

"Right on time!" said Joshua's partner, who answered the doorbell. There was a bottle of hand sanitizer by the door, which I spritzed onto my hands. Joshua was sitting on the couch with one of the twin girls, swathed in a blanket and resting on his chest. The other baby was sleeping in her crib in the nursery, attended by the soft-spoken grandmotherly woman Joshua and his partner had hired as a nanny. The room used to be Joshua's partner's music studio. Now it was mostly furnished with stuffed animals, diapers, and a rocking chair, though a poster of Julie Andrews in the movie *Star!* still hung over the two cribs.

"So I have some news, too," I announced. "Anthony and I are engaged."

"We are, too!" said Joshua.

For Anthony and me, it had happened spontaneously, as we watched the gay marriage news together on our living room couch. Suddenly we turned to each other, and I popped the question I'd been considering how to ask ever since it looked like the bill might pass: "Will you marry me? I want to spend my life with you."

He burst into laughter and said yes.

Asking the question was the easy part. Now we had to decide, how would we do it? Since we'd been together over a decade, the idea of throwing a lavish wedding to mark our commitment to each other seemed superfluous to us. It was also out of our price range. However, drawing up a guest list for a tiny celebration was impossible. "There's no such thing as a small wedding," I'd always heard my mom say, and in this case, she was dead-on. How could we leave this person out? Or that one? And yet if we didn't cut the list somewhere, we'd end up with a hundred, and then two hundred people, which meant renting out a hall for a thousand or two thousand dollars, exactly the scenario we wanted to avoid. Also, when would we do it? If it was on a Friday night or Saturday, my Orthodox Jewish brothers might not be able to come. But if we did it on a Sunday, that would be inconvenient for everyone else. And what kind of food would we serve? What type of officiate would we want?

And where would we find the time to plan all this?

For years, I'd had dreams of registering at Bed, Bath, & Beyond for fancy silverware, fine china, and a waffle iron. But now it seemed simpler for us to buy any presents we wanted for ourselves.

"Let's just go to City Hall," said Anthony. "One day when we move to a big house in the country with two dogs, we can have an anniversary party there."

Over lunch in their shady garden, Joshua, his partner, and I talked about all these issues. They, too, were planning to get married, but not sure of where or how or when. Despite the expense, Joshua was hoping for a traditional ceremony, in a synagogue. With tuxedos and little appetizers on trays with doilies. The main difficulty was choosing a synagogue that was affiliated with a good school for their two girls. In New York, you couldn't plan these things too early.

As my friends and I munched on mozzarella and figs and drank sparkling water on that balmy summer afternoon, I took in the easy domesticity of it all in wonder. Who knew this was what gay life in New York City would look like ten years before, or even ten weeks before? Suddenly there were all kinds of possibilities, and with them new responsibilities. Even more remarkably, this strange new life resembled nothing so much as what some might have called the mainstream hetero-normal fantasies I'd brought with me to the city back in the mid-'90s and had worked so hard to abandon.

So were we selling out, or merely settling in?

THE PLACE
I PARKED MY CAR

G. WINSTON JAMES

I OWNED A USED, SECOND generation, gold Toyota Celica GT lift-back in the summer of 1985. It was purchased for me by my father. My parents, two sisters, brother, and I lived in the three bedroom/two bath first floor and basement sections of our corner two family white house. Our home sat on a hill surrounded by a meticulously maintained lawn and green, chain link fence. We lived on the very northeast edge of the working class Riverside section of Paterson, New Jersey, just one block away from the 5th Avenue Projects where almost none of my then-current friends resided. My girlfriend was Vickie Miller, a young woman I'd met at Governor's School the summer before, whose mother belonged to the Order of the Eastern Star and worked at the same Eastman Kodak processing plant at which my father was a maintenance engineer. I had recently graduated

from Paterson Catholic Regional High School and looked forward
to beginning college at Columbia University in the fall.

To most of the people in my world (and, to a great extent, myself)
I was a heterosexual in 1985, occasionally messing around, purely
sexually, with men on the side. At seventeen, my driver's license
and Celica gave my interest in males a range far greater than it had
previously enjoyed, having been limited before then by how far I
could walk or ride my bike, or the routes along which the P4 and
other New Jersey Transit buses ran. Columbia gave me a plausible
excuse to visit New York throughout the summer; my car gave me
the freedom and the means to explore the city at will and begin
to discover just how limited my sexual and social desire for, and
expectations of, men had been. The lives with which my own would
eventually intersect on Christopher Street ultimately redefined the
term gay for me and would inspire the authenticity still present in
my work today. The advantages of the middle class and proximity
to New York City were beneficial to facilitating my entry into this
forbidden yet alluring world. There was hardly ever a question for
me of whether I would embark on this odyssey, but only of when
and exactly why.

Late one evening, unpremeditated, I decided to make my first
trip to Manhattan alone. I drove southeast on 26th Street one block
then made a left onto 5th Avenue. I drove down the hill, past the
sprawling factories on the left and the projects on the right, then
merged onto Route 20 South, running along the western bank of
the Passaic River to the interchange with I-80 East then I-95 to New
York City. After paying the $3.00 toll and crossing the upper level of
the George Washington Bridge, I entered a world entirely different
than the one I'd known since age three in Paterson; an island I'd
experienced chiefly with chaperoned groups on field trips to museums, Grant's Tomb, or to Radio City Music Hall. I headed south

along the Henry Hudson Parkway and West Side Highway until, after a total journey of just over twenty miles, I reached Greenwich Village—the vibrant, bohemian, homo-friendly place I'd heard about so often—and its fabled, notorious Christopher Street. If memory does not deceive me, I parked my gold Celica at the foot of Pier 45 ("the Pier") where, in many ways—after I'd gathered the nerve to open the driver's side door and step out—the timer on my gay life truly began.

I can only re-imagine the sense of wonderment and anxiety that I experienced on arriving. I recall cracked, worn concrete merging with faded asphalt along the ground, misaligned concrete Jersey barriers, and rectangular planters in need of weeding and other aesthetic concerns. I dimly recollect noting the presence of the river, the length of pier jutting into it, and of skyscrapers and lights glowing further south in Manhattan and in New Jersey on the Hudson's opposite shore. What I captured most permanently in my mind, though, were the boys: mostly Black and Latin teenagers like me, gathered boldly together in public, apparently without an apprehension in the world. Due to our similarities in age, build, and carriage, I instantly knew that they were not males whom I'd imagined being with sexually, but whom I just as quickly knew I wanted, and perhaps had secretly yearned for years, to be around.

Before that night I'd literally never been in the presence of more than one (if any) self-identified gay person at any one time, though the block on which I lived in Paterson had been extraordinary. There was Blake, one of the neighbors' sons two doors down: a white boy a few years older than I with whom I occasionally walked to the town of Fairlawn to buy yarn, and from whom I learned to knit and crochet. He later nearly burned down their house and lost some stabilizing part of his mind. There was Pamela who lived around the corner on 25th Street: a Black woman seven years my senior who we all presumed, based on stereotype, was a butch lesbian. Fists clenched she bobbed, slid, ducked, and jabbed as she beat up my older brother like a boxer. There was Robert, one of the sons of the postal worker across the way, whose gender reassignment to female (including a complication that resulted in her vomiting blood on their landscaped walkway) I witnessed with the passing days. And Brandon, our next door neighbor's son, at least eight years older than I, who rode me on his motorcycle then boastfully showed me pictures of himself having sex with a pre-operative transgendered woman in New York.

These neighbors and their parents had shown me by example that the world was more diverse, complicated, full of possibility, and potential acceptance than my immigrant Jamaican parents, the teachers at my Catholic school, or even I might have preferred. Despite their presence in my world, though, their lives seemed in many ways like an adult program on WHT (an early subscription movie channel) that I'd been attempting to watch and make sense of without the decoder box required to remove the snaking bands that, while piquing my curiosity about the censored and verboten transpiring on the screen, all but completely obscured the display. Unaware of what transpired in their lives outside of the flashes of their reality that I was able to witness, they were not peers or real gay or bisexual people to me so much as characters drawn of gossip, supposition and hearsay. With no out friends or mentors for guidance and fortification, as a teenager I was agreeable to having sporadic sex with men, but completely uncomfortable with the notion of considering myself a homosexual, much less labeling myself *gay*.

On the Pier that first night, however, the memory of my childhood neighbors was with me and allowed me to consider that despite my distress around the notion of my own potential homosexuality, I had benefited throughout my adolescence from the knowledge that

I was far from unique in deviating from the societal norm. That recognition had gone largely unrealized before I found myself standing on the Christopher Street Pier faced with an evidently unselfconscious crowd that seemed intent on establishing itself as a jubilant new norm.

Moving cautiously further from my Celica I heard intensifying music (that I would later learn to identify as "House") thumping from beat boxes and saw dozens of young adults, some just milling about, but others laughing, gesturing, dancing, prancing, and posing. As naïve as I was, I remember thinking to myself. "Wow! All of these guys are models!" Even the least attractive or most heavyset of them was made striking and statuesque by the ways in which they moved and the finger shakes and praising calls, "Worrrrk!" that they inspired.

Consistently a somewhat reserved person, I've also always been possessed of a bit of Princesse Tam-Tam: unable to resist the call of a beat. Like many urban Black children, I grew up dancing. The Hustle, the Freak, the Patty Duke, the Smurf, the Cabbage Patch, the Roger Rabbit, the Bus Stop, the Running Man—you name it—I did all of those dances for the love of music, rhythm, and motion. For people like me, music that makes us dance creates an atmosphere, a space, a connected energy of brotherhood that is difficult to explain. Melody constructs a venue in which spoken language becomes unnecessary; wherein sound, sight, and movement are the sole requirements for successful articulation. There was no better scene upon which I could have stumbled that night. Inadvertently I'd chosen well for myself the point at which to enter and ease into lower Manhattan's gay world. There, at the concrete and asphalt foot of Christopher Street among gay folks my own age, I had the strangest sense that I'd been abducted as an infant and had finally found my way home, to other brothers, to another extraordinary block.

I don't remember how long it was that I stood around watching and surreptitiously taking Voguing lessons from those dancing denizens of the Pier before I decided to venture east across the West Side Highway to further explore the Village on foot. The farther away I walked from the music and my Celica the more my initial apprehension, sense of inexperience, solitude, and the vulnerability of my youth returned. I had, before that night, only been inside one bar. I'd gone into the heterosexual bar connected to the corner store at 5th Avenue and 26th Street in Paterson to buy cigarettes for someone from one of those old, pull-knob cigarette machines. It was a dark place, even in the daytime, with only one or two patrons that I recall.

Keller's Bar, at Barrow Street and the West Side Highway, while also a dark bar at a crossroads, was a completely different experience. When I pulled open the faded black metal door, I found an enormous pool table inside a tiny bar packed with what I saw as old, tough-looking Black men through whom I'd have to push and shove in order to fully enter. Looking back, while I wish I could say otherwise, I remember feeling quite simply afraid. I was put off by the run-down look of the bar, the density and uniform Blackness of the patrons, and the comparative seriousness and maturity of the assembly as compared with the teens on the Pier. I believe I flashed back to a brief visit I'd made as a young teen to the rough and tumble Alabama Projects in Paterson where I was threatened that if I stayed, the bike I'd ridden there—and was still sitting on—would be taken from me by force. I'd felt like a weak and fearful outsider who'd failed at blending in. I may have stepped one foot inside Keller's then pivoted and walked away.

I then headed north across Christopher Street to yet another crossroads bar: Badlands, at the northeast corner of Christopher and the West Side Highway. Despite being underage, as with Keller's, I was not carded and crept my way in. Perhaps because the space was larger than Keller's, and due to the fact that its clientele was a mixture of races, more like the Riverside section community in which I'd grown up, I felt at first more at ease. The longer I stood there, however, the more my youth seemed at odds with the advanced age of the other customers. Some part of me liked the fact that the space felt seedy, almost damp with the musk of old liquor and the potential for sex—the type of brief, emotionless cruise-and-do sessions I'd had once or twice in my Celica on Paterson's ho stroll—but even that seamy potential was not enough to mitigate my discomfort at being confined with so many older gay men as a smallish, teatotalling seventeen-year-old.

My experiences in New Jersey with men who had sex with men had always been one-on-one and most often in the great outdoors or on some other turf that I'd selected where I had the option to stab (if necessary, since I had at times pretended to be a girl) or run. Furthermore, the vast majority of those involvements had found me somehow disguised (as I just mentioned) or otherwise incognito. Wearing a wig or shrouding my masculinity under large hooded jackets was never an expression of transgender identity for me, but a practical costume that, along with disguising my voice, allowed me to perform oral sex on men whom I'd procured by dialing strategically located pay phones, through random calls to homes within the Paterson exchange, or by calling men (or other teenagers) I already knew. Many of my earliest homosexual experiences were fraught with and heightened by danger, carried out in an atmosphere in which hiding and the constant awareness of my surroundings and the whereabouts of my partners' hands was of the utmost importance. I'd rarely approached, or been approached by, men for sex instances in which eye contact and total self-revelation were involved. Even the hustlers who later made it into my

Celica in Paterson contented themselves with never meeting and holding my eyes.

It also occurred to me, as I found a corner in Badlands in which to isolate myself (with a good view of the door) and think about my brief interaction with Keller's, that of the homosexual sex I'd had up to then little had been with Black men. Inside empty cargo semi-trailers, in parking lots, in the wooded areas behind factories, the men with whom I'd had sex (only oral up to that point) had most often been white or "Puerto Rican" (the then current Paterson catch-all term for Latinos of any extraction). I realized that I had for most of my life been uncomfortable around my father, my brother, and almost all masculine or gathered Black men. While I didn't give it much thought at the time I accepted and was comfortable with my on-sight rejection of Keller's, even sensing that some level of rebuff and fear of men of my own race had been involved.

I spent the entire time I remained at Badlands thinking on the one hand about having a raunchy experience with a white guy, while on the other hand fighting my discomfort and the increasingly over-whelming urge to leave. If music that I liked had been playing, I've little doubt that I would have stayed longer, but Badlands didn't offer any of the sounds that would have allowed me to conjure a greater sense of belonging. After less than a half hour I was headed back out the door.

Like a barhopping Goldilocks, neither of the first two brick-and-mortar establishments I'd sampled had been to my liking. While I could easily have returned to the Pier and enjoyed myself, I realized that though I might frolic there at the water's edge, I was unlikely to feel compelled to do anything erotic. Those other young men reminded me too much of myself at the time for me to find them sexually attractive. Admittedly, I was eager on some level to happen upon one of the stereotypical Village fantasies that I'd previously imagined, one in which I'd find myself either cavalierly removing some guys chaps in an alley or tracing some rich, preppy guy's cum on my chest as I relaxed against his plush pillows.

Race and class played a huge role in my fantasies back then. The first few years of my life in America were spent in a rented apartment in a tenement on Hamilton Avenue in Paterson—a poor, almost completely Black neighborhood, seemingly plagued with drugs and violence. In contrast, when we moved to our white house on 4th Avenue, the street had been all middle class Caucasian-owned and occupied until my father's purchase and our arrival. There was an obvious sense shared by my entire family that we had done as the Jeffersons had: we'd succeeded in "movin' on up." A green-eyed son of one of those Caucasian neighbors soon provided one of the earliest of my same-sex experiences, though he was an older teen at the time and I was still years from entering puberty. I imprinted on him like a duck. By the time I'd sat down in my Celica to drive to New York, I'd long ago bought into the advertised campaign that white was right and the more money someone had the better.

With that mindset, I was specific about the types of intimate encounters I wanted to have in the city. Based on my limited knowledge it seemed likely to me that in New York—in the Village—bars (as opposed to street corners, phone booths, or factories) were the places in which such scenes were initiated. Nevertheless, while I tried to resist the impulse to head back to the Pier and instead push further east on Christopher Street to test yet another watering hole, I ultimately had to admit to myself that I wasn't bold enough yet to venture into the heart of the Village. Besides, I still lived in my parents' house and had to head home.

A few minutes later my Celica and I were alone once again. On the drive back, the whir and push of her engine seemed to assure me that this was only our first time and that I shouldn't despair at having failed to have my first sexual experience in New York. I'd merely peeked behind the gay curtain, seen the very edge of the West Village and we'd return before too long to push the salacious, social gay hunt into the interior.

True to my background, in 1985 I considered homosexuality ("messing around") to be purely a question of sexual curiosity, gratification, and servicing, wherein verbal communication was not required. "Gay"—the images and clips I saw on television—seemed to be a social lifestyle that went beyond intercourse, if only to the extent that gay socializing (and the venues created to harbor that fraternization) facilitated and/or celebrated the sought-after homosexual sex. I'd driven to New York more inquisitive about gayness and its institutions in combination with sex than in pursuit just of sex. While my experience on the Pier with the other young men affirmed the non-heteronormative attributes and same gender attraction I had for the most part successfully downplayed in my life in Paterson, the absence of obvious sexual cruising or even desire among them (us) left me uncertain how to classify that particular situation; where to place the idea of confraternity among homosexually inclined men for the ostensibly sole purpose of platonic fellowship.

On my drive home I was puzzled and disconcerted by the fact that, while I'd enjoyed the Pier, I'd been ill at ease in the very bars in which I'd hoped to be inspired by and impelled (as if by some homoerotic force) into the gay lifestyle. Truth be told, the social milieu of the Pier was a variable I'd never actually anticipated, since the media of the 1980s hadn't widely publicized or yet reported on the existence of such a youth-based minority scene. Still, had I had foreknowledge before setting out I would have laid odds that, assuming my age didn't stop me from entering the bars, I'd have enjoyed them both—though the bars, for sexual reasons and my intended goals, by a measure more. That had not, however, turned out to be the case. It did not occur to me as I drove back towards Paterson that there on the Pier I'd had a brush with the reality of a notion referred to by some as "community."

Over the weeks that followed I made various forays back into the city and the Village—always starting at the Pier. I eventually made my way east on Christopher Street to Two Potato Bar at the corner with Greenwich Street and discovered, as I'd suspected, that music and dancing were the combined elements that had been missing for me at Keller's and Badlands. As a nondrinker, I observed (as I had similarly on the Pier that first night) that dancing was fundamental to my ability to relax and to lose myself in the environment; therefore becoming more attractive to others as I arched, spiraled, and allowed myself to smile. The sex I'd been seeking quickly followed.

Before long I learned, however, that the pleasure I derived from sexual interactions was more fleeting than satisfying and (while distinctly different) paled in comparison and fascination to the connections and observations I'd continued to make on the Piers and on the sidewalks of Christopher Street. Nearly invariably, the people who captured my fascination were not men with whom I ever found myself having sex. As I learned more of the history and then current reality, I realized that the individuals I admired (some from a distance) were often "the Children" from the Houses that oppression and irrepressible creativity had built out of the ballroom scene during the 1960s in Harlem. They were the people who I felt dared to express aspects of themselves through their bearing, dress, language, cosmetics use, or other embellishments that could and did cause some of them to be shunned by "respectable" homosexuals and heterosexuals alike. They were the individuals who, whether for financial or personal reasons, remained outside the bars and, without actually verbalizing it, by their comportment shouted, "I don't need your fucking bar or your permission to know that I belong!"

As I had initially turned my back on the Black men of Keller's, similarly I had not originally considered the young men and the scene I'd first discovered on the Pier to be a viable gay option. Despite originally finding those teenagers "so like me," I'd continued for a long time to use them and the Pier as little more than a landing point, a parking spot for my car, a place from which to draw pluck before setting off for "better," more middle class, more promising horizons. Each time returning there to mingle a few moments and gaze at the river, before heading home.

I don't recall—whether it was the evening I witnessed a young man struck and tossed like a puppet by a car as he attempted to cross the West Side Highway to the Pier, or the night I heard the loud pop as I saw another young man bashed viciously in the head with a bottle, or the day a drag queen hastily tied her hair into a bun and fearlessly told a muscular Black man who was threatening her, "I fights down!" as she briskly led him to the Pier to stand her ground—the incident that forced me to acknowledge the risk these "people like me" were taking to reach the Pier, a place where they felt more or less safe and could convince themselves, for a few hours among comrades, that when they eventually left the Village they would still matter.

Courage, audacity, authenticity, and the strength (alone or in numbers) to back and defend those virtues (or vices) were the requirements and lessons of life on Christopher Street and the Piers that I'd managed to disregard for months, if not years, as I sheltered myself in the bars, overestimated the value of the hunt and of sex, and considered the lives of so many to have scant worth and interest beyond that of spectacle and entertainment. Once my eyes were opened I noticed that the challenge to know, be, accept, celebrate and defend oneself (myself) and one's choices was nearly everywhere I looked, not so much in the bars but outdoors on Christopher, in some ways great, sometimes petty and small.

As harsh and cruel as it was, when Smiley Pendavis pulled a pass-erby's toupee from his head I later drew a lesson for myself about self-acceptance and the ways we sometimes make ourselves unnec-essarily vulnerable to various forms of violence as a consequence of our insecurity and our hiding. I imagined her chiding him saying, "You can't hide anything on this street. So don't even try it! Don't make things worse. Own the balding man that you are." When I wore biker shorts to the Village only to have someone directly in front of me say to his friends, chuckling as he pointed at the flat sur-face of my crotch where I'd self-consciously tucked my penis, "He don't have no kind of trade!" I was understandably embarrassed, but took it as a sign to either confidently let the penis I was born with show or do away with the biker shorts I had donned, ill-advised and ill-suited, in the name of conformity and fashion.

These instances of social challenge and peer inculcation, though, were not confined to the ball children. When Rodney Dildy, Editor of the former Pyramid Periodical, near death from AIDS as he was, took short, pained steps down Christopher Street as he made his way to Keller's, his gaunt, determined figure dared onlookers to ignore him and testified that he was still alive, and was evidence of a cer-tain life before and during the worsening onslaught of HIV/AIDS. His presence proclaimed that he yet remained a part of his com-munity and fully refused to be shut in. When Roy Gonsalves set up a lone table on the Christopher Street sidewalk near Hudson Street to sell his collection *Perversion: Poems and Three Stories* to a public little concerned about the Black gay literature of AIDS, he demon-strated an unshakable and shameless commitment to his truth and work that continues to inspire me to this day. When writer, editor, and activist Bertram Michael Hunter recounted to me outside of Keller's that his good friend Michael, with whom I'd so often seen him, had reasoned that allowing himself to become portly would extend, if not preserve, his life from AIDS, Bert highlighted for me the fact that none of us was safe, tomorrow was not promised, and myth was no path to salvation.

The question of what we do in the face of adversity and in response to being called out and rejected was answered in multiple ways around me every hour I spent on Christopher Street. The act of arriving on that street, in and of itself, was an adventure for some, an operation of temporary escape from an unfriendly world for others, and for a variety of individuals a huge step towards liberation. For any number of people on any given night Christopher Street belonged to an alternate universe where, in some bar or on the Pier or on a chosen corner, they were allowed to be, and express, for a period of time, whoever they actually were, or any aspect of their complex identities that they chose. Outside of the bars this self-expression and determination were not limited to individuals standing isolated, but extended to groups, cliques, chosen families that were drawn together out of common attributes and shared circumstances to create stronger, far less disheartened, more easily defensible, units.

When I parked my Toyota Celica at Pier 45 in 1985, I happened upon the result and continuation of the organic and crucial process of acquaintance making and community building among gay folk for the sake of fellowship, self-celebration, definition, and defense. At the time, though I'd observed, participated, and benefited in a palpable way, I had not known quite what to make of, or take away from, the congregation. I'd not before then considered men who had sex with men to be the stuff of friendships, but as objects to either veer away from or engage as the action suited the protection of my social standing or my libidinous satisfaction. As I reflect on more than twenty-five years of my life in association with Christopher Street and the West Village it is not the sex that I most quickly remember, but the outspoken, original, and sometimes activist individuals I observed and with whom I connected in a completely platonic manner, some of whom came to be important members of my constructed, non-biological family. Doubtlessly, and in spite of the human tendency to romanticize bygone eras, the associations I made on Christopher Street were critical to grounding my gay identity and to refocusing me on a personal and artistic path conscious, most importantly, of the fact that, as is said in John 8:32, "And ye shall know the truth and the truth shall make you free."

BAD BOY

FELICE PICANO

WHEN I WENT TO WORK at Rizzoli in the Fall of 1971, I began one of the strangest and most extreme double lives of my existence. I'd already completed my first novel, and it had already been read by several people and deemed extraordinary—even if no one had offered to publish it. By day and sometimes after midnight, I continued writing: stories, poetry, short plays, and fictional fragments that would eventually become my first two published novels. Clearly, I was already on my eventual life-course as a writer. But I would need to hold tightly onto that tiny speck of a sense of almost-achievement, as my life quickly veered out of my control and into other people's.

Because in my new life, by late afternoon and all night long, I was working six days a week at Rizzoli, possibly the most elegant bookstore, record shop, and art gallery and with the most glamorous trade to ever exist in Manhattan. During those times I would be dressed in jacket and tie, acting like a gentlemen, or at least like a grownup, meeting and greeting on a daily basis the famous and the rich: writers, rock stars, actors, playwrights, the best known and most sought after people in the world. Maria Callas, John Lennon, Abba Eban, George McGovern, Gregory Peck, Igor Stravinsky and Robert Craft, Jerome Robbins, I.M. Pei, Phillip Johnson, Mick and Bianca Jagger, Mrs. John Rockefeller, and Greta Garbo were in the shop on a regular basis. While Elton John, Salvador Dali, Jackie Onassis, and Rose Kennedy, among others, soon became my personal customers.

Yet I intuited that this would become one of the freest, if at times loneliest, periods of my life—and so, outside of writing, outside of work, I threw myself into another world too: a nighttime world of easy pickups, group groping and anything-goes casual sex.

When I first moved to the West Village in 1965 it was already known as the center of New York Bohemian life; and to a degree, also of gay life, what there was of it open in New York.

At the beginning, Greenwich Avenue, from 6th Avenue up to around 12th Street, was the hub. There were several bars and a few restaurants that pretty much catered to what was called in magazine articles of the time the "third sex." Further west and south was a section around Sheridan Square—held in place by the longtime, tough-dyke bar, the Duchess, and by the newer Circle Repertory Theatre nearby, an area that would, after the Stonewall Riots, become the new, real gay center of town, arrowing right into Christopher Street.

Note that up till then, ever since I'd come out seven years earlier, I'd been either getting myself into, or attempting to recover from, one all-consuming romantic episode after another. Three of them in a row, Mark Hobbs, Bob Herron, and the most recent, Ed Armour, had left me in a state that can only be compared with a jetliner making an emergency landing without a runway, no visibility, running lights, or landing gear.

Having realized exactly how major and how consistent this disastrous pattern was, I somehow found a smidgen of self-respect and survival instinct and called a major time-out. Next I made a harsh but resolute decision to completely switch gears and to give up romance altogether. Along, of course, with any chance of finding that soulmate whom I'd thought might exist out there somewhere for me.

Having dismissed romance from my life meant that I was opting for a life of impersonal sexual gratification, which I was aware existed sometimes just beyond my building's front door.

Unlike the East Village—where I'd lived throughout my college years, 1960-1964, and which had become the drug culture's hangout area and then a very seedy and dangerous Alphabet City—the West Village, where I now lived was quiet, residential, and even boring... unless you knew when and where to look.

I'd moved a half-mile north of Christopher Street, to Jane Street, in a primarily residential area. And that's where I ended up playing the most for the next twenty-five years.

I'd been warned by new neighbors and especially by an older gay man I'd met to stay away from the West Village tenements close to my brownstone apartment and their mostly working class, Irish-American inhabitants. Some of those young men belonged to a rough and powerful gang known as The Westies, a holdover from a century before. But as a ten year old I'd also been warned off from my local suburban Catholic School playground—because, as I'd soon figured out, that's where all the bad boys were!

So, out at age twenty-one, that's exactly where I headed; because, like my ten-year-old self who had gotten into glue sniffing and all kinds of preteen sex, I wanted to be a bad boy, too. I was older now and that late spring and summer, I'd begun cruising for sex. Not to my surprise, the local Irish hoods, when approached solo, were amenable to smoking grass and getting blown. More than one of them reciprocated, and several did a lot more, teaching me sex tricks they'd picked up in Juvie, i.e., Juvenile Detention Hall. I would "see" some of these redheads for decades, one long after he'd moved to Queens, married, and had kids themselves old enough to do time themselves.

Among the gay bars in the Village then, the one I preferred was the Roadhouse on the southwest corner of 11th Street and Hudson. It had been a spaghetti and meatballs Italian restaurant, and the new owners never got rid of the red leather booths—I liked them because they were comfy for flirting and especially for some nondiscreet foreplay. The Roadhouse only lasted three or four years before it became a restaurant again, and then another and another. But I found The Roadhouse to be a comfortable neighborhood bar and a *primo* cruising ground. And it was close to home. Before either me or my new pal knew it, we were in my bedroom, undressing.

Six blocks south, on and around Christopher Street, were many more gay bars and restaurants, from The 9th Circle (younger guys and hustlers) at the 6th Avenue end, past the venerable post-grad hangout, Julius (even then a New York institution), way over to Keller's (older guys and lotsa leather) at the Hudson River end of Christopher.

A new bar between the latter two opened called Boots and Saddles, with a semi-western theme. My friends quickly enough renamed it "Bras and Girdles." While on Christopher Street's other end, at the Hudson River, up West Street from Keller's, a whole bunch of new places opened in that decade, Sneakers, the Ramrod, the Vault, and Badlands. Later on, Ty's would open on Christopher Street to anchor the "Seventies Gay Broadway."

But even those places soon cloyed with their omnipresent country music or hard rock and the cigarette smoke that clung to your clothing for days after you'd been inside, not to mention the often overpowering stench of cheap beer that assailed you as you stepped in the door.

For a change and for alfresco fun there was a nearby building with a front door always unlocked, and so gay tenanted, it soon became known as "Leather Flats," with a rooftop perfect for summer fun. The nearby Hudson River front held a dozen huge, crumbling, wooden piers, where guys took to hanging out day and night.

Many of these had been there a hundred years or more, as this area of the Hudson became a later, secondary port, especially for the larger ocean liners of the early twentieth century.

Even before that, however, shipping had overfilled the South Sea Port at Manhattan's opposite, Lower East Side and Fulton Street, and shipping had straggled west, over to an area only newly incorporated into New York City, the Village of Greenwich. First settled in 1664, the Village had been independent of New York City until the Civil War, before becoming just another Manhattan neighborhood. Fitting the village's more angled streets into the city's more rigidly geometrical grid, however, accounted for most of the strange angles in the Village. Seventh Avenue cut right through buildings, making for triangular apartments, and then there was the odd fact that, for example, West 4th Street actually now crossed West 12th Street!—a seeming mathematical impossibility!

An elderly neighbor of mine on Jane Street, who coyly admitted to being ninety when I moved in, and was as active as ever, once said her grandmother would often tell her about growing up on the old Edmunds farm, where West 11th Street now runs, west of Abingdon Square, a block from where I lived. The farm's property began at the old Hudson Highway (now Hudson Street) and at its most prominent corner had been situated the White Horse Tavern, owned in those days by her ancestor Edmunds, along with another man.

That tavern had been amid open land for grazing, with rooms for hire overnight, a taproom, as well as a little independent hostelry. There also as the highway was much traveled, opened another, smaller tavern, a bit further south along the Hudson Highway, owned and run by French Canadians who had been forced off their land in Quebec, part of the massive Acadian population disruption at the end of the French and Indian War in 1764, made popular in the poem *Evangeline*. Known for two centuries as Chez Sazerac, in later years when I lived there and went in almost weekly, it was the only Creole cuisine restaurant in New York, called The Sazerac House.

My neighbor's grandmother was a girl of twelve when George Washington and his aide de camp, a very young Alexander Hamilton, stopped for water for themselves and their mounts. She told her grandchildren how she'd helped them get it at the farm well on what is now Greenwich Street at 11th Street (where, later on, I resided for thirteen years) and she was thrilled to speak to the dashing "American" soldiers. Hamilton had liked the area so well that in later years, he bought a portion and built himself a little country homestead—two blocks away from where I lived on Jane Street.

My neighbor's ancestral farm had spread in that Federal era from 14th Street down below Christopher, and had extended west— not as far as West Street, which didn't exist then except as ragged water's edge. The names of the streets even today—Jane, Horatio, Charles, Christopher, etc.—were all names of the children of the Edmunds family.

Her grandmother had been a grown woman with children when the Pacific Clippers began arriving at the new Hudson River west side docks, easily seen from their farmhouse. The family boys would run over to see Chinese and Malayan wares unloaded: incredible exotic animals and treasure! During the nineteenth century, the river frontage was slowly filled in and raised and a cobblestone street was laid down too — named West Street—and then the Edmunds leased the land out to various shipping companies.

But it was the steamship lines from up north arriving laden with corn, wheat, cattle, and hops coming from the Midwest territories and new states abutting the Great Lakes via the Erie Canal and the upper Hudson that really exploded the growth of this western shipping pier area. The Hudson River was wider and less turbulent than its counterpoint, which despite its name as the East River, is in reality geographically only a strait between Manhattan and Long Island.

Anyway, that eastern waterway was by the mid-nineteenth century so busy it was overfilled with boating, including private yachts, and a score of private line ferries constantly moving daily commuters between the burgeoning city of Brooklyn and Manhattan. When poet Walt Whitman was a cub reporter for the *Brooklyn Eagle* newspaper in the 1840s, one of his jobs was to write about frequent ferry collisions with rescues and fatalities on the East River.

Several fallen signs on the northernmost of the dozen decayed piers, not at all far from my West Village apartment, still held the partial or full names of shipping lines, the White Star Line and the Silver Swan Line prominent among them. The White Star Line was, of course, parent company of the Titanic, among other gargantuan ships. The end of the street that I'd all unwittingly moved to, Jane Street, was the official North American arrival dock of that huge, doomed vessel. In fact, the tottering blackened brick building that faced the decaying pier, which was—when I moved there—a single room occupancy residency known as the Jane Street Hotel, had been where the survivors of the Titanic actually stayed their first few nights in New York. Its decaying lobby, filled with listless unemployed men whenever I would pass by on the way to sun at water's edge, had been the scene of that first great American media frenzy, when hundreds of reporters converged to meet, interview, and photograph those survivors.

Only two blocks further up Greenwich Street, as I wandered after midnight, I came across other monuments to this earlier and more glorious era. The blue-gray stone, Beaux Arts style Customs House on far West 13th Street, on the river side of the old Chatham Square market area, all boarded up, for example. That was where Herman Melville labored for the last twenty-five years of his life, checking in steamships and those early liners. It's also where he is believed to have written his late masterpiece, the novella, *Billy Budd*, when the slips were vacant and he had time on his hands.

I was generally on less literary and more lurid errands there, looking to meet someone else wandering the streets or, failing that, joining the often writhing mass of anonymous strangers who would risk the broken floors of the unlit, abandoned piers to have group sex in what remained of their upstairs offices. Some people became so fond of these piers they would go out during warm summer afternoon, find a spot to sunbathe on towels at the farthest dock edge, and languidly wave to the surprised out-of-town tourists on the Circle Line tour boats who passed by.

North of where I lived, just south of 14th Street in the old Meatpacking District, a new place opened named the Zodiac. Up a long flight of stairs and with a rooftop terrace, it offered the first publicly shown gay porn movies I'd ever seen. It closed after a year and reopened on two floors, without the rooftop level, as The Mine Shaft. It would become one of the most infamous places in Manhattan; a place I seldom went to unless I was asked to bring curious out-of-towners. These were many, however, and as the decades slogged on and I became well known, they included my dinner guest, brought by Giles Barbedette, (and done up in leather, head to foot) that trendy *philosophe,* Michel Foucault!

A few blocks north, in a motel at the very edge of the city that looked like it belonged in Fort Lee, New Jersey, and I believe was much utilized by Manhattan office workers for their daytime trysts, another club opened, the Anvil, a.k.a. the "Twinkie" dance palace. Later on this venue got a lot more glittery and a lot more publicly lewd. It also somehow attracted uptown jetsetters and one could see society women like Mrs. Guest and Princess Radziwell in their haute couture and fox furs watching gay men dance naked and have sex on stage.

That area is today home to multimillion dollar celebrity lofts surrounded by Armani and Barneys emporia and little cafes with $200 tasting menus. But in those days it was *the very last place* in the city you wanted to be seen. Unless, that is, you were an unattractive half-way-there transvestite hooker—or a bridge and tunnel Guido looking for exotic head.

I called it "Beat Me Fuck Me Country." And I also called it home.

Only a few blocks from me and from the Anvil and Mine Shaft, beneath what was left of the elevated West Side highway, dozens of empty meat and produce trucks would be parked over night and on weekends. Poorer gays and their furtive, usually suburban-Dad admirers would have sex inside those trucks. And, as the day follows the night, the NYPD used to raid them. I recall hanging around chatting one night and seeing a cop car way up the road; I yelled a warning. Within one of the trucks, I heard someone holler "Run, Mary!" and someone else respond, "No names! Please!"

But once the city went bankrupt and the police no longer cruised by, gangs of teens from the projects above 14th Street began to swoop down to beat up queers, which was an unsafe precedent for everyone in the area. Some of us neighbors ended up forming ad hoc vigilante protection squads. A semi-famous, tall, African-American tranny named Marsha P. Johnson and I usually took the Thursday night midnight to 3:00 a.m. trucks shift. Marsha kept three sharp-ened-to-a-stiletto-point Afro-combs in her huge 'do, and I kept steak knives hidden in each cowboy boot. One time we trounced four kids so badly I was running and literally repeatedly kicking one in the ass as I chased them back across 14th Street traffic, screaming and waving my shivs. When I got back to the trucks, Marsha announced, "Chile, I ain't *never* having sex with *you!*" Adding, "Either you got too much testosterone, or you just plain *pissed off!*"

But that fight had gotten me around more exploring the West Side, which I did fearlessly. A few blocks north in the Twenties along West Street I discovered two grownup leather bars, the Eagle and the Spike. Soon, a very well-attended sex club called the Glory Hole opened nearby, and briefly a bathhouse too.

Along that Chelsea-through-the-Village stretch of West Street east to 9th Avenue, several famous bars and discos would open and close in the '70s. Among the latter were three dance clubs I used to go to regularly. Furthest south was Mel Cherin and Mike Brody's Paradise Garage at King Street, occupying an actual, two-level park-ing garage during the week. Twelve West—at 12th and West Streets, as its name implied—had been a lamp factory. There was for a few years, a fun, mostly gay roller disco at 16th Street off West Street, and another place in a converted warehouse around the corner from it with a big, half moon concrete bar atop which one cute, short-shorts-dressed, hetero bartender/waiter/actor would dance solo at 3:00 a.m. promptly every Saturday night. He later hit it big with a role on a TV show called *Moonlighting*, before becoming a man's man action hero in the movies.

And then there was that anything-goes place, The Strap, set amid a bunch of late-night-only Jazz Clubs at 18th Street and 10th Avenue where there are now chic bookstores and restaurants and the High Line. One time I lost my clothing in the darkened back room of the Strap and had to nakedly beg a flashlight from the amused barkeep, only to find it all neatly folded and hung on a nail.

The only nighttime taste I ever got of the lifestyle that poshly surrounded me daily at Rizzoli took place just beyond West 23rd on West Street. Up a braided uniform-manned elevator on the top floor flourished one of the most unique '70s clubs of all—and one of New York's best kept secrets. Allegedly financed, opened, and hosted by one of Europe's most famous madams, the glitzy, very private, members only, two-star restaurant, bar, and dance space was named Les Mouches—The Flies. Was it in honor of Jean Paul Sartre's play? Or was it The Flies as in "the flies around rotting meat," i.e., decadence personified?

I can't recall how I got into the place the first time—at its official opening yet—probably an invitation or membership card was slipped into my denim pocket in some backroom while I was otherwise preoccupied. I thought it would be far too high end for the likes of me. But the first time I tried to pay for a drink at Les Mouches, I found that it was either complimentary or someone else at the central, squared horseshoe bar had already paid for it. In fact, I don't think I ever paid to get in, to get a drink, or even to get a late-night snack at Les Mouches. One night, an older man in a good suit with a strong, unidentifiable accent (Bulgarian? Serbian?) and a shock of silver hair told my very attractive friend Don Eike and me that we were "wonderful for the club's atmosphere."

Maybe *he* paid? Or maybe he was the manager and he ordered us to be comped whenever we showed up?

The clientele—aside from a dozen or so All-American gay boys like us—was mixed gender, bisexual, affluent, and distinctly Eurotrash! Were some of them customers at Rizzoli by day? It was more than likely. A few years later, when my lover and I began vacationing in the Turks & Caicos Islands, I'd recognize them at the airport or in the swankier resort cafes. More than once, after dancing under that lighting system designed to resemble a giant housefly, Don and I would take a time-out and crash on the big-pillowed sofas.

There, dressed in denims and sneakers, shirtless with our Tees strung through our belt loops, we invariably met and were wooed by a brace of tuxedoed young oil sheiks with bedroom eyes and Oxbridge accents just in from Riyadh or Tehran or Abu Dhabi for the weekend. They always came in pairs and were always named Ali, or Dariush. They claimed to be fascinated by America (and, apparently, by its young men). So they invariably took us back in separate limos to their penthouses at the Waldorf Towers for a "nightcap."

As I would leave at dawn, the older male person who saw me out of the suite (the bodyguard? the majordomo?) would invariably slip a hundred dollar bill into my hand, whispering that it was "cab fare home." Home to Chicago by jet in those days, (and four-fifths of my monthly rent)—not down to Jane Street in the Village via a Checker.

But maybe those frequent, often quite wild, dates with foreign men and the subsequent "tip" explained why we guys were comped into Les Mouches: we were good for repeat business.

I slowly discovered this for myself because when I wasn't working or writing something, especially on the weekends, and now that I'd begun to have a bit more disposable income, I'd also begun patronizing a few other, more mixed venues around Manhattan.

Le Jardin was one of the first of these clubs, located below ground level in a midtown hotel, and resembling nothing so much as an old time ballroom, or 1930s speakeasy—which might have been the case. With its large white-figured statuary and enormous ferns and tropical plants, its white wrought iron and wicker tables and chairs, it was summery and yet after hours, too, with a Deep South kind of decadence. The music was contemporary (i.e., disco), the drinks were strong, the crowd was attractive, and from what I could see, it hailed from various levels of New York society. One time, after dancing with them, I got into a heavy necking/petting session in a dark corner with a very pretty girl and a beefy, handsome midwestern young man. Years later, an acquaintance assured told me that he had been one of President Ford's sons. We were all stoned enough that it might have been true.

Downtown was The Loft, a far larger club, run by David Mancuso, who'd been one of the Three Davids, owners of the legendary Tenth Floor, made famous by Andrew Holleran's *Dancer from the Dance*. I first went there thanks to my friend Ray Yeates, the DJ, and had remained to party until it shut its doors. Mancuso's Loft had women members, as well as a good-sized contingent of Latinos and African-Americans, and thus it was another place where you might easily get into a three- or four-way before the night was over. My pal Dave Frechette once summed it up as "exotic poontang of all colors and genders."

The World opened in another huge factory space, this one way over on 254 East 2nd Street between Avenues B and C, which at the time was utterly isolated and empty at night. At another very mixed dance place, I once exited with a friend to see a straight couple having sex right outside the door against a parked car, oblivious to whoever was watching.

This was also the period of Plato's Retreat, which opened up inside the Ansonia Hotel, and while my agent Jane and I kept threatening to go together, we never did. The Ansonia's other claim to fame is that it formerly housed the Continental Baths, the site of some of Bette Midler's earliest shows.

The truth was, sex was in the air all around me during those years. Whenever I would leave Rizzoli upon shutting it down after midnight and walk to the subway, I would pass what I assumed to be high-class working girls. (We were on 5th Avenue, between the Pierre and the St. Regis Hotels.) One girl especially used to say something to me virtually every time I passed her. She was pretty, with a very statuesque body, and a few times I had seen her talking up a client, usually some older, well-dressed man, who was probably staying at the nearby Plaza or the Yale Club. One night when I'd closed out the cash registers and gotten out of the bookstore just before 1:00 a.m., there she was again, on a corner of 5th Avenue, and again she said something to me.

I'm not sure what possessed me, but I responded: "I'm a bookstore manager. Sorry. I just can't afford you."

She laughed. "That's usually true of younger guys."

I shrugged, she shrugged. But she followed a little bit alongside me as I headed down to the subway.

At the next street she stopped me. "Tell you what," she said. "I'm in the mood for young and cute tonight. For you it's free."

"I live downtown. And I don't even have cab fare there and back tonight. Maybe another time?"

"Hold on," she said, as we reached the corner, "I've got an idea." I looked on as she went up a short flight of concrete stairs to what I thought was a little side entrance to a church. She pushed at the big wooden door and it opened. She gestured me to join her as she went inside.

More curious than anything I went up and she pulled me in. The area was no more than five feet by three feet, and there was a wooden bench built into one side, and another door, leading, I supposed, to the church itself.

She threw herself at me, loosening my shirt and belt, her hands everywhere all at once. I thought: this cannot be happening. Then she pushed me against the bench. When I wasn't sure what she wanted me to do, she told me to stand up on the bench. The minute I did she pulled down my pants. I had a brief moment where I wondered if I could get hard. Until I saw that, sensation-junkie that I was, I already was. Everything happened very fast and suddenly she was done, outside the still slightly ajar door, spitting. Instantly she was gone.

I almost fell, I collapsed so totally, but I managed to catch myself and ended up athwart the bench.

But if all that was a scene, you can easily imagine what a shock it was when a little slot in the brick wall at eye height next to the door into the church suddenly flapped open. A plastic package of some material was shoved through it and out. As it fell on the bench, I couldn't figure out what it was. I stood up and quickly pulled up my pants, zipped and buttoned them. Then the slot opened again and this time I could see an elderly male face, framed by dimness beyond. He whispered, "Are you hungry?"

The very last question I expected to hear.

"Have you eaten today?" the voice asked.

I nodded my head and managed to utter, "Yes."

"Well, then good night," and the little door flapped closed and I heard it locked shut.

I remained still until I thought I could hear steps receding beyond the door. Then I redressed myself less haphazardly. I slowly opened the door to the street and in the light I looked at what had been handed to me: it was a packet containing—and I quote from what was typed on a little attached card—"one sanitized pillow plus one sanitized blanket." What the...?

Then I understood. Someone—a sexton, a caretaker?—within the church, must have been going around checking up on things for the night and heard me and the pro making noise and had thought I was a homeless person. If I was, he would ensure that I could sleep in the little room, on that bench, with a sanitary little pillow and blanket. I'd even be fed if I had been hungry.

I ripped them out of their packet and arranged them on the bench as though used—fewer questions that way—and I carefully looked out to see if anyone was coming. When no one was, I sped across the street and into the corridor and stairs leading down to the E train.

When I arrived, breathless, at the subway's upper track it was empty; I was the only one there. About five minutes later some guys joined me from the other end of the long stop. I wonder if they heard my absolutely whacked-out laughter as I got on the train headed down to Christopher Street.

TWO NEAR WATER— AND ONE VERY QUIET

THOMAS GLAVE

OXFORD ROAD (KINGSTON)

BUT THEN WHEN I AM in New York City—a place I often loathe these days, but also often love, and from which I know myself to be from as much as or even more than, sometimes, I am from here—I think more often than not of here, and long, I mean really long, to be here; and when I am here, as I am now—when I am here in my apartment five stories above bustling and traffic-thick Oxford Road; in my apartment looking out at that southward view without which I cannot live for long in Jamaica, which is the view of the Caribbean going south, toward Curaçao and Aruba and Bonaire, and then South America; in my apartment watching the planes across the waters of Kingston Harbour landing and taking off at Norman Manley

Airport—one of the planes that will, regrettably, eventually take me away from here—when I am in my apartment in that white, not well-maintained building on the corner of Haining Road, only a few steps from my beloved Emancipation Park and the rest of this area that is New Kingston, and feeling upon my skin and hair the brilliant burning midday sun and smelling the smells of Jamaica, of *Kingston*, of *capital* and *daily work* and *very busy people*, I remember that, although they are here—the men who, as I remember them from New York, kiss each other in different public places, and reach for each other's hands along certain streets—I yearn to see them walking out and swaying their hips, here, as I do in New York. Here, not far from that warm bluegreen water without which my Caribbean memory cannot long either survive or prosper; here, summoning in my longing memory a distant Manhattan's 7th Avenue South, where I have often glimpsed them hip-swaying, and Washington Street, where, on a humid summer evening, I once saw one man squeeze, then massage, the blue-jeaned buttocks of the man with whom he was walking (who immediately, after a sharp intake of breath, exclaimed, "Fuck! Jesus Christ!"—though you could clearly see that he seemed not at all displeased). Here in Jamaica, if not on Oxford Road, those of us who are so inclined do, like others elsewhere, squeeze each other and press ourselves into and against each other's hard and soft parts—but rarely, if ever, do we do it in public; at least not yet. In that regard, I would love to be that sort of New Yorker on Oxford Road. I would love to throw my many-fingered hands in the air, right in front of my apartment building near the park, and shout, "Look at me!" and then, with him, that only-and-no-one-else-but-him next to me, I would love to shout to everyone passing by, "Isn't he pretty?" and "Isn't he unbelievable?"—as, once upon a time, upon emerging from a coffee shop with him in New York City, in a state of similar exhilaration caused by something I could not believe he had said (and he had actually indeed said it), I shouted similar things to the faces of mostly indifferent, or amused, or sometimes alarmed passersby.

But then here is a true story about New York that, whenever I am in Jamaica, and sometimes especially when I am walking on Oxford Road, I remember; a story, which—for its faint suggestions of sadness, but also for its beauty and hope, at least—I wish very much to share with you. Its events are of course more well known in the Northeast Bronx than in any other part of New York City, although, if you yourself were in the city at that time, not so long ago, you would have read about these happenings in the newspapers, or seen them reported—though not entirely accurately—on television news. And, well—do you remember the story about those stunning pin oak trees that used to line most of Baychester Avenue, in the Northeast Bronx? (For the record, the rather large area of Baychester is now more of a Jamaican enclave than ever; but this fact is of no consequence, really, when it comes to what happened with the trees themselves.) Whenever I am back in the Bronx, visiting the family members who still live there, I remember those trees, and often weep over their destiny; and whether I am ultimately crying tears of joy or envy even I can't say, even now, although I would prefer to think that my tears indicate a deep and limitless wellspring of joy.

But the *trees*: and so it was that these particular trees were in fact the spirits of seventeen long dead, or at least disappeared, Jamaican men; and these men, as it turned out, had been men who had spent a great deal of their lives kissing and moving their bodies against those of other men; they had done this either in Jamaica, or in North America, to which they had all, for vastly different reasons, emigrated at some point, and died (or disappeared) there.[1] How exactly they wound up as seventeen huge, thick-trunked pin oak trees planted one exactly following upon the other all the way down that part of Baychester Avenue still is not completely known nor understood, this

information somehow having eluded city records; but what is definitely known in the realm of public witnessing is that one day—in
early June, in fact, of that recent year—all seventeen trees in question
apparently suddenly "decided," in the words of one Baychester woman
who was present, sweeping the sidewalk in front of her brick home,
that they were going to uproot themselves. "Uproot themselves," one
of my older brothers told me—my favorite, who had always had a
passion both for Byzantine stories and for eloquence—"and at long
last, after decades, become the broad-chested, ripple-armed men they
had always known themselves to be." On the face of it, I initially had
thought this ridiculous, and impossible, of course, and had suspected
my brother of attempting yet again to tease me to a point that would
reveal what he had always believed to be my great gullibility; but this
time the story was true, as the New York media would shortly dis-
close. The Seventeen Pin Oak Tree-Men of Baychester Avenue, as they
later became popularly known, indeed uprooted themselves from the
confinements of their planted squares that morning; and, fantastical
though it appeared to all who saw (and by that time more gawkers
had gathered along the Avenue), they flew rapidly into the air, up into
the June Bronx sky, in fact, taking on all at once, as they ascended, the
unmistakable shape of men: men astonishingly holding each other's
hands, each of the seventeen holding the hand of the man next to him,
and letting fly all sorts of obscene remarks in patois about what they
would do, do, oh *do* to each other once they arrived back in Jamaica.
(More than one person that day was convinced that he or she had
seen several of the men passionately kissing and embracing some of
the others, and doing even more things along the route of passion, but
most of those who directly witnessed the event were too shocked by
its ultimate drama, or concerned about what it augured for Jamaican
men of the future, to believe or even begin to acknowledge the facts
registered by their own eyes.) Is it too obvious to state that they left

behind seventeen enormous holes along that part of Baychester Avenue beneath which, only a few moments before, their thick, twisting roots had stretched? And is it too fantastical, though utterly true, to say that only six hours later, seventeen men, each holding the hand of the man next to him (and in a state largely of great undress, some people observed), descended out of Jamaica's sky over the most densely vegetated section of the Cockpit Country in the dead center of the island, so sparsely inhabited, where, as far as anyone knows, they live to this day, doing God knows what sorts of things with each other, as men, trees, or who knows what yet to be seen? It is certainly not too fantastical, being a story that—especially as those in Baychester, Northeast Bronx, and particularly as the Jamaicans there know—is completely true, and has been documented and, for more than one skeptical statistician, re-documented ad infinitum. As I walk along Oxford Road now in the fleeing Jamaican twilight, recalling trees and other living things shaped like men near the spreading bluegreen sea of here that is also my sea of primeval memory, I find myself wishing that what happened on that June Northeast Bronx morning could also have happened someplace else; happened in some other part of the world where, as on Baychester Avenue, perhaps, or some other part of New York, or in the Cockpit Country or Kingston, such things have happened throughout time, and will not soon (if ever) be either forgotten or dismissed by human beings, nor trees, nor anything in any way in between.

CITY ISLAND AVENUE

ONCE, IT IS ABSOLUTELY TRUE, once upon a time—

Once upon that time that was mine but that also wished so much to be yours—really to be everyone's, but the world as it was then did not permit such roaming—the Northeast Bronx, in a fever of cycling but always deeply lucid dreams, wrote a letter to itself: a letter scrawled—scrawled!—on parchment and the brittle skins of pin oak leaves that had decided to live forever, for once, and not abandon themselves to the gray pavement, come October, so far below their realms. The Northeast Bronx wrote that letter to itself telling itself and all its voices and sighs, listeners and everyone, including insects, including birds and still-unnamed things low and higher still, that it would, in its own honor (for no one else loved it, and in fact few in the great city of which it was a part even knew that it existed), create an avenue that "would end at the sea," the Northeast Bronx wrote to itself, "and begin at a bridge, a small bridge…in fact a low-rising bridge over an inlet or something like that, from which a traveler on any day, and on a day of leisure in particular, might glimpse the masts of tall boats at anchor; might glimpse"—the Northeast Bronx reflected, then bent again to its pen—"the towers of the other bridge, the enormous one, that spans that water in that place and goes to the long island, over there."

And so it was: that letter in which the idea for an avenue was born soon thereafter descended to earth by way of ten thousand snowflakes or more, and made its way into the dreams of both the living and the dead: and while the avenue that became City Island Avenue, at the very end of the Northeast Bronx, in fact, did not end quite at the sea, it did end at the Long Island Sound; and from it you could, as you still can, see the towers of the "other bridge," by which the Northeast Bronx meant the Throgs Neck Bridge, that to this day spans the Sound waters from Fort Schuyler to the "long island," Long Island. And indeed, the Avenue does begin at a small, low-rising bridge, that permits traffic from the mainland to cross over onto the Island, City Island; but how could the Northeast Bronx know—and in fact it never did know, not even up to now—that, years ago, a small brown boy with beginnings in another island entirely—a much warmer, brighter one, where people's language really did sound like a distant relative of the music for which the island would become

famous—would walk now and then upon that Northeast Bronx avenue that ended at the Sound, if not the sea? The avenue that ended
where seagulls clamored for leavings from the waterside diners at
Johnny's Reef Restaurant. He would walk on that avenue, the small
brown boy who would grow into a teen and then into a man, and in
his deepest, most secret dreams, he would yearn for them: for the
people whom he never, as far as he knew, saw moving along that
avenue and others near it in that part of the world, but who—as he
could not quite discern or know with certainty at the time, as a boy
and a teen—were indeed there. He would yearn for them because he
was, of course, though he could barely know or understand it at the
time, one of them. One of them about whom so many never wanted
to know about or see, one of them whom so many would still rather
not ever see. To see them—the men who walked alongside each
other and *looked* at each other (yes, he remembers them), and the
women who did the same with women—he would have to cross that
other water, over to the narrow island of tall buildings, fewer trees,
and many, many people; on that island, along certain leafy streets
lined with old houses hewn from brown stone, he would gradually
see those whom he had so longed to see on the City Island Avenue
that he had always loved, that water-to-water stretch of cheap sea-
food restaurants and boat repair and tackle shops, that led down
to the almost-sea. Trains that made a great deal of noise, with steel
snouts that burrowed their way underground and under water from
the Northeast Bronx to the narrow island, took him there; desire and
loneliness and longing took him there; the need to see and understand and (perhaps most of all) to belong took him there; and now,
when he walks on City Island Avenue down to what might have been
the sea but is not, he remembers, with a smile, but also with great
longing, those people of the leafy streets on the narrow island: the
men who touched each other in those ways and looked at each other,

and some of whom touched and looked at him; and the women who had mostly merely had to turn their faces one to the other to reveal that the single word revealed in their eyes just then, and maybe some other time, would be—would have to be—"Yes."

Years ago, the discarded face of a young brown boy (though he might have been older) was found at the far end of City Island Avenue—placed carefully in a trash bin as though left for the most cunning of seagulls. The face looked as if it had been carefully, even lovingly, removed from the person who had owned it, and deliberately left behind. To this day, no one in the area has any idea to whom it had belonged, or why—*why*—someone would have chosen to remove his face and leave it there, of all places. At length, someone among the inquisitive dared to take the face into his possession, and, illegally, even vindictively, tossed it into the waters of the Sound, which, miraculously, managed to carry it all the way to the actual sea. Out there, upon those infinite gray waters, it drifted, and drifted and drifted, beneath dark moonless nights and brilliant ones; and finally—at least so some people I know believe—it sank down, down, down to the darkest, most irretrievable place out there. Some of the people on the narrow island of tall buildings and occasionally leafy streets lined with homes hewn from brown stones remain convinced that he whose face that face had been walks among them still, somehow, on the narrow island—walks and, with great pleasure, some of them believe, every now and then kisses and holds the hands of other men. I do not tell them about the sea, nor about his lonely sojourns on City Island Avenue; I do not tell them about how much, way up in that other part of the vast and reaching city, he yearned so much, so much, for all of them, for years. I do not tell them that, though they may indeed believe that he or some other form of him walks among them still, the fact remains that, whether he moves upon this earth as one of the living or as one of the very many dead, there can simply be no telling.

GILLESPIE ROAD (LONDON)

Now—

But now it is evening, and already, at summer's end, nearly dark; now, in this part of North London, along this mainly residential road lined with the sort of two- and three-unit attached houses that are commonly seen in London (though these are not "posh," they are not grand and imperious like the proud homes in Holland Park or Kensington or Bayswater), the air is, as usual, quiet, very quiet; now, filled with joy, filled with the great anticipation of seeing that dear friend whom you truly do love, you emerge from the Piccadilly line tube station—out of the Arsenal station in this part of the city that has in recent years become very much yours.[2] The tube station exits onto this quiet road, Gillespie Road, and from the station it is but a short (though actually surprisingly long) walk, past small gardens filled more often than not with roses and nodding hydrangeas, to the farther busy main road, a road of red buses and restaurants and Halal shops, where your beloved friend lives.

But then why mention this road, rather unremarkable in and of itself except for, perhaps, its proximity to the Arsenal stadium, home of the cherished team? Perhaps because something about it, particularly in these twilight hours, reminds you of those certain New York streets where, with but the merest turning of the briefest corner, you suddenly find yourself strolling along a narrow street quieter than quiet—a tree-lined street of what savvy up-market realtors have sometimes called "elegant" brownstones: smart and smartened residences quite unlike these Gillespie Road houses; a street in one of those leafy quiet New York neighborhoods where you have always wanted to live—one of those neighborhoods where, it seems, so many men (although, you have noticed, mostly white men) walk comfortably enough quite closely alongside another man—alongside him, perhaps holding his hand; perhaps feeling gently, so gently, in that place where the pulse beats truest; perhaps pressing their face into the warmth of his neck where it is lovely, oh it feels *lovely*, because it might be, yes, absolutely, it might be love. You have wanted to do things like these on certain New York streets, on certain London and even Kingston and Berlin and Addis Ababa streets, but you have rarely done them anywhere, although you have, on a few occasions, done them; but Gillespie Road, quiet like those particular New York leafy streets, streets of nineteenth-century brownstones and (mostly white) men snuggling against one another and occasionally holding each's hand, reminds you of something else: the quiet-quiet New York streets where men lean into each other and sometimes kiss each other on brownstone steps, yes, but also this friend: the one who lives in a top floor flat in a building on the busy road just beyond Gillespie Road; a flat with a view at its front door of rooftops and nineteenth-century houses; he is the friend who, above all others, reminds you of the men in New York who, along those quiet streets and others, kiss each other in boldness or shyly, and reach for each's hand. He is the friend who, himself a steadfast kisser of men, makes London more. Who makes it love: who makes it a place worth traveling to, into, once one has again descended to earth from the journey across the sea that raced through a great many clouds, from that other city where men and women still kiss each other and grasp hands on leafy and sometimes not-leafy streets; who, with his friendship, makes Gillespie Road, like those certain streets in that brownstone-ish city on the other side of the ocean, something to look forward to, espe-cially at dusk; especially when lights in modest homes are just com-ing on; especially when hydrangeas are nodding off to sleep, roses no longer beckoning (and they are such *sultry* flirts, the houses above them mutter), and red buses have not yet ceased their runs for the day. The fact is that, up to now, you have not ever seen men kissing each other or holding each's hand on Gillespie Road, admitting some lonesomeness and sadness because of the fact; but then the other fact is that, to your great surprise, though it would indeed be nice to see them here—bracing, embracing—you do not necessarily have to. Not knowing that you have this friend. Not knowing that you do, finally, possess the great gift of looking forward to seeing him, which makes the long (but short) walk down Gillespie Road from the tube station to the busy road of red buses deeply worthwhile. For you know that, like him, they all are there somewhere, even if (like him, sometimes) still mainly unseen; there somewhere, in Finsbury Park or Highbury, the men who kiss each other and reach for, and hold, the other clasping hand; there, pressing against that brownstone wall on that street of trees as he feels the other's warm face against his own and doing all that to his neck, doing those things to his (and it feels so good, my God, it feels so unbelievably good). There are so many of them in that city across the wide water, that city at whose center presides a narrow island of tall buildings and many, many people, and not many trees. Once, as everyone knows, some people in that city— especially certain men deeply fond of kissing each other—believed that if they had lived for a time as trees, as so many at one point had done, they would eventually have to uproot themselves as they abruptly made their way back to the pulse and desire of human flesh, and, so fleshed, clasp as if clasping the heart of life itself the hand of the beloved one planted in solid earth next to them; then soar up into the air in order to fly back to their original country, where, perhaps, they might live, unmolested, in peace, in quiet, forever. A quiet place was all, it seemed, they sought. A quiet place where, if all did go well, no one would ever need to leave his face behind. *Tonight, in whichever city I may find myself, find myself literally or otherwise, I know for certain that, at least this once, I have not left my face behind.* Now, as twilight enfolds me as it has enfolded me on Oxford Road and on so many streets of the vast city across the ocean, I can see them again: the men who were trees, the women who might have been trees, kissing each other. Moving. Perhaps, as, on this city's Gillespie Road, I come finally to the busy road of restaurants, Halal shops, and red buses, soon to ascend to the top story flat of my dear friend, I understand that this is what that city across the ocean means, in part, to me: movement, excitement, and just being able to know that all of those people are there, and will be there. The people whom the young brown boy who loved City Island Avenue wanted (and needed) so much to see. The people of whom the Baychester Jamaican tree men were (are) inevitably a part. The people of whom I often think when I walk slowly—yes, so slowly, at a more Jamaican pace—along Oxford Road; and later, at twilight, gaze out at the Caribbean from my top story apartment; just gaze out, that is all; seeing once again that sea of primeval memory, and all those people. Seeing distant cities, and one in particular, bound by memories that bind me to it; pull me to it. Seeing all of them walking there, breathing. Still being. Still being and—at least for now—eclipsed neither by memory, nor by time.

1. You will know from the story itself and the circulated researched reports at large that these men had origins, between them, across the fourteen parishes of Jamaica; that several of them lived with another man exclusively for more than twenty years, and, in one case, thirty-seven years, and more than six of them raised children with that other man; and that the first of these men officially documented was born in Aenon Town, Clarendon Parish, in the year 1877, only a few decades after Jamaican Emancipation, and died in Baychester, Bronx, New York, in 1986 (most of the seventeen men were born between 1901 and 1946, with the youngest man having been born in 1956 and on record as either "expired" or "disappeared" from Baychester in 2004).

2. "Yours"? But why? But then things make sense visually here, everywhere throughout this sprawling city, you have often thought: things such as tin coffee or tea containers stacked in triangular displays in shop windows, or the word "bookshop" instead of "bookstore" displayed on a pendulous sign above an unprepossessing street entryway; they make sense, these small things, partly, but not only, because of the British colonial-Empire past you have inherited from your people, from your Jamaican-Caribbean people. Yes, you know it: colonialism makes possible—demands—familiarity, even (especially) alongside uneasy intimacy, revised or completely rewritten history, and the strangeness of affection in the grasp of repugnance, contempt; the deep distrust that understands (or is at least acquainted with) the pulse and quickening of hatred.

GOODNIGHT, NEW YORK: A SERMON ON THE MOVE

RABBI ANDREA MYERS

WORLD AIDS DAY, 2011
PARSHAT VAYETZE, 5772

"My heart is in the east, and I am at the end of the west."
—Yehudah Halevi, Jewish philosopher
and poet of medieval Spain

MY HEART TOOK ME TO the east. I was a Long Island girl who grew up Lutheran and then fell in love with Judaism. It didn't hurt that my first college girlfriend was a nice Jewish girl who introduced me to religion as I had never known it before. Though the girlfriend came and went, I graduated from college and got on a plane to Israel with nothing but a duffel bag full of clothes and the determination to become a Jew.

In Jerusalem I was introduced to the line from Yehudah Halevi: "My heart is in the east, and I am at the end of the west." While Jerusalem entranced me, when I first heard Halevi's poem, the city I thought of was New York. I had traveled all the way to the east, only to discover that my heart was still in the west. I remember wondering whether Jerusalem could ever become as special to me as New York. Jerusalem certainly has a longer history in terms of its hold on humanity; but in terms of my personal history, there was no doubt that New York had pride of place.

For me, as for many others, New York is the place where I found myself. In Halevi's poem, the word chosen for "I"—"anokhi" in Hebrew—is somewhat unusual. There and in the Bible, it is possible to read "anokhi" as suggesting a kind of revelation, some realization or actualization of self. Jerusalem was central to my journey, but I never would have gotten there if not for New York.

Growing up, New York City was always a place of both possibility and caution. Trips into the city were an event. My family would take the Long Island Rail Road into Penn Station, then take the subway to wherever we were going; usually, down to Chinatown. Before getting on the subway, my mother would instruct me, "Be careful who you look at, because they might look at you back. Just look down at your shoes."

As a result of this sage advice, I have vivid memories of the shoes I wore on New York subways for decades, and the memories that go with each pair.

I am sitting on the subway, looking down at my black patent leather Mary Janes.

My mother made me wear them into the city, all dressed up to meet with the relatives who weren't close enough to invite to our home but whom I apparently still needed to impress. The number of Band-aids needed to buffer my feet from the assault of the patent leathers was substantial. I remember sitting on the subway looking down and thinking: "Maybe one day, I'll be able to wear comfortable shoes."

My family moved from Queens to the safety of the Long Island suburbs before I was five, but even then I knew I was different from other girls. When we played house, I didn't just want to *be* a wife, I wanted to have one, too. Whatever role I wanted to play, I knew the shoes had to fit.

I am sitting on the subway, looking down at my sandals.

A few years later, I found myself looking at sandals. These were for trips to Coney Island to see Aunt Rosemary, one of my mother's best friends, in the Mermaid Parade. She had long red hair, and a fantastic sense of adventure. As teenagers, she and my mother created an Elvis Fan Club, getting together with friends, singing along loudly to Elvis, fawning over pictures, and wearing pasted-on sideburns in homage. Perhaps, not surprisingly, Rosemary ended up with a lot of gay friends and became an institution at the Coney Island Mermaid Parade. Every year, she would sew her elaborate costume herself. She was a bride mermaid, the Star-Spangled Mermaid, and any number of years, she was crowned Queen. She would show me the pictures afterward, and now, I have no doubt they were censored. Now that I'm a parent I have jumped across the table to intercept Rosemary's pictures from reaching my own young daughters—but the creativity and playfulness of the parade never ceased to amaze me.

I am sitting on the subway, looking down at my white leather boots.

The white leather boots—with heels—were part of my straight girl drag in high school. I grew up in the land of football teams and the big hair of the 1980s on Long Island. It was not the best environment for a budding young lesbian, so my eyes were always towards Manhattan, including weekend excursions to clubs like the Limelight and Tunnel, with our highly suspect IDs. Those of us who were gay knew that the people who lived in the city were part of a whole world that was different, a world in which they could be themselves. It was just a matter of time until we could get there.

I am sitting on the subway, looking down at my Doc Martens.

They had black and pink laces. I was nineteen, home from college, going to the New York Pride Parade for the very first time. I was with my girlfriend, and I was clad in my ACT UP T-shirt. I was angry about my cousin Mark, who had died of AIDS not long before; I was angry about all the people who were dying of AIDS, and the deafening silence of our government.

Mark was, in many ways, the epitome of a Southern man: well-mannered, genteel, with a very sweet drawl. He also was a hairdresser, and gay. Mark was HIV-positive before anyone knew what it was. He ended up in New York staying with my parents for a summer, when it was clear that Arkansas was not ready for him. That summer, he took me from my parents' home on Long Island to spend time with him in the city.

It was Mark who showed me Christopher Street when I was in sixth grade, saying, "This is a place where you can be yourself. Just be careful who you go with." Mark was lost along with a generation of creativity and progress in the LGBTQ community. Outrage at the lack of care and services given to him and so many others fueled my activism for years. People like Brenda Howard and Larry Kramer were my heroes. New York City gave their voices a much-needed public platform, and I wanted to be part of it. My boots were made for marching.

I am sitting on the subway, looking down at my Timberlands.

After the Docs came the Timberlands. In these years, as a girl who looked like a guy, I was especially careful not to look up for fear of being beaten up. I no longer had my fellow activists around me; now I was a rabbinical student, realizing that the identities which felt so integrated to me—lesbian, rabbi, Jew—were contradictions to others. At the same time, I was coming into my own: a kid who grew up Lutheran in the highly heterosexual suburbs, to a visible queer sitting on the subway, on the way to her Talmud class.

I am sitting on the subway, looking down at my Fluevogs.

These shoes frequently walk the Upper West Side. Now, I am on my way to a board meeting of Keshet, a national grassroots organization working for the full inclusion of LGBTQ Jews in Jewish life. After years as a congregational rabbi in the Catskills, my focus is back on the city, where my partner is a rabbi and our kids go to school. I have just published my first book, and so these shoes also are taking me through airports to book signings around the country. Although I am still sure to keep my eyes on my feet, more and more, I try to look up.

I look up from my shoes, and I see change.

Gay life in New York City has changed over all these years as I looked at my own shoes on the subway. Now I am old enough to need to wear sneakers to Pride. What a contrast the 2011 Pride

Parade was compared to 1991 in my Docs. This time, the parade was just after same-sex marriage had been declared legal in New York. I had been in Albany the night the legislation passed, as part of Pride in the Pulpit, a group of liberal clergy, vastly outnumbered and outspent by members of the religious right. Until the vote was taken, we had no idea if it would pass. With Pride Week around the corner, we knew it would be a celebration or a riot, depending on what happened in Albany that night. As it turned out, I have never seen such a celebration. We marched with the Governor of New York, carrying signs reading "Promise Kept," our T-shirts proclaiming victory, couples all along the parade proclaiming their intentions to marry.

When I was marching this year, I thought again of Mark. I have a Christmas card from him with the words Happy Holidays at the bottom, surrounded by pictures of pine cones and ribbons. The top of the card is a picture of Mark, wearing an ACT UP T-shirt saying Silence=Death, and standing, gaunt but proud, behind a sign for AIDS awareness. On the back, he wrote:

Dear Andrea,

This picture was taken on World Aids Awareness Day! In front of the Arkansas State Capitol there was a group of people trying to join hands around it. Two years ago, twelve people showed up. This year there was well over 1,000, which was many more than needed to circle the capitol, and it is a large building. It was one of the most moving experiences of my life.

Hope you have a wonderful holiday and may all your dreams come true,

Love Mark

P.S. Let the family read this note and tell them I love them

We have come so far. How proud Mark would have been to see some of our shared dreams coming true.

I look up from my shoes, and I see possibility.

As much as things have changed, so much of what I love about New York is timeless. This has always been the city to which people come to find a sense of possibility, and the hope of happiness.

I remember a discussion I had with Mark over coffee in Provincetown. At that point it was clear he was seriously ill, but his sense of humor and great advice were always on target. We were talking about an awkward romantic situation he had gotten himself into, and how he was being forced to choose between two people. I asked him how he could possibly make such a hard decision. He leaned over, took my hand, and said to me, "Andrea, I only have to ask one question: Does he make me happy?" Then he smiled his big Southern belle grin and leaned back, knowing that his decision was made.

My experiences as a lesbian, as a Jew, and as a New Yorker all have taught me that life is not just about subsistence. Do we choose to be who we are? No, we choose whether we will be miserable by pretending to be someone else, or whether we will allow ourselves the happiness of being at home in our own skins. An essential part of my theology is that God wants us to live fulfilling, joyous lives. "Choose life," we are told in the Torah, "so that you and your descendants may live" (Deut. 30:19).

The Talmud teaches that when we die, we will be held responsible for all the pleasures we might have enjoyed and did not. New York can certainly be a tough place to live, but it also is full of pleasures. Years ago, I lived briefly in Manhattan, followed by a short stint in Brooklyn and a much longer tenure in the Bronx. But it was in Manhattan that Lisa and I had our first apartment. In true lesbian style, we moved in together the moment we were living in the same city, after over a year of long distance love. We lived in a brownstone on West 69th Street, a few steps in from Central Park, with two kittens and the requisite assortment of herbal tea.

Best of all, there was a short-lived but fantastic business called Urban Fetch. You could place an order on your computer—hypothetically speaking, for a pint of Ben and Jerry's Chubby Hubby ice cream, and a video of k.d. lang's first movie, *Salmonberries*, that 1991 lesbian underground not-quite-classic in which lang plays an Alaskan pipeworker who falls in love with a librarian. Half an hour after you order, these choice items would appear at your door, delivered by someone on a bicycle who looked like he had waded through a lake to get to you, bearing not only your order but also a T-shirt and fresh-baked cookies in appreciation of your patronage. You were strictly forbidden to tip. We never figured out how the company sustained itself, and before long, it didn't. But it was glorious while it lasted. It was a very small microcosm of the city in which anything was possible.

The only catch was that our apartment was an illegal sublet. Just how illegal it was, we were not aware—at least until we received a warning under the door from a private investigator who the landlord had hired to follow us. This put a damper on things, but until we had to move, the rent was the stuff New York real estate fantasies are made of.

I look up from my shoes, and I see community.

Despite my outer-borough credentials, for me, as a gay New Yorker, the rainbow always leads back to Manhattan. It was there that Lisa and I were married, in a synagogue around the corner from the sublet that had been our first apartment. The wedding was a month after 9/11. The city was still quiet. A number of our guests' flights had been cancelled due to increased security and caution. For most of us, it was our first celebration since the tragedy. I could still hear the sirens of the fire trucks racing past our Riverdale apartment on their way to the city that horrible morning, the sound seared in my memory by the knowledge of how many firefighters on those trucks never came back. There was a moment where we thought about postponing the wedding, but we realized: what better way to fight terrorism than hold a big gay Jewish wedding in New York City? And so we did.

What was most beautiful to us, however, and most representative of New York, was how many worlds came together at our wedding. Our guests crossed the spectrum of Jewish denominations as well as other religions. We had people from all the chapters of our lives. It was as if I took people with me from each of those moments on the subway, on the move and looking down at my shoes.

What I love about my life in New York is how integrated it is, how often my different worlds come together. The life I have lived in New York has been far from the Christopher Street that I saw so many years ago with my cousin Mark. Connected to a synagogue and school on the Upper West Side, we are a married couple with kids like the other parents, straight or gay. When we go to the Village, it's to visit friends or get our hair cut. Yet we know that in our freedom, we are indebted to Stonewall and the courage of those who came before.

I look up from my shoes, and I see home.

As I write these words, I am preparing to leave this city that has been my home. Lisa's work is taking us to Montreal. Yet again, as in Jerusalem so many years ago, I will be a functionally illiterate immigrant, existing only because of the beneficence of the Jewish community. We are excited about the move, but I will miss New York terribly. There will be times when, as for Halevi, my heart is in one place, and the rest of me is in another.

What I will take with me is a sense of possibility and change, and the conviction that beauty, happiness, and community all are essential to human life. What I will take with me is a belief in integration, that we really can bring with us all of who we are. These are the blessings I have discovered from my life, and these are the gifts New York has given me.

What I take from Halevi's poem, though, is that it is never so simple as being at home or in exile. Wherever we live, we are always in motion, back and forth between these different states of mind. What New York City has taught me is that home is in community; home is in relationships; home is in people. Home is where you can be yourself, with the people that you love. Home—and holiness— can be anywhere. "God was in this place," Jacob says in the Bible, "and I did not know." Here too, as in Halevi's poem, the word for "I" is "anokhi." I am who I am because of New York City. My heart is in New York, and New York is in my heart. Good night, New York—and thank you.

IN THE HOUSE OF STRANGERS

OCEAN VUONG

IT'S A RAINY NIGHT IN Brooklyn. I'm lying in bed, waiting for her
to cry like she does every night it rains and thunders. Sure enough,
by the third crashing thunderclap, I hear her, her faint voice rising
with each boom until I can feel the tremor of her wails through
the springs on the bed. I bury my face into the blanket and curl
into myself, hoping she will calm and return to sleep as she tends to
do on calmer nights. Unfortunately, this is not one of those nights.
Within minutes, my bedroom door bursts open and the silhouette
of a small woman collapses into the room, screaming and trembling.
I leap from the mattress and gather her frail body into my arms.
I stroke her back, my fingers frantically rubbing the length of her
arm, trying to coax her back to the present, to herself.

This is not a nightmare. The woman is eighty-four years old and suffers from severe dementia. Her name is Grazina and she is my landlady—well, sort of. I take care of her in lieu of paying rent. It's the only way I manage to live and write in New York City on my own. How did I get here? You can say I'm naïve, or, an aspiring poet—overly ambitious and very broke. The answer is simple and, of course, a bit complicated: I needed a place to study and write and go to school. My single mother, being an immigrant from Vietnam and living in a housing project, cannot afford to pay for my education, let alone support my ambition to become a writer. Sure, I could write in my mother's apartment in Hartford, Connecticut, but as the oldest son in a Vietnamese household, it's my duty to obtain an education and provide a house, a *home* for my mother to grow old in. I am able to attend university only because of a generous scholarship from Brooklyn College. Unfortunately, the scholarship does not come with an apartment to accommodate living in one of the most expensive cites in the world.

WHEN I FIRST ARRIVED IN New York City in the fall of 2008, I had exactly $764.00 in my checking account and a backpack jammed-full of handwritten poems. Other than a handful of acquaintances in the city, I knew nobody. However, through the generosity of a few kind folks, I managed to set up an intricate couch-surfing map indicating where I would stay on which night of the week. I ended up sleeping on three different couches and in one kitchen per week, showering wherever and whenever I could. Of course, there were nights when my host could not accommodate me: relatives were visiting, landlord checking in, vacations, illness, etc. But I was usually quite crafty and found last minute accommodations from other friends, sometimes even strangers.

But on some nights when I was not so lucky, I ended up in Penn Station, a major underground railroad station on 34th Street and

8th Avenue in Manhattan. There I would hole up for the night and do my homework or write poems, often side-by-side with the regulars: homeless men and women who stay at the station, sometimes for months or years at a time. I eventually had to stay there for two weeks straight. I knew it was coming, I knew I couldn't crash on couches forever, especially without paying any rent and with people I didn't know very well. It was February—one of the dreariest and coldest I could remember. It was impossible to walk four blocks without my fingers growing numb and my cheeks stinging from the wind. *How can any homeless person survive a single night in this weather?* I thought. I soon found out. On the first night of my homeless existence, I left Brooklyn College at 5:00 in the evening after my last class and took the 2 train up to 34th Street/Penn Station. Upon entering the station I saw them almost immediately: rows and rows of amorphous shapes lining the halls of the old station, their clothes soaked with rain and filthy to the point of rendering their original colors unrecognizable—everything was the shade of soot and ash. You would think the city had been burning for months and these people, slumped and crumbled in the corners, were its unfortunate refugees. It was hard to believe that actual human bodies, that warm tender flesh actually lived inside those thick layers of fabric, plastic, and dirt. Even when the station cleared around 8:30 p.m., the corridors were still lit with the shadows of their bodies, and as the night wore on, more and more came in to keep from the cold. Unlike at Grand Central Station, where the police would corral the homeless into a small corner by the entrance where it's often not much warmer than the temperature outside, the guards at Penn did not seem to take the initiative to bother them. Maybe there were just too many people, maybe they were sympathetic—I don't know, but I was glad because, suddenly, I was now one of them. I spent most of my time in the Starbucks inside the station, working on my school assignments until it closed at 11:00 p.m. Then I would try to get comfortable in the waiting area where there were chairs. Sleeping was difficult. There was constant noise: a steady stream of Long Islanders coming home from bar-hopping, often intoxicated, hanging around, eating, drinking more alcohol, shouting, sometimes even fighting. This cacophony would last anywhere from 12:00 a.m. to 3:30 a.m., when the last train would leave the station for the night. After that, the other homeless folks would stumble over to where I sat and try to settle in.

The homeless in New York City, as I assume is true in most places around the world, are not all drug addicts or criminals. In fact, most are far from it. Some are sufferers of severe mental illness whom their families have either abandoned or simply lost touch with. A few are even escapees from metal institutions or hospitals whom, apparently, no one bothered to find. Many have been abused and taken advantage of, both sexually and financially. Some seem to have lost their sanity simply through the isolation of being homeless. What I discovered, even during my brief two-week existence at Penn Station, was that, as a homeless person, you tend to disappear. Your body, the space around your body, blurs into the landscape, you are seen less and less until you actually *become* the landscape. No one looks at you, even as you shout and beg, even as you scream for help. No one will look you in the eye. No one will look at you except the other homeless, who often do not have the most amiable intentions. The psychological effect is striking mostly because it is not all external. You are an outsider not only because others deem you as such, you are an outsider because you begin to truly see *yourself* as one. That's its power of total social isolation. You see people come and go, how they speak on their phones with anticipation and excitement, how they hold each other, how their faces light up as they make plans according to some promised order, promised future. You begin to envy their concerns: taking the dog out, what to wear for the party, where to go for the holidays, and you begin to see, through your idleness and lack of destination, how utterly alone you really are, a refuse to society, a pair of eyes watching from the margins.

I also learned to wear a perpetually disgruntled face, to furrow my brow and look "tough." The more vicious and crazy you appear, the less the chance someone will try to rob you or even mess with you out of sheer boredom, which happens more often than you would imagine. So I often sat brooding, trying to look "hard." Sometimes it worked. Sometimes it didn't. Throughout all this, sleep was nothing short of a luxury. If I was lucky, I'd get four sporadic hours throughout the night.

But despite the obvious difficulties, not all was ugly. By the time I started my two-week stint at Penn, I had already slept there dozens of nights and had come to know a few regulars by name, even befriended a couple. One night I was writing in the waiting room when a very well-bearded man came over. He stood in front of me for about two minutes before inquiring into what I was writing. When I told him I was working on a poem, his eyes lit up and I saw him for the first time. His face was dark and leathery as his bright eyes squinted out from a furrow of thick eyebrows. He was thin and a bit frail. I thought he must have been at least sixty-years old. He told me his name was Sage and that he wrote poems, too, except his poems "never end."

"What do you mean never end?"

"They just don't. I write and write and I can't stop. It calms my nerves though—when I'm feeling blue I'll just start writing. Fast-food bags, food wrappers, heck I even write in the blank pages of books! See?" He takes out a worn copy of a real-estate book and shows me his poems written in the margins and blank pages. "I can be an author, too!"

He sat down and we started to talk. He told me how he used to be married and even had three children he hadn't seen in nearly fifteen years. He thought he had grandchildren but wasn't sure. He was lugging around two large black garbage bags mostly filled with clothes, rags, and blankets. He put his head into one of them and gathered an armful of paper tattooed with what looked like hiero-glyphics. Pen and pencil of all colors slashed and swirled through-out the pages.

"Here, look at this one. This one's my best." He held a crumpled McDonald's bag in his hands and carefully peels it apart, the way an historian would unravel an ancient text for the first time. From what was legible, they appeared to be prayer-like: a lot of "Dear Lords" and the constant anaphora of "mays": "May the light shine in my heart again, may the wind find itself in my voice, may I never grow too cold and hungry etc..."

"Now it aint finished yet. I'm not done with it. I told you it aint never done." He took it back and glances, suspiciously at me, almost worried I would steal or damage it. He tied up his bag, rubbed his beard and looked at me sideways, his head cocked slightly back. "So what you writing, son? Go on, let me see. No, no—matter fact, *read* it to me. I like to hear. Seeing other people's words gives me headaches."

I read him one of my novice poems (something probably plagued with abstractions and most likely an imitation of Rimbaud or Lorca).

"Ha! Yous a romantic, huh? Okay. Okay. Go ahead, son. Write that love shit." Suddenly instilled with a sense of pride, he started, like an older mentor, to dish advice. As he spoke, he grew more and more excited and started to lean forward, his beard trembling around his lips. He kept telling me that I should write only to satisfy the soul, to "murder" demons with words. He spoke of healing the mind with the pen, that every stroke of ink was dagger to the heart of evil. I wanted to assume he was crazy, but his charm and charisma were simply mesmerizing. And since I was utterly alone, I felt very unsure of myself. What he said was intriguing solely because he harbored such devout faith in it, and that alone gave it the highest measure of credibility. There was no one to turn to and say, "Can you believe this guy?" and get a reaffirming shrug or nod or eye roll. I found myself losing the ability to measure normalcy against the rest of the world. Was I crazy? Were we both crazy? I asked myself the questions but had no way of answering them. We were surrounded by thousands of people and yet I found myself enclosed in a booth, just me and Sage, our own words and our own minds. What was sane or insane suddenly had no bearing—we simply were and that was, well, alright.

He rambled on for a good half hour while I nodded and "uh huhed" throughout. Then, as if from some sort of distant dream, there was music. Just like that. Not the light and bland train lobby instrumentals—it was real music, it was Motown. If I wasn't crazy before, I thought, I must certainly be now. Growing up in a black neighborhood, I have Motown running through my veins. I mean, you can dance to music, but you can only *get down* to Motown. Marvin Gaye, Luther VanDross, and Sam Cooke were the first to bless my little immigrant ears. I didn't know what the country I was born in looked like, but as soon as I heard that music, I knew America would be alright. Some might find it odd that I had such an immediate affinity to Motown and Soul. But Motown, in its essence, was also the Vietnamese lullaby. The Vietnamese folk song was the first song I ever heard. From my mother's vocal chords, it reverberated down into her womb and literally hummed inside my body, syncopating with my heartbeat. You see, like Motown, the folk song consists of a sort of wailing, an elongated and mournful cry even before the lyrics can make sense of anything. The pain and sorrow of generations could be understood in a single note of sound and I think when I heard Marvin cry out "ooooooooooh ooooh" for the first time from my friend's mother's stereo, my body knew it, it knew to the bone. To me, it was Vietnamese, it was pain hammered into song, and it was glorious.

I stopped and listened. The voice was clear, pristine as it echoed through the corridors. "Sage, what's that, man?" "That sweet thing? That's good 'ole Rupert. Some sort of aspiring soul singer. I tell ya, I didn't think there was any more soul singers nowadays, but some of these young kids got the itch for that sweetness I guess. And I don't blame 'em. Come on, let's have a listen." We picked up our bags and walked, following the music to a large clearing in front of the now empty ticket counters. And there, a man, somewhere in his early 30s, his face shadowed with a low fedora, swayed and crooned into a mic hooked up to a portable amplifier and an iPod loaded with instrumental Motown hits. He closed his eyes and sang, he sang as if he was smiling out the words. There was just so much joy on his face, the sight itself was enough to lift you. But his voice—what a voice! It was smooth, rich and utterly flawless. If velvet cigarettes had a sound, that was it. You could feel it thrum beneath your feet. I stood in awe and soon found myself swooning to its duende. The song? "At Last" by Etta James. Sage started to sway and I could tell his bones knew this familiar work as he gyrated and shimmied, his fingers snapping to the beat not unlike one of the original members of the Supremes. "Man! How he gonna do me like this? This song gonna kill me tonight. It's the saddest song in the world! But it's got that sweetness." I nodded in absolute agreement. People were already gathering, mostly other residents, but there were some drunken stragglers of the night who were waiting for their trains, standing with their last beers, sometimes a pizza or a pretzel in their hands. We stood like that, we danced like that. I saw the other home-less men and women begin to cheer up as they gathered and lay down around the song. Their limbs started to move and gesticulate as they warmed up to one another. As if through the song's familiar landscape, they were able to see each other as human beings again, maybe remember a brother's or cousin's face in one another. The whole scene had the effect of tremendous warmth and melancholy. I started to think of my mother, how, after my father left us, she and I would stand in the long lines outside churches to receive a loaf of bread and dented cans of soup. How we warmed ourselves by making up a song and dancing as the line moved along the snowy parking lot. I was suddenly stricken with a fierce urge to weep. I wanted to weep fully and hard. It seemed like everything was hopeless and tomorrow and the day after that and the day after that were going to be bleak, and I was too tired to think about anything else. But I busied my lips and my jaw with the song, I let the words find their way in and started to chew out those bittersweet lyrics as the night wore on and on: "At last. At last, my love has come along…"

ONE DAY AFTER CLASSES, I was making my way into the Starbucks at Penn to charge my phone when I saw a missed call. It was from a friend who lived on Long Island. I had met him at various poetry readings I've been to throughout the city. After the readings I would usually head to 34th Street as everyone else went home or to another bar for drinks. I wasn't keen on telling anyone about my staying in the station, but eventually I told him. Shocked, he suggested I just return to Connecticut, or at least call my mother. But neither was a plausible option. Calling my mother and telling her I was homeless would only cause her to worry. She would frantically wire me the little money she had and spend days preparing my favorite dishes to welcome me home. And although I was often tempted to do so, the semester was already in its fourth week and I figured I could "tough it out" and at least get twelve credits closer to my degree. Besides, my mother was so proud of having a son attend college—she would tape a picture of Brooklyn College at her table in the nail salon where she worked and, not being able to pronounce the name of the school, would gleefully point to it when customers and co-workers inquired about her oldest son.

I called my Long Island friend back. "Dude! I have a deal for you," he said, "take care of my grandmother in Brooklyn and you get a room for free..." The words "room" and "free" were all I heard, they struck my mind like shards of light. I heard nothing else. "Can I come now? Okay. I'll be there in an hour. Wait, wait—what train do I take?"

The building was an old Brooklyn brownstone: two floors and three rooms, only one of which was occupied. The children had long moved out and the husband long passed. When my friend opened the door, a little puff of white hair hovered behind his shoulders. An old woman timidly peered from behind him. Then, she stepped out from behind my friend and started to smile, apparently relieved at my small stature. "Oh, he's just a small one! That's good! That's good. Come in, we have tea." She turned in and I followed them inside the house. "Labas!" (Lithuanian for Hello) "I'm Grazina!"

"Labas! I'm Ocean!" This one word would play a major role in our exchanges with one another. To make her feel at ease, I would always use her native tongue and say "Labas" instead of "Hello." For some reason, she never trusted herself calling me Ocean, perhaps because my name is a bit unique. And, being self-conscious about her dementia, she would say "Ocean" and quickly look down at the floor, thinking she had done something wrong. Eventually, she just called me Labas and to keep it simple, I called her Labas as well. From then on, we would greet each other by saying "Hi, Labas!"

She reached out and held my hand with both of hers. I almost pulled back at how cold they were. She led me through the dark hallway, which opened to a stuffy living room furnished with what seemed to be everything made before 1965. The walls were plastered with some sort of faux woodgrain. There was an assortment of odd, Victorian style chairs that seemed to be facing in no particular direction. Everything, save for the rug and our bodies was coated in a thin or thick layer dust. What was most bizarre, however, was a glass armoire in the dining room that housed a fleet of sad-looking owl figurines also filmed with dust. In fact, there were owls everywhere. Apparently, Grazina is an avid collector of all things owl: owl clocks, owl paintings, owl lamps, towels imprinted with owls, even owl slippers. Everywhere I went, I was watched by hundreds of mournful yellow eyes. She had my friend and me sit down in the old kitchen while she made tea. Fumbling through the drawers and opening and closing the cupboards, she tried with great difficulty to find the proper cups. Her breaths grew heavy and her poof of white hair trembled in the effort. "I know they're here. Don't—don't worry. I know....I know. Please..." Growing uneasy, I looked to my friend who looked equally confused. Finally, she turned to us; a wooden spoon and a sponge in her hand, her forehead jeweled with sweat. Her eyes had the look of a child's who's just been caught drawing on the wall, waiting for either an affirmation or scolding. She was clearly lost. And I suddenly realized how lonely she must be. Her husband had died nearly four years before and she had had no other permanent company since. I began to realize how utterly real this would be, that it was not going to be easy, that whatever it was, I was mostly likely not prepared for it, and I was right.

My friend took me to a room on the second floor. When I opened the door, I was immediately plunged into a thick musty odor. It was the scent of air trapped for way too long. My friend said it would dissipate and went over to open the window, which had a picturesque view of the brickwork on the side of the next building. Of course I didn't mind any of this. After all—I wasn't actually living in luxury at my previous residence. And then, I saw it: an old wooden thing with only three legs, lit by the ochre evening light falling through the window. "Can I keep that?" I asked, pointing to it. "If you want," my friend replied, "I don't see why not. It'd be a pain in the ass to move it anyways." I walked over and touched it, ran my fingers across the surface, the dust, the wood, the cracks and seams and knots in the wood, I opened the drawers, I sat down and placed my hands on the table, testing the height for writing. It was fake oak—laminated to look natural, but it was perfect. Perfect not because of its quality (or lack there of) but because it was *mine*. My *first* desk. It didn't occur to me until then that having a desk of my own, something I did not have even in Connecticut, legitimized my identity as a writer. It was a badge, a label, a dedication, my vehicle. And having no publication and barely any respectable poems, the desk was an anchor, it was the promise of possibilities, that good work would be done, and it would be done right *here*.

A THUNDERCLAP SHAKES THE FLOORS of the apartment, and in a small room in Brooklyn, Grazina's mind is firing a memory from 1944 in Dresden where, as a young girl, she witnessed the gruesome scene of a city being firebombed. The genesis of my family began in the very nucleus of bombs. As a product of the war in Vietnam, my mother is a "con lai" or "mixed child" whose father was an American vet. Without the war, I would never exist. It's a hard pill to swallow and I'm not sure I've got it down. When heavy fighting tore through her small farming village, my grandmother took her two young daughters and fled to Saigon, the most heavily fortified city south of the seventy-sixth parallel, the line that divided North from South Vietnam. The city was a merciless place in time of war, especially for a young woman with no education and two small mouths to feed. Along with many other young women from the countryside, my grandmother took to the streets where many young American G.I.s were starving for affection and had plenty of money to pay for it. When my mother was born in 1968 and the family grew to four people, her father was already long gone: transferred to another city? Discharged? Killed perhaps? No one knew and frankly, no one cared. He wasn't meant to stay and her life was merely the byproduct of a means for survival.

I remember the first few years after immigrating to the U.S. We had no TV, no radio, and no one knew how to read or write in Vietnamese or English. The war disrupted everyone's education and upon coming to the States, all the adults in my family rushed into nail salons to earn a quick buck making other people beautiful. But even without books, we were filled with stories, and after dinner, we would all gather around my grandmother for "talk story." She would close her eyes, the words coming slow at first, but soon they sputtered and surged, always growing into a song. It was as if pain could not be told in any other way, that only through singing, could the memory exit the burden of a body and flourish as something abstract and therefore tolerable, even beautiful. Within minutes, every wall in the room would melt into fantastical landscapes of terror and wonder. Someone would start to cry, my grandmother would begin to cry, the song still coming between her gasps for air. Her daughters would join her where they could, as fresh snow started to crackle against the windows and wind rattled the beams of our tiny apartment. We would sit deep into the night like this; the tea pot emptied and filled a dozen times over.

WITH GRAZINA, MOST OF MY duties are manageable. I am in charge of her pills, which means I have to know what they look like and remember their names—all fourteen of them. She needs pills for everything from cholesterol, to arthritis, to nerves, to dementia, and even one for "general pain." I have to allocate the pills into a giant plastic organizer labeled with the days of the week, making sure she takes them at the right time. Missing one dose risks the possibilities of a dementia attack. But eventually, I get better at reading her body language and emotions. If she starts to talk to herself while watching TV, or if she just starts wandering around the house, putting owl figurines into her pockets, I know we were heading down the slippery slope. Most times, I can see an attack coming ahead of time and will try to talk to her or put her to bed for a nap. But sometimes, it is a lot trickier. One morning she was watching the news or *The Price Is Right* as I was leaving for school and as I walked past her to leave the house, she leapt up from the couch and grabbed my arm.

"Eric!" (the name of her forty-eight year-old son), "you can't leave me like this! What did I do to you! I raise you! I come to this country with nothing for you and now you run away like this!" This was followed by a slew of what I assume to be very harsh Lithuanian. No matter how much I tried to tell her I was not her son, she didn't stop. She was so deeply stricken by the attack, that there was nothing I could do to convince her that I was, in fact, her twenty-two year old Vietnamese caretaker. I ended up having to call her daughter who promised Grazina that Eric was at her house in Long Island (which wasn't even true. Eric lives in Boston) and that he was fine and that he would be coming home soon.

"Are you sure, honey? Oh. Okay. I see my son later then." She hung up and turned to me, wrenching her hands, "I'm so sorry, Labas."

Other times, it can be quite eerie: I will find her sitting in the kitchen late at night having an easy conversation with an empty chair. When she sees me she'll say "Why don't you make some tea for this nice little girl here?" This will be followed by me silently freaking out and ushering her to her bed. Sometimes, to make sure her mind was working the way it should be, I would check on her by asking her who the president is every few hours. Other responsibilities included showing her how to use the microwave and cooking for her, shoveling the sidewalk and driveway, getting groceries, fixing the cable when it went out, teaching her how to use the TV remote, which was something I would have to do at least once a week as she would forgot nearly every time. Sometimes I would be working on a poem, and, in the midst of figuring out a metaphor, would walk to the staircase and shout, "Grazina! Who is the president?!"

"My God! It's ughbama!"

"Okay, thank you!"

Some of my favorite moments are at breakfast when she reads old Lithuanian magazines, sometimes stretching back to the '80s, while sipping her coffee. I will be reading poems or working on some of my own at the table and she always asks me to read one to her: "Labas, read me a love poem please." She stares out the window as I read as if lost in the past, the future, or perhaps simply blanking out. Whatever it is, I am always glad to see her pleased. She looks at me from beneath her glasses and says, "Very well, then. Very well, then, Labas." I'd take that as a good response. It's in these moments that I think: this isn't so bad, she's actually getting better. I have a place to sleep and shower, not to mention the luxury of writing in a warm room. What more can I ask for?

And yet, here I am, the thunder growing louder, the rain relentless. Grazina is clinging to my shirt and between gasping breaths, begs me to save her brother whose charred limb she sees poking out beneath a pile of rubble. She points into the darkness and her hand is swallowed by it. I can hear her wet eyelids blinding rapidly as the memory flashes behind them, so clearly that her hands reach out for it. I try to calm her with words:

"It's okay. It's just a dream. Please. I'm here. I'm here. It's Labas."

But her terror is shocking in its vigor and determination. In my panic, I forget that she barely understands English. So I do what I know best, what my grandmother did for me on those hot summer nights when I would lay awake wheezing and sweating with nightmares, I start to sing. My voice unsteady and crackling, I guide the dirge of my grandmother's lost country into Grazina's ears and through her buckling body. I sing, the long sad notes shared between ancient Vietnamese poets and the soulful crooners of Motown. After about thirty seconds, Grazina begins to wilt from her body's long and tarnished history and returns to the present. I keep up the song and can feel her breathing slowing, her clutch easing. My singing softens into a whisper and I ask the crucial question: "Grazina, who is the president?"

She looks at me, her face exhausted, nearly pleading for something to stop or begin. "I am," she says, "I am the president of this God-damned country." She chuckles and asks politely to be brought to bed, and we go down the hall and I assist her in. I sit by her and sing softly the same song until I can hear her breathing evening out, lulling into sleep.

Despite the confusion and difficulties of living with Grazina, not once have I considered it impossible, in fact, I see myself as lucky, even blessed. Here I am, an immigrant son whose family, or what's left of it, has been living below the poverty line for over twenty years—I shouldn't be writing in New York City while having zero income, I shouldn't be going to a great college and studying with some of the smartest and most passionate professors in their fields. I shouldn't have the luxury of making art, giving readings and lectures. And yet, here I am, doing it all and more. Not in my wildest dreams could I predict this outcome. And I am even more grateful for the opportunity to help someone else.

So I sing and I write—until singing and writing are no different, until the sound of the words themselves are song. Because, at the risk of sounding naive, I believe in the unquestionable power of words, that poetry can change lives, maybe even save them. I close the door to her room save for a crack just in case she panics again, as she sometimes does.

"Labas?"

"Yes?... I'm here."

"Will you have a new poem for me at breakfast time?"

"Of course I will."

"A love poem, okay?"

"A love poem."

"Good...Good."

"Goodnight, Labas"

"Goodnight, Labas"

A 1986 BRONX STORY

CHARLES RICE-GONZÁLEZ

1986. AIDS WAS LIKE A machete slicing down lives all around New York City and the world, and I was taking a sledgehammer to my closet. Slamming against its concrete walls, chipping away at my Puerto Rican culture, breaking down my Bronx bravado, and hacking at my fear that had kept me sealed inside. I was disconnecting from the girlfriends I had had in order to throw the world off my queer scent, knocking down Catholicism, Jehovah's Witness doctrines, and born-again fundamentalism to set my gaze to a gay world—a world that was in a fight for survival. And in a way, so was I. Whereas the gay community and its allies were rising up to stop the tidal wave of AIDS, which was having a devastating effect here in the US, I was in a fight to wrap my arms around myself so that I could embrace another man and love him. By the end of

1986, eighty-five countries had reported 38,401 cases of AIDS to the World Health Organization, and 31,741 of those were in the US, mainly New York City and San Francisco. But instead of using AIDS as another reason to keep myself imprisoned, I picked up the sledge-hammer and continued to bang, bang, bang.

I was twenty-one years old and had graduated from college the previous year, but had no social life because—returning to my Soundview projects in the Southeast Bronx after being away at Adelphi University in plush Garden City, Long Island—I was no longer connected to my childhood friends who had either become drug dealers, were in jail, or were already married with a kid or two. I worked at Human Sciences Press, a publishing company located on 13th Street and 5th Avenue that produced a plethora of jour-nals and publications about mental health, depression, Alzheimer's, Post-traumatic stress disorder, violent adolescents, and ways to cope with all kinds of emotional and mental challenges, but not one about dealing with AIDS. I suppose they didn't find it marketable, or perhaps the psychologists hadn't figured out what to offer us.

I remember the previous fall, shortly after I had started work-ing at the publishing company, I came in and heard some of the journal editors speaking about the breaking news that Rock Hudson had died. The media described it as a one-two punch to the general public because 1) he had AIDS and 2) it was revealed he was gay. Gay was synonymous with AIDS, but I still pushed on to see who I was and who I was to become as a Black-Puerto Rican working class gay man.

I shuttled between the Bronx and my job in the Village. I'd browse through bookstores, mainly Barnes & Noble on 18th Street, where I discovered Andrew Holleran's *Dancer from the Dance*, Edmund White's *A Boy's Own Story*, Andrew Tobias and John Reid's *Best Little Boy in the World*, Mary Renault's *The Persian Boy*, Rita Mae

Brown's *Rubyfriuit Jungle*, and Jane Rule's *Hot-Eyed Moderate*—even Anne Rice's *Interview with the Vampire* offered a connection to my gayness. I spent my train rides and my evenings reading books.

On the weekends I'd drive out to dance at clubs along Hempstead Turnpike with my Adelphi classmates. Straight clubs, of course, because all of my former classmates were straight. We danced to Cyndi Lauper, Depeche Mode, and Dead or Alive: "You turn me right round, baby right round."

But by 1986 I had done enough turning around and was ready to come out. No more trying to deny my desire for other men or wondering whether I could go through with the marrying/double life thing. The books offered worlds full of romantic longing but also satiating sex. They spoke of men in San Francisco, Key West, and Fire Island, but also of men in New York City's Greenwich Village. Men whom I'd see walking the streets of the East and West Village, on my lunch break in Washington Square Park or walking along 14th Street. I'd avert gazes as I rode the train. I'd looked at hot guys indirectly. In the *Village Voice* I saw personals of men seeking men and read about orientations at the Lesbian and Gay Community Center on 13th Street. I'd buy a stack of magazines and slip in *The Advocate* so that I could read more about the gay worlds and learn about Christopher Street with its gay bars, shops, and the infamous pier. And it was all right around me like ripe, heavy-hanging fruit.

I started to save money, just in case my family chose the stereotypical route and demanded that I leave home. But I wasn't coming out to them just yet. I was coming out to myself. I was embracing my desires and shedding the shame that had accumulated throughout my life. I read more books like Christopher Bram's *Surprising Myself*, which offered a beautiful story about a young man finding love and discovering himself in New York City. On the other end of the spectrum were Gordon Merrick's trashy novels about rich white men fawning over young bucks with tight bodies and sandy blond hair. My gay experience was not flesh-to-flesh but eyes to page. I was ready for more, so I called up friends who I thought might be gay.

Ricky was first. Ricky had grown up with me in the Soundview projects. We used to play a prepubescent version of Carol Burnett's Momma and Eunice. We talked to one another in bad, twangy southern accents and constantly yelled "Momma this" or "Eunice that" to one another. I wished we could have put on dresses and wigs as part of the fun. "Hmmm," Ricky said, sizing me up from across the small table at the 7A Café in the East Village after I made my confession of being attracted to men. "There's nothing wrong with you, Charlie. If this is what you want to do I am still your friend. Wanna take a stroll?" He gave me a walking tour of the East and West Villages, pointing out gay bars as we passed them. "You might want to visit one of those sometime." Ricky worked at a small boutique in the West Village and I met him there often. Soon he was taking me to Uncle Charlie's on Greenwich Avenue, the *Rocky Horror Picture Show* at the 8th Street Playhouse, and shopping in thrift shops in search of long, vintage men's overcoats. Then we'd walk down 7th Avenue and let the wind billow our coats. He schooled me on how to work my coat while serving up my Diva Reina face. We went into bars in the West Village and under the 59th Street Bridge and drank amaretto sours and listened to news reports about spacecraft Voyager 2 revealing the secrets of Uranus and watched the Marcos flee the Philippines as the new president Corazon Aquino took the reins. I cheered her on even though I didn't really understand the politics. I just thought that it was cool that she was a woman and that her first name was heart. And I also thought, *What the hell, Imelda can be fabulous somewhere else and not on the backs of her people.* That much I knew.

Ricky and I expanded the "girlfriend" relationship we had as kids and supported one another in many ways, and we still do, but still no flesh to flesh for me. Even though Ricky was sexy with a tangle of wild, big '80s hair and a cocksucking pout, he and I were decidedly sisters.

Next was Kenny. He was part of my born-again brigade. We'd met at John 3:16 Pentecostal Church on Prospect Avenue when I was fifteen. It was 1979 and I had abandoned disco dancing (because Pentecostals only dance in the spirit and all other dancing belonged to the realm of the devil) to be saved from homosexuality by Jesus. I'd find refuge in the Lord's arms and press my face to his sacred heart to obscure my crushes on Carlos, Elias, Steven, and just about any teenage boy at church and a few of the hot elders, too. But by 1986 Kenny and I would be sauntering around the West Village. In one of our promenades we ran into another former churchmate at Uncle Charlie's on Greenwich Avenue, then the three of us headed to Uncle Charlie's on Christopher Street and the West Side Highway to meet up with some friends, and by chance we ran into another former churchmate. One of the friends who I was meeting asked what kind of church was it. *Church of the Poisoned Mind*, I thought.

My big "I got these feelings" confession to Kenny was met with "Charlie, please! We always knew. Me and David and some of the other guys at John 3:16 would say that we should just take you into the church bathroom and rape you." Several weeks later he and his friends took me to my first club, Better Days. Looking back, the name of the club fascinates me because it encompassed the past, present, and future. Although we were there in the present, many of the men dancing and rejoicing in that club were experiencing a time they'd later recall as better days, a time when they were healthy, strong, beautiful and young, not HIV-infected or if so, at least asymptomatic. Then, again, although we were in the present, the name suggests that there were better days in the past and I could feel the collection of human energy, the years of men and women who had danced with body and spirit, leaving some of their essence to add to the next night's joy. It is, was, and will be a place that folks recall from better days.

Kenny had told me that his friend Paul, who I had already met, and Luis, who I'd be meeting for the first time, would be joining us. He warned me that Luis was into him then he rolled his eyes with disgust. When Luis arrived at the Soundview Projects to pick me up, Kenny and Paul were already in the car. Luis had a bright, dimpled smile and he didn't seem especially interested in Kenny. When I had first met Paul, he and I argued about politics but it was a subtext to our sexual attraction. I sucked Paul's dick on the second date. I was by no means a virgin. I'd had sexual experiences since I was thirteen years old, but that is another story. When I got my mouth around Paul's dick, I sucked it raw and I didn't think twice about AIDS. I didn't think about all the men who were sick and dying right that moment. I was just savoring the experience, feeling the heat of his cock, relishing the sounds of his moans, riding the thrusts of his hips. I was completely lost in the pleasure, in the smells and the flavors. Paul and I had this modus operandi. He would call me up after work. Ask me if I wanted to go out for some frozen yogurt (because I was hooked on it at the time). We'd get yogurt and then drive to some Lover's Lane spots out at the end of Soundview or over by Orchard Beach. There, we'd suck and fuck and come and laugh and never worry about AIDS, never introduce a condom.

Most of the men I had seen in magazines, newspapers and news reports who had AIDS were white men, and part of me rationalized that as long as I didn't sleep with white men I was safe. The other rule Kenny had once shared was, "Don't go for the old trade because it's mostly them who are sick. Stick with the young trade 'cause we're still clean." So, my new crew was young and "clean."

That night of my first club outing, Luis was in the driver's seat and Kenny was beside him. Paul sat in the back with me. His eyes sparkled and with each glance we connected on our sexy secrets.

Luis found a parking spot on 49th Street right up the block from the club. I barely let the car stop before I opened my door and popped out. I wiped my palms on my overcoat and shook out my hands. I would have run up to the door, but felt foolish even considering the act. Standing outside the club I could hear the music. I was instantly in a trance. I couldn't wait to start moving my body. Who would be inside? Would there be a giant disco ball, flashing lights and couples dancing like they did back on the TV show *Disco '77*? Once inside, my questions were answered. Better Days was wild because it was mostly macho Black gay men dancing with each other. They looked like my friends from the projects with their loose clothes, and Jheri curls, their gold chains and corn rolls, their do-rags and high tops, except these guys were grinding groin to groin on the dance floor. They smiled and hugged. Some kissed deeply, oblivious to the audience they'd attracted. I recall the lighting in Better Days being low. And after I came into the entrance there was a bar with a little lounge area with the dance floor beyond it. I don't remember it being all that large but it felt massive. The lighting system was simple and the sound was decent, but it was the house music and the people that had me hooked. I had never been in a room with so many amazing, beautiful gay people. There were butch women wearing fedoras, white shirts with ties and vests; voluptuous sisters with gold hoop earrings wearing tight, black strapless dresses that showcased every curve; drag queens with high hair and gold sequins; young dark men with cut off sleeves waving arms with ample biceps and some guys in business suits; young women and men in track uniforms and headbands; and slim people wearing thick framed glasses with asymmetrical afros.

They drank, grooved, grinned, and shared intimate conversations whispering into one another's ears as Carl Bean sang, "I'm happy, I'm carefree, and I'm gay. I was born this way. From a little, bitty boy." Kenny, Paul, Luis, and I took to the dance floor, and we danced. Oh, we danced, testing the flexibility of our young spines as we swayed our torsos, discovering new ways to wave our arms. "Proud to tell it," Bean professed, and we responded with our hips, swinging them side to side, back and front, pounding them into one another. I watched how the others danced, how some raised both arms over their heads and waved them quickly side to side, and others grinded their asses into their partner's crotch, and the music, the beats were nonstop, so we released any worries and gave in to them. I shut my eyes and delighted in the House music vibrating through my body. I didn't care about getting caught by someone from my building or catching herpes or AIDS. If being gay meant dancing in the middle of a crowd like this and feeling the euphoria of the movement, then I was signing up for a lifetime membership.

Paul put his hands on my shoulders and brought me back into the room. We danced staring into each other's eyes. Paul grinned. He was all teeth and gums. The flashing lights made him pink and blue. I wiped sweat from my brow and flicked it into the air. I looked for Kenny and Luis and saw them sitting by the side. I didn't want to stop dancing.

As a weekend warrior, prior to that night I'd danced for hours at spots like Danceteria and The Pyramid Club. Those crowds also knew how to get down, but it was this crowd who looked like me, who looked like the people I knew, who made being gay feel normal. That it wasn't just muscled white men and flashy queens, but also guys who looked like they were from the Bronx, and who just like Paul, Luis, Kenny, and me, most likely were.

After what seemed like hours, I headed to the bar to redeem my free drink ticket, which was handed to me when I paid my admission. As I tapped my foot and waited for my rum and coke, I felt a hand on my shoulder. It was Carlos, a friend who lived in the house on the corner across the street from my projects. I knew it! "What are you doing here?" he asked. I didn't need to answer and we both just laughed. It was fun to see someone I actually knew. I pointed out my friends and we talked a bit. Then, he got closer and slipped his arm around my waist. I relaxed and enjoyed connecting with Carlos in this way. I was crazy horny and wanted to make out with Carlos even though I was never into him. But I was in view of my friends and I was feeling like I was "with" Paul, even though we were all just out with each other. I brought Carlos to meet my friends and then he left us and continued cruising the club.

Kenny pulled me aside and complained that there were so many hot men and that Luis wouldn't leave his side. I looked over to Luis who smiled and laughed with Paul. He looked over and saw me looking at him and raised his eyebrows in a greeting and continued his conversation with Paul. Luis seemed like a nice guy, accommodating, good-natured and nice looking in an average kind of way. His most winning aspects were his mound of curly hair and his wonderful smile. As Kenny continued to complain about Luis, he stared at a tall very dark guy with braids who was staring back from the dance floor. "Check him out," Kenny said. The music thumped and the lights flashed as bodies writhed and swayed around him, but the guy stood still and continued staring. "Carajo, that guy is so my type, but I better not mess with our ride."

Paul interrupted our powwow. "¿Qué está pasando aqui? How can you two be chitchatting when 'Move Your Body' demands our presence on the dance floor!" He pulled on my belt loop and wiggled toward the lights. Luis came up beside Kenny, who smirked. The club seemed like it would explode as every single soul in the place, past and present, crammed onto the dance floor. Bodies pressed up against me and strangers instantly became dance partners as they sang along with Marshall Jefferson. I'd soon learn from a drag queen that night that "Move Your Body" was the national anthem of House Music.

We danced past last call and right to the point where the lights came up to reveal a sweat-drenched, disheveled room of revelers who groaned that the night had come to an end. Paul and Luis went on ahead and I stood in the coat check line with Kenny who was being stared down by the tall guy with the braids again. Kenny turned to me. "Torture! He looks even better with the lights on."

I laughed and saw a reflection of a guy in the mirror. "He's pretty cute."

"Who?"

I pointed to the mirror at a guy wearing a white jacket.

"Charles? That's Luis!"

"It is?" I looked away from the reflection and over to Luis who was talking to Paul. Somehow in the bright soft light, Luis looked cuter. His brown skin looked smooth, his eyes expressive and his smile was downright seductive. "Holy shit," I said and Kenny and I laughed.

Kenny winked. "You can have him." And we laughed more.

We did a lot laughing in 1986 while some gay men worried about dark spots appearing on their skin and others lay dying in hospitals. Once, while waiting for a drink and laughing heartily with Kenny at the bar at Better Days, I noticed a solemn-looking drag queen staring at me. She had on a red, highly teased wig and mammothly long eyelashes. I recognized the stale, flowery Jean Naté she wore because one of my aunts used it, too. She called me closer with one long, black-painted fingernail. "C'mere, sweetie." She whispered so close to my ear I could feel the warmth of her breath and smell the rum on it. "Enjoy yourself because you never know what can happen. Did you see that space shuttle explode? And all those little kids were watching as their teacher was killed inside it. One minute she was zooming up to space and then next—" she paused and snapped her fingers, "you explode and you're dead."

I didn't think much about it at first. *She's just a drunk, sad drag queen.* But I watched her later, still sitting in the same place, nursing her drink. She looked about forty years old and I remembered Kenny warning me to stay away from the older trade. Was she clean? Was she possibly talking about her life as a drag queen, how one moment she can be on a ride to heaven and then the next get punched down?

As I continued to come out and embrace my desires, I was on a celestial ride of a sort—focused on friends, clubs, books, which I never gave up, and meeting men and feeling desired. I was laughing as the world around me was changing and I was entering a community of gay people who were in the midst of one of the largest transformations since the gay revolutions of the 1960s. I had sex with Kenny at first and continued having sex with Paul, while I longed for Luis. It wasn't long before Luis and I were staring at each other on car rides and he was making me mix tapes of Madonna music. He and I were well aware of the tangled relationship among me, Paul and himself. Kenny was a free agent and his fucking circle went way beyond us. My attraction and desire for Luis grew from a steady simmer to a full boil, and I had to let Paul know that I wanted to date Luis exclusively. No more going out with Paul for yogurt or sex in parked cars. Paul, being a devotee of the nighttime television soap opera *Dynasty*, did not take my news of wanting to stop fucking with him well. He even made his car jerk forward when I crossed in front of it as if he would run me over. I glared at him, but he didn't make eye contact. Just stared into the night. There is a Buddhist saying that aggression comes from deep sadness. I'd like to think that Paul was sad, but if it was sadness it was fueled by pure anger and hurt from being rejected. I really liked Paul and sex with him was amazing, but Luis made my heart stop.

Anita Baker was our songstress. Luis and I listened to her *Rapture* cassette over and over again in his car. We sang along and to each other in falsetto and held hands. Sex went to a whole new level with Luis. We'd make out and suck each other off in his car at first, just like I did with Paul, but soon he would take me to his room and I would take him to mine. We both still lived at home, but being two young men it was no big deal. We were just buddies, just friends going to listen to music or watch a videotape. Once the door was closed we'd peel off our clothes and explore our bodies.

I loved touching every inch of him and running my fingers through his thick hair, which was turning gray even though he was only twenty-three. It was one of the characteristics that added to his sexiness. I loved stroking his smooth brown back and pressing my face against his furry butt nuzzling it before my tongue lapped at his taut hole. I kissed the back of his thighs and behind his knees, his calves and feet. And I held him for as long as I could, which was sometimes only minutes because his mother would call us down for dinner, or hours when there was no one home. I loved Luis's eyebrows. They framed his eyes so perfectly and he made them dance and wiggle. I kissed them every chance I got.

In the hot summer, we'd rub ice all over each other and I liked to take a cube in my mouth as I sucked his cock. Luis's cock got so hard it pressed up against his belly and I loved peeling back the dark foreskin to reveal the lighter colored head with the brown pink slit. I didn't use condoms when I took him in my mouth nor those few times when he fucked me after playing with my hole so much that I felt I could climb the wall and crawl across the ceiling. We were both clean, I thought to myself. We both looked healthy, and what was the point of getting tested, there was nothing that could be done. I just wanted more of Luis.

We'd meet after work. Drive to Pelham Bay Park and walk

around in the dusk, then go park somewhere and make love. We'd meet up for a movie, then go home and make love. We'd go shopping, then make our way to one of our beds. When we didn't see each other, we talked on the phone and made plans to meet up, and we wrote love letters. Countless love letters, greeting cards, and notes sharing our feelings and thoughts. We were every clichéd idea of two young men in love....stuffed animals as birthday gifts, spontaneously showing up to the other's house with flowers, mix tapes of our favorite songs, candlelight dinners, and strolling along the Christopher Street Pier, staring out into the black Hudson River or watching young queens vogue and cavort under a streetlamp while beats thumped out of a suitcase-sized ghetto blaster. "Go Nelly! Go Nelly! Go! Go! Go Nelly!"

Everything was perfect until I felt a small growth on my asshole while showering. It didn't hurt or sting, just itched a little. I'd never had a hemorrhoid and figured that must be it. Within a week it had grown to twice its size and was hanging out of my ass. I got nervous. I remembered that a neighbor had had a growth in her rectum that had become cancerous and she died.

With no health insurance, I quietly went to the emergency room one evening after work. I was diagnosed with anal warts and had to have a colonoscopy to determine if there were more inside of me. At that point, Luis had only fucked me once and I had only been fucked by one other person, Kenny. And I knew that Kenny had had genital warts. I was ashamed to tell Luis. I thought Luis would dump me, but he didn't.

The doctor said she was concerned, not because of the warts. That was easily treatable, but she said the obvious. "This indicates that you are not using protection. Or at least not all the time." Not at all was more like it. She looked away and said there was a test available. Then she looked me in the eye and suggested that I get tested.

I refused her offer and said that I would get tested anonymously. I had read that if there was a record of a person being tested, that an insurance company could refuse to insure him.

I got my first HIV test in the fall of 1986. This was the first time that I felt pulled directly into the AIDS crisis, and 1986 was also one of the turning points for AIDS. In May of that year the International Committee on the Taxonomy of Viruses issued a ruling that settled the fight between the US where researcher Robert Gallo called it HTLV-3 (human T-cell lymphotropic virus, type 3), and the French insisted on LAV (lymphadenopathy-associated virus). The dispute was solved with a new name, HIV (Human Immunodeficiency Virus). That fall was also when the first flurry of news about AZT trials came out, one of the first glimmers of hope in this dark time for people living with HIV, and for the rest of us living under the specter of being infected. But we'd soon learn that AZT prolonged the life of some people, killed others, and was highly toxic to all. When I tested negative, I vowed to use protection. But since I was with Luis and he was negative and wart-free, I didn't.

AIDS was this looming threat on the periphery of my life. I didn't know anyone personally who was infected, at least not anyone who was out about it. There was the wife of my cousin who was an IV drug user and she got sick very quickly and died, and the husband of an aunt who became ill and died of pneumonia, but our families were not using the word AIDS.

For the most part I felt safe. As long as Luis and I were monogamous and both negative, I was fine. And the friends in my immediate circle, Kenny, Ricky, Paul, and his new boyfriend, Jay, were also negative. I wasn't burying friends or going to memorial services. That would happen later. In 1986, I was focused on embracing myself as a gay man, going dancing, and falling more deeply in love with Luis.

I switched jobs and went to work for an ad agency on 90th Street and Broadway, so I was no longer in the Village every day walking side by side with the greater gay culture. I spent most of my time with Luis, who liked to go to City Island, to movies, go shopping, watch videos and walk along the Christopher Street Pier. And we'd dance at Hatfield's in Queens, the aforementioned Better Days, and at the Paradise Garage in Tribeca. If there was a gay heaven, it was the Garage. The long ramp to get to the ticket booth was like a portal to another world. I could hear the House music echoing in its cavernous walls. My heart would start thumping with excitement and my entire body tingled. My palms always sweated from excitement whenever I was about to enter a club, so I wiped my palm on my pants before I held Luis's hand. We paid and then turned and went inside the club.

The main floor was an active ocean of people dancing beneath flashing lights. "Follow me, Follow me." The synthesized strings swirled around me and wrapped me up. They pulled me to the dance floor and within moments Luis and I were dancing with a group of strangers as if we had been friends for life. We looked one another in the eye, gave high fives to our new tribe, and shook every possible part of our body. The lyrics were simple and easy to sing along with. We raised our hands as if we could touch the clouds in the sky and swing from stars.

I wiped sweat from my brow and face constantly, but I didn't want to stop. And didn't for hours. Then, Luis and I went to catch our breath and drink from the punch bowls set up on the bars. There was no liquor served, so the club stayed open way past the NYC 4:00 a.m. curfew. We traveled up to the rooftop garden and cooled off in the autumn night air. We were still in our honeymoon phase, winking at one another, sitting close and sharing small gentle kisses. Clubs were one of the few public places where we could be

physically affectionate. We often left the club in the early morning sunlight feeling more alive than when we walked in the night
before, even though we hadn't slept.

In 1986, Janet Jackson joined Whitney Houston and Madonna
at the top of the pop charts with her album *Control*. The title song of
her album was about taking charge of her life and her career. And
for my now twenty-two-year-old self it was about taking charge of
my love and trying to figure out what kind of life I wanted to live.
How out could I be in the Bronx, with my friends, with my family?

Luis and I spent a lot of time driving around in his car listening
to news of the US attacking Libyan terrorist centers, Desmond Tutu
being elected as the Archbishop of South Africa, and the nuclear
accident at the Soviet Union's Chernobyl power station. On some
level I was aware that there was more to life than love and clubbing,
but I preferred to listen to Patti Labelle and Michael McDonald
sing "On My Own"; Steve Winwood sing of a "Higher Love"; hear
Cyndi Lauper croon about "True Colors," and shut my eyes in angst
as Simply Red wailed about "Holding Back the Years." I held Luis's
hand tighter with each song and each moment.

As in love as I was with Luis, I was still attracted to just about
every guy I'd meet, but I didn't cheat on him. I thought it was a
sense of duty and commitment, but in hindsight it was also the fear.
I knew plenty about safer sex, but the operative word for me was
safer. There was no guarantee that I would not be infected if I so
much as sucked a dick of someone who may not have known he was
infected. I knew that sucking dick was low risk, but it wasn't no risk.
Besides, my love for Luis was new and burgeoning. And even though
my libido was out of control, Luis had my heart.

I often thought of that drag queen in Better Days who talked
to me about the Challenger exploding and how quickly life can
change or literally end. So, Luis became my world. We found time

and places where we could share our love. One chilly fall night we went to the Christopher Street Pier. It was the day after the Mets had won the World Series, and it seemed like all of New York City was one big party. The buzz was about how the underdog New York City baseball team had overcome all the odds and won the big prize. Even though I was a Yankee fan from the Bronx, I too got behind the Mets, because I was also an underdog trying to hold on to love when there was so little support for it to exist, and trying to stay ahead of a disease that was swallowing up my people. While New York celebrated the Mets, no one talked of the craziness that was happening in the world, or the crime in the city, or knew that a week later it would be revealed that President Reagan had secretly facilitated the sale of arms to Iran, putting the Iran-Contra affair on the front pages of the newspapers. And no one talked of AIDS which, it was said, would increase by 1,000 percent in five years. And Reagan didn't publicly say the word "AIDS" until 1987, six years after it was first reported in the *New York Times*.

On that chilly fall night in 1986, Luis and I straddled a large cement block and faced each other. "What do you want to do?" Luis asked.

I shrugged my shoulders. "I'm good right here."

Luis chuckled, "I don't mean right now, I mean with me."

It was one of the first times I felt my heart swell and expand in my chest. "With you? I want to be with you forever." I shivered as a cold breeze swept across us.

Luis smiled and opened his jacket. "Come inside." I slipped into his jacket, wrapped my arms around him and he wrapped his jacket around me. We just held each other, feeling our chests rise and fall with each breath. The night was clear and there were a few distant stars trying to add romance to the scene with their feeble twinkle. I felt his warmth and I moved in for a tighter squeeze.

PERRY STREET REDUX

CHRISTOPHER BRAM

I AM BACK ON OUR front stoop again, at the end of the first decade of a new millennium. I am reading—as usual. It's a lovely late afternoon in the spring and Draper is upstairs at his computer editing a friend's documentary. I am waiting for him to finish so we can go for a walk before dinner.

I'm reading *Exile's Return*, Malcolm Cowley's lively, impressionistic account of his generation of writers in the 1920s. Greenwich Village was a major site of their comings and goings. I recognize many of the streets he mentions.

Suddenly Cowley is describing the address directly next door. The brownstone on my left was the home of Squarcialupi's Restaurant in 1924. It was a spaghetti joint, located in the basement. Cowley, Hart Crane, Allen Tate, Caroline Gordon, and others used to come here to eat cheap pasta, drink red wine, read their poetry aloud, and play songs like "Too Much Mustard" on the piano.

"We were all about twenty-six, a good age, and looked no older; we were interested only in writing and keeping alive while we wrote, and we had the feeling of being invulnerable," writes Cowley. "We didn't see how anything in the world could ever touch us, certainly not the crazy desire to earn and spend more money and be pointed out as prominent people."

I sit up and take a deep breath, amazed. The building is now the home of Cynthia Rowley, owner of a chain of pricey dress shops. You can't get more prominent or earn and spend more money. She installed a swimming pool out back for her two daughters—we hear them splashing and screeching in the summer. There are more children in the neighborhood than there used to be, which has its charms as well as its annoyances. Back in the 1980s, the Rowley building had a crack den in the basement, its windows broken and stuffed with mattresses. I don't miss the mornings when I left for work and found blood splashed on the pavement like paint and a police car at the curb. But in eighty-odd years the address next door has gone from poets to crack addicts to Cynthia Rowley.

Our neighborhood has changed. Our building has changed as well. Our stoop isn't nearly as sociable as it once was. The chief reason for that is our good friend and neighbor, Cook, is no longer here. He died in 1991. Cook had thought his multiple sclerosis might protect him from AIDS—there were rumors and superstitions regarding MS and immunity—but it didn't. We visited him regularly in St. Vincent's Hospital around the corner. He wasn't our only friend who ended up there. Sometimes we had to decide which of two or even three people we would see on a given day. Cook's family was often in his room with him. His sister took his dog Fred home with her when he became sick. Nobody else holds court out here on the stoop the way that Cook and Fred once did.

Only a few of us old-timers remain. There's Sam upstairs with us on the fifth floor, and Bo on the first floor. Bill, the straight know-it-all cabdriver and lawyer, is still here, too, but a different version of him. I will tell his story in time. Our four apartments are the only ones still rent stabilized. The rents are so high for everyone else, however, that new people come and go before we can get to know them. Even Jenny, a smart and pretty photographer from Sweden, stayed just long enough for us to want to know her better, and for her cute husband to fix a broken spring in our oven door.

In the window of the empty basement apartment to my right is a large white placard advertising condos for sale. It's a non-eviction plan, which means protected tenants can stay and continue to rent. We certainly can't afford to buy. We were sent the offering package and learned our three-room, five-floor walk-up is worth $650,000. Our landlord's decision to condomize could not have been more badly timed, however. The apartments went on sale a month before the real estate market crashed. He has not sold a single unit.

Cowley writes that Greenwich Village in 1924 was a mixed neighborhood of bohemian artists and Italian working class families, with a few posh residences stranded here and there like islands of money. The working class is gone now except for a handful of rent-stabilized holdouts, including an elderly couple who live on the top floor of the Rowley brownstone. The Italians poured in around 1900 and poured out again twenty years later, leaving behind cafés and bakeries and Catholic churches. The rich people who recently poured in are sure to pour out eventually, too, but it's hard to imagine they will leave behind anything of value, only swimming pools that will need to be filled in, and overpriced restaurants that will go out of business. We are already seeing a lot of the latter.

DRAPER AND I HAVE LIVED in this building for thirty years now, longer than either of us have lived anywhere else. But other neighbors lived here longer.

Nina, of Tom and Nina, the parents of Sam the Baby, grew up in that same apartment with her parents and *three* siblings. When she and Tom had a second child, they moved to Westchester. She and I were talking about living space before they left and she confessed that the hardest part was that they had only one bathroom. "But how did you manage with six people when *you* were a child?" I asked. She looked surprise. "I don't know." Then I remembered I too grew up in a house with six people and only one bathroom. Did folks simply have bigger bladders in the old days?

Wendy, the little old lady with the German shepherd, grew up in this building, too. Her father was an opera singer with the Met. She loved music herself. Draper put her in one of his movies, strolling down a street singing "Most Gentlemen Don't Like Love." Wendy claimed to be in her eighties but was actually ten years older. She became confused in her last year here, wandering the building and knocking on doors. Draper opened our door one morning to find Wendy standing in the hall wearing only a sweater, naked from the waist down. "Hello, Shreeve," she said. "Uh, Wendy, you need to get back to your apartment and get dressed," said Draper and he gently took her by the hand and led her downstairs. A niece eventually put Wendy in a nursing home. After she died, her ashes were scattered under the niece's rose bush.

Bill, too, has been here longer than we have. But we don't know how much longer he will remain.

When I last wrote about Bill, he was still married. His daughter Regina was ten and Bill had just finished law school. I frequently ran into him out front, coming home in a light blue seersucker suit with a briefcase in his hand. But then Peggy left him, taking Regina with her out to Queens. We never learned the details, but Bill could not have been an easy man to live with. Regina frequently stayed with her father on weekends and he helped her with her schoolwork and her applications to college. Bill often told me what Regina was reading and how smart she was. He was very proud of her.

Then Regina stopped coming to visit. Bill spoke less about his law work when I ran into him—until one afternoon I spotted him on the street behind the wheel of a taxi cab; he ducked so I wouldn't see him. Apparently his legal practice wasn't working out.

When Bill caught me reading on the front stoop, he would still ask to see my book, then share his own experience or memories about the author or topic. But his stories grew less coherent, his cheeks redder, his garrulity louder. "You know, when I grew up in the city, my mother wouldn't let us sit on the stoop. She said it was low-class. Ha!" I knew his talk was fueled by alcohol, and it was no longer entertaining or always friendly. He once testily asked what I'd done with the Victorian sheet music he'd loaned me. I'd never borrowed it, but I played along and said I'd see if I still had it, trusting him to forget the next time he saw me, which he did.

Sam was closer to Bill than we were—each had helped the other in times of crisis. He admitted Bill wasn't doing well, but he didn't know what to do. Finally I put in a call to a good friend, a psychiatrist who'd begun a new job with the city making house calls for psychiatric emergencies. He promptly got in touch with Adult Protective Services and they sent a team over. In a fictional tale, that would have been the happy ending, but it was only the beginning of a long, long, messy drama that is still going on. Bill's wife and daughter became involved in his life again. Police have visited more than once. One night, a trio of surprisingly sweet street toughs brought Bill home after finding him drunk and badly hurt in a nearby park. Bill went into detox twice, and was in a clinic for six months. While he was away his wife and daughter went to work cleaning out his apartment to make it livable again. He had become a pack rat while living alone and his rooms were knee-high in debris—far worse than Wendy's apartment had been the night of the burning mattress. For weeks our hallway was full of fat garbage bags that were later taken down to the street. Since Bill returned from the clinic, he has been a ghost of himself, a pale old man with a wispy beard and baggy jeans who nods and says hi and little else. A caregiver comes by for a few hours each day. His wife says she has washed her hands of him, but we still run into her at the mailboxes.

BO JOINS ME ON THE stoop and asks what I'm reading. "Malcolm Cowley?" he says. "I don't know him. But the Twenties? That would've been a fun decade to live here. *Before* the Crash."

Bo is a tall, lean, handsome man a few years older than me, a former sales rep for a fabric design house. He loves opera, movies and history. We regularly recommend titles to each other, mostly books about the Third Reich. It's a peculiar predilection. Neither of us read it for horror or indignation, but out of a sad need to understand the world. Our need predates the invasion of Iraq, although my fascination with Germany deepened when I first understood that we, too, might be the bad guys.

"Nice weather," says Bo with a weary sigh. "Which means summer will soon be here and the Rowleys will be having pool parties directly outside my window."

"Hello, all," says Sam, bringing his feisty little terrier, Raqui (short for Raquel), down for a walk. Sam looks better than he did fifteen years ago, trimmer and healthier. He lowers his voice to ask me, "Could you call your psychiatrist friend? I think Bill might be drinking again but I don't want to confront him."

I explain there's little my friend can do now that Adult Protective Services is involved.

"Well, then, could you ask if he has any advice for how *I* might talk to him?"

It's curious that, of the five old-timers, the four gay guys do what we can to look after the straight guy.

But I don't find our building particularly sad. Stay in one place long enough and you follow a score of life stories to their end: all lives end in death. William Dean Howells famously complained that American s want tragedies with happy endings. But you can follow any story past the tragedy to better times, if not for the dead then for the survivors.

Look at our city, for example: we survived September 11.

The World Trade Center was not visible from our apartment upstairs, but could be seen from the roof. Half a mile away, those stark twin posts, like two surveyor stakes, were never pretty, not even at sunrise when gold light sometimes glittered on the sides like fish scales. Yet the structure was reassuringly homely.

As everyone now remembers, the morning was lovely, clear and mild, with no humidity. Draper and I were home, sitting at opposite ends of our sofa, each reading a book—I was rereading *Buddenbrooks*—drinking coffee and enjoying the silence. We never turn on the TV in the morning. We heard a loud crash outside, like a car wreck on 7th Avenue, followed by a collective gasp from a crowd. Wondering why so many people were on the street at that hour, I stuck head my head out the window. I saw nothing, so I raced out to the hall and upstairs to the roof. The twin towers stood downtown with a gaping hole in one and two long columns of smoke slowly blowing to the east. We had heard the second plane hit—we didn't hear the first. Tiny white specks like cigarette ash danced around the hole—we later learned these were thousands of sheets of paper blown into the sky. Time stood still.

When I ran back downstairs, I found Draper on the phone with his sister. The TV was on, locked on the very image that I had seen upstairs. Time continued to stand still. Draper's sister, watching TV in Kentucky, knew more about it than we did. But nobody knew very much that morning.

We made repeated trips between our apartment and the roof during the next hour. People stood on the rooftops all around, gesturing to each other and pointing at the towers as they spoke on cell phones. A young straight couple joined us on our roof, two drama students from California.

Then, at 9:59 a.m., the middle of the south tower swelled out a little, as if turning into smoke. The top section sank down into the smoke and it all dissolved in a black column of cloud. It was unreal. Not bad-movie-special-effects unreal but unthinkable unreal, unbelievable. The silence added to the unreality. Then the young woman beside us broke into loud sobs and it became real for us.

"We have just witnessed mass murder," said Draper.

Shortly afterwards, I was downstairs on the phone talking with *my* sister when the second tower collapsed. I raced back up. But seeing it with the naked eye made it no more believable than seeing it on television.

The wilder reports on the news—that forty planes were unaccounted for, that the Mall in DC was on fire—were soon put to rest. It looked as if the worst was over. Then the newscaster said that hospitals needed blood. Draper and I hurried downstairs to go to St. Vincent's. The streets were full of people, but the city was strangely hushed, as if during a power failure. There was almost no traffic. Doctors and nurses stood at the entrance to the emergency room with wheelchairs and gurneys, waiting to tend survivors. Neighbors were already lining up to give blood. We followed the line around the block to 6th Avenue, where we ran into my cousin, Maureen, and her lover, Meg. We all decided we could donate blood later, when they would still need it. But one of many sad facts about the event was that there were so few survivors for the doctors to look after and the blood was never needed.

For the rest of the day, for the rest of the week, it felt like life would never be the same again. We waited for the next terrorist attack. We waited for full-scale war. Our friend Geoffrey, an abstract painter and teacher, had been a ten-year-old boy in London during the Blitz. He assured us this was bad but he had seen far worse.

The young couple who had stood on the roof with us moved out of New York by the end of the month. But everyone else remained. And the city slowly became itself again, with an enormous hole in it, both literal and cosmic. Our hour of chaos and death was eventually projected overseas in six years of chaos and death inflicted on a country that had had nothing to do with the attack. After watching three thousand innocent Americans die, I was sickened that we could turn around and kill a hundred thousand innocent Iraqis.

Bo and Sam and I are still chatting when the two twenty-something gay boys from the third floor burst out the door and bound down the steps with their frisky new dog, an adolescent Weimaraner. The boys nod hi, but they're not as curious about us as their dog is about Raqui. We're invisible to them, which I don't mind.

"Ah, youth," says Sam irritably, watching them bounce down the street. I don't even know their names.

Draper joins us. "Hello, boys," he says. "What a beautiful day."

"How's the film coming?" I ask.

"Oh, it's getting there."

Draper looks awfully good for a man in his fifties. He does yoga twice a week and he eats wisely—more wisely than I do. His hair is as grey as mine, but on him it looks good.

I stick Malcolm Cowley into our mailbox so I won't have to carry the book. We wish Bo and Sam a pleasant evening and head down toward the river.

Our block is quite grand now, with renovated stoops and pretty shrubs and an expensive restaurant on the corner. Next door to the restaurant, however, is the meeting room of a local AA group, one of the toughest in the city we hear from a friend who knows. Folks stand outside before and after meetings, smoking cigarettes and drinking coffee, a wonderful assortment of gritty New Yorkers. We like having them at our corner. It keeps our street real.

Because much of the street has become artificial. In the next block is the brownstone used for the exterior of Carrie Bradshaw's apartment in *Sex in the City*. She's supposed to live on the Upper East Side, but Draper and I were watching an episode on tape one night when I said, "Hey, I know that corner in the background." We rewound and, sure enough, it was the corner near the AA meeting. Walking past the brownstone a week later, we saw a woman out front watering her flowers. Draper struck a conversation. "Oh yes," she said. "They asked if they could use my stoop and front door for exteriors. They pay me something. I figure there's no harm in it."

A year later, tour groups began to arrive, busloads of young women with digital cameras. They lined up across the street to take each other's picture at Carrie's front door. Now and then a pissed-off neighbor told them that the real Carrie, Sarah Jessica Parker, lived just around the block. Why don't they go take their pictures on *her* stoop? The tourists only looked scornful, refusing to be taken for fools. Finally the woman in the brownstone strung a chain with a "No Trespassing" sign across her steps, a chain and sign she has to replace every few months when they are stolen.

(Carrie Bradshaw never hung out on her stoop on TV, but one evening Draper and I passed Sarah Jessica Parker, her baby and a couple of friends hanging out on *hers*.)

I tell Draper about my discovery in *Exile's Return*.

"Right next door? God, I wish there was a cheap pasta joint there now. Remember when there used to be cheap Italian places all over the neighborhood?"

Malcolm Cowley's Greenwich Village has disappeared behind facades of money and make believe. It still exists in pockets, like the AA meeting or even our stoop, but is invisible to tourists. We are afraid it might die away completely. Draper and I frequently complain and sigh during our strolls. "Do you remember Sazerac House?" "Or The Front Porch?" "Is that another nail salon?" "My god, are they opening a *sixth* Marc Jacobs store on Bleecker?" We probably sound like two old Russians pining for Moscow under the Tsar. Bo works in a nearby antique shop and says none of these new stores do much business except for Marc Jacobs and a bakery famous for the lines of suckers waiting to buy its mediocre cupcakes.

At the end of Perry Street stands a trio of glassy Richard Meier structures that Draper compares to giant ice trays. These luxury condos look awfully cold and dead, especially when half the floors are still empty. The crash that followed the housing boom has left us wondering what will happen to all these high-priced high-rises not even foreigners can afford to buy into. The West Village could become a futuristic ghost town.

But then we walk between the glass towers and come out to the river and our hearts lift a little. The Hudson is beautiful, wide and open—the new waterfront is actually a change for the better. Where old green warehouses used to sag into the river, or open piers stood crumbling in sunlight, there is a wide walkway with flowers and shrubs and young trees. Two new piers covered with grass reach out toward New Jersey. The bigger pier attracts swarms of sunbathers in warm weather, gay and straight, shingling the grass with a landscape of skin and swimsuits and underwear. They are replaced in the evening by gay Black and Hispanic kids from uptown who come down here to a place where they feel safe to be themselves. They mix with the locals and everyone usually gets along.

The evening is beautiful. The blue sky overhead softly changes and the lights of Hoboken come on across the river. "And there's Czechoslovakia," says Draper, pointing out Ellis Island in the distance with its steep roofs and baroque towers. The Statue of Liberty stands diminutively beside it.

At the end of the bigger pier is a pavilion with a twisty canvas roof like a piece of non-Euclidean geometry. Under the roof tonight, a tango club is meeting. We hear accordion music as we approach. There must be two dozen couples dancing, every kind imaginable: a short Asian man with a tall blond woman, an old woman with a young man, a young white woman with a young black woman. They slowly move clockwise around the center post where a large boom box plays. All around the dancers stand a friendly assortment of curious New Yorkers. Even the kids from uptown are silent, with one willowy boy standing off by himself, trying out a new dance step alone.

"It's like *Last Tango in Paris*," I say.

"*Last Tango in Manhattan*," says Draper.

We watch, fascinated, admiring the way dancers improvise turns and gestures, stick a foot backward, pause, then dip and twirl a partner. We don't dare dance ourselves—these people are so good, so graceful—but it is a privilege to watch them perform this old-fashioned dance translated to a very new world. We lean against each other, shoulder to shoulder, and watch the circle of couples slowly come around one more time.

AN INTERVIEW WITH MICHAEL MUSTO

KATHLEEN WARNOCK

MICHAEL MUSTO HAS BEEN CHRONICLING nightlife and pop culture in New York City since 1984. First, and still, in his column, "La Dolce Musto," for the *Village Voice*, then as a broadcast and online commentator, he's a latter-day Samuel Pepys, recording and reporting the fire, floods and pestilence of twentieth- and twenty-first-century life. From Lady Bunny to Lady Gaga, he writes about the people, politics and parties of the day, reporting with a distinctly queer and distinctly New York point of view on the things that matter. Musto is the author of four books, most recently *Fork on the Left, Knife in the Back* (Vantage Point Press, 2011), a collection of some of his favorite *Village Voice* columns and original essays. I spoke with Michael about growing up and coming out in New York City.

KW: *Unlike many New Yorkers, you're a native. You grew up in Brooklyn, which was like a different world than Manhattan back then, wasn't it?*
MM: I grew up in Bensonhurst, Brooklyn…and it was not trendy. Bensonhurst was an old world kind of Italian-American residential neighborhood. It's a little more mixed now. A lot of the Italians moved out to Staten Island; now you see Asians, all kinds of people. We almost never came into Manhattan. We might have come in once in awhile for the Feast of San Gennaro, or an occasional school trip, but basically, when you were in Brooklyn, you were just in Brooklyn. I didn't get to taste a lot of Manhattan culture. I gradually started going to Broadway plays and things of that nature. I knew I wanted to go to college in the city. I got into Columbia, and there was no turning back.

KW: *Did moving to Manhattan and going to college give you the impetus to come out?*
MM: I wasn't quite out yet in the first few years there. I entered college at sixteen, and I hadn't had any experience of any kind. But another friend of mine, Arthur (who was also a burgeoning homosexual), and I would spend weekends in the summer just walking up and down Christopher Street, absorbing the gay atmosphere, without ever commenting on it, or taking part in it. It felt like we were both really obviously drawn to it; it was an unspoken thing. Christopher Street was just such a magical destination for the two of us. After college, I caught up with him, and he had come out. Big time.

When I got to school, the second I started joining theatrical groups it was clear that some of the people in them were flamboyantly gay, and some of them were really okay about it. And that was a good influence on me. I still wasn't ready to say that I was gay myself. I'll tell you the best thing that ever happened to me: There was sort of a gayish mixer at a nightclub and I went, hoping people wouldn't think that I was necessarily gay. A really outrageous, flamboyantly gay guy grabbed me and pulled me into the middle of the crowd and said: here's the latest addition to the Columbia gay community. And no one even rolled an eyeball. His outing me that way was my indoctrination. And again: there was no turning back… maybe that's why I out celebrities today.

KW: *At the time you came out, how difficult was it to be out in New York City?*
MM: I came out at the peak of gay hedonistic culture of all time; there was so much excitement, so many clubs and bars, and everybody wanted to be gay or be around the gays. We were at the forefront of the cultural life, like fun explosions. When people talk now about how gays are just starting to get a place at the table, I have to say it really wasn't bad in the '70s, it was fabulous to be gay. Things like DADT and gay marriage were not even issues then. We were flourishing as people, citizens, partygoers.

KW: *It was also when you began your journalism career. How did you get your start?*
MM: I've always been painfully shy, an only child who hardly spoke at all when I was growing up. The most comfortable form of expression for me is writing. When I was young, I would go see movies by myself and come home and write reviews on index cards just to have them. It was great experience, my form of writing a diary. It was a way to cathartically express my feelings. So it was only natural that I pursue writing as a career. I started working as the theater editor for the *Columbia Spectator*. I started at the highest level, going to Studio 54, gay bars. The original productions of *Chicago* and *A Chorus Line* both opened the same year. It was a high-water mark for a theater queen.

And I was also attracted to performing. So when I get to do TV nowadays, that becomes a form of acting and getting my yayas out, performance-wise.

KW: *As you wrote, how did you develop your style; what kind of voice were you trying to develop?*
MM: Well, initially I was too nasty, I cut down everybody and everything; and then I learned you have to be more willing to show your fan mentality, because I do love celebrities. It helped that I was really, sincerely, interested in every scene that makes New York tick. I didn't have to force myself to go to a show, movie, party, premiere. I started writing these ziggy, first-person romps around town. I still do. I always felt like the original blogger anyway. I've had a blog over three years now. At this point, the blog becomes more the receptacle for the shorter bits on the breaking news and the column is more about interviews and theme pieces.

KW: *You also arrived as a journalist at the start of the AIDS crisis; how did that change what you wrote about and how you went about it?*
MM: It immediately politicized me. Nobody was doing anything about the crisis except us. The religious right people were saying that people with AIDS deserved it. PWAs were getting doubly oppressed. I immediately took a break from parties to write about it. I was one of the first to write about ACT UP, to protest in the streets, writing screechy columns, and I alternated that with the stories about parties, because I felt it was still my job to report on the fun as well. It was a kind of a weird, schizo time for me.

It made me very impatient with anybody who was even vaguely homophobic, so I would really use the column to scream, for example, at Pat Buckley, who wouldn't openly disagree with her husband (William F. Buckley) on his views about AIDS. People protected her in the media, but I didn't have any patience with that bullshit, and I would go to town on these people. When David Geffen got Guns N' Roses to do an AIDS benefit, I thought it was horrible. Axl Rose had said horrible things about AIDS. I went to town on him. Looking back now, maybe I should have had a little more compassion for these people…maybe I should have said: let Guns N' Roses atone for their sins and raise money for AIDS. I don't think they did it to atone for their views. I think it was more of a PR thing to save their image. It's hard to take the right point of view in a war zone.

KW: *How did that change the perception of your work?*
MM: A lot of people were pleased that I had given some heft to the column by writing about issues. I don't know if it reached a wider audience; I don't know how many people wanted to read about AIDS and gay identity. But now, take a look at things from that era like Tony Kushner's *Angels in America*…these are epic works that you can look back on, and they're being revived now. Everything they said was right on the money. That's why they're getting more awards than they did originally. Larry Kramer was right, Tony Kushner was right. Larry has been criticized for only attacking certain people…but he's attacking the community itself, as well as Ed Koch. He's a good antidote to the giddy stuff, people saying how far we've come. Even now, he's saying: you know gay marriage still has a long way to go.

KW: *As New York City headed out of the twentieth century, how did what you write about change?*
MM: Well, you have to preserve your voice and be consistent about that, you can't be a whore, or too much of a chameleon. Nightlife is one of my big things. As I watched, the crazy club kid culture I chronicled imploded, and New York City became all about people flaunting their credit cards and sitting around these boring bottle

KATHLEEN WARNOCK

service lounges in the Meatpacking District: that was my new target.

At the same time, the gay community started going to the gym a little too eagerly and that became another form of boring oppression. If you didn't have a big muscly body you were invisible, which started out as a reaction to AIDS: as in, I'll beef myself up so I'll be invulnerable (which of course didn't work), but it didn't continue as a fight against AIDS; it became peer pressure to work out or pump up or you weren't a viable entity.

KW: *Do you think that kind of thing represents some people being left behind in the mainstreaming of the gay community?*
MM: I've always celebrated the transsexuals, lesbians, drag queens, people who are usually the ones driving the bus, even though everyone else wants them to sit in the back. I've battled that my whole life, where I'm not the "right" kind of gay. There's an idea that you have to be a button-down shirt "masculine" type of gay male. And it becomes ludicrous to face oppression from your own community. We can be our own worst enemies at times. And we're mirroring the same stuff that we get from everyone else.

KW: *Where do you see yourself heading from here?*
MM: The two things I least wanted for myself were to get married and to be in the military. But I see the value in the community of having these things, things that have happened in a world I partly helped create and dreamed of. I never dreamed there'd be this much gay rep in the media, gay topics being discussed, gay rights being offered. One of the great things about being around so long is to see how society evolves and advances. Ages ago, I found the ultimate job. "La Dolce Musto" is the ultimate Michael Musto position. It's a wonderful home base where I can do other stuff, go on TV, and write my books. At this point, I'm planning on continuing to do what I do.

NEXT YEAR
AT SONNY'S

EDDIE SARFATY

"Finished with the tablecloth?"

"Not yet."

"I wish you'd hurry up with it, Ed. I still have a bunch of things I need you to do."

"I'm almost done."

Though my attention is focused on the steam iron in my hand, I'm aware of the faint gurgling in the kitchen being quietly stifled by a pot cover, and I can detect the vibration of my mother, with her hunter green slacks and frosted hair, as she pads up behind me. The flutter of the blood in my temples accelerates with each moment she stands there watching me press the cross-stitched, slightly stained Passover cloth that my Aunt Syl embroidered fifty years ago. Her silence exacerbates my irritation, and when she punctuates her exhale with a faint puff, I bark at her. "What?"

"I'm just looking at what you're doing "

"I'm ironing a tablecloth."

"You know you have to turn it over when you press the embroidered parts?"

"Yes, I know. Thank you."

She continues watching. "You know the steam button is adjustable?"

I blow up. "I know how to use an iron, Sonny! Go away! You're making me crazy."

I only call my mother Sonny when she aggravates me. Nobody calls her by her given name, Sonia.

"I'm sorry. I'll leave you alone. Don't forget you still have the napkins to do."

"I did them already."

"All of them?"

"Yes."

"You're a good kid."

"I'm forty-six."

"You'll always be a kid to me," she says as she pats my cheek. "When you're done ironing, wanna get the leaves?"

I finish the cloth, put down the iron, and open the closet where the oak planks are stored while my mom reaches underneath the dining table and unclicks the brass fasteners that hold it together. Once the leaves are in place, we stand at opposite ends.

"Ready?" she asks.

"Push your end toward me."

I'm wary of pushing my end of the table toward her. She's seventy-seven, and I don't want to knock her over—a mother with a broken hip, I don't need. We relock the fasteners and spread out Syl's cloth. It's just big enough to cover the table that can now seat twelve.

She sizes things up. "I think we're gonna need the card table too."
I'm a step ahead of her and have it unfolded in a minute.

"When you're done, I need your help getting the china down."

I return the iron and board to the closet, get her good dishes down from the cupboard (that I won't let her stand on a chair to reach), do a quick run with the vacuum, change two light bulbs, and set the table. "What else?"

"That's it for now, Ed. What time do you have to pick up the fellas?"

"Their train gets in at 6:40."

The phone rings. My mother makes her prediction. "I bet that's Arlene."

She's right.

"'I said it was you…Happy Pesach…I can't complain…Ed came out last night to help me…Well, I have brisket, sweet-and-sour meatballs…Yes, you've had them. I make them every year…No, with rice and the tomato sauce mixed with grape jelly…Right. And there's chicken, broccoli, Brussels sprouts…What can I tell you? He wanted Brussels sprouts. There's the concoction you like with the matzoh and onions, mashed potatoes, kugel, soup, yams, and carrots…Oh, and I baked some of my matzoh muffins."

Arlene is having Passover at her daughter's. My mom's friend Esther has a new boyfriend, and their friend Leona's "not doing too well," and so, this holiday, Sonny will be the only widow at the table. She continues listing what—and who—Arlene is going to miss: "This year we have Mark. He's the set designer, and Bob and Michael… Bob's the one with the new novel and Michael writes plays…Right. I showed you the review in *Newsday*…Very enjoyable…And Peter from the museum… Jeffrey you know, Danny you know…Yes, you do—the one with the mouth…I know it's filthy, but he's such a sweet guy…Then Jaffe…No, that's Andrew. He's Jewish, too. Jaffe's a comedian. He performs with Danny, Bob, and Ed in the Funny Gay Males…No, Joe and Tony can't make it this year. Neither can Tom. But Gregory's coming again…The tall accountant who sings the country music. And Court's coming…Oh, Arlene, he's a doll. The first time I met him, I told Ed, 'He's a keeper.' And he's so polite—he's always thanking me…What do you mean, 'Is that it?' That's eleven plus me and Rita and Shelly…No, they're going to their son's tomorrow night…I agree, it is a lot, but I love having the boys here. When else do I get to have dinner with that many handsome young men? They treat me like a queen, and they're all so well-mannered."

I emerge from the bathroom, drying my hands on my pants.

"Except for my son."

I protest. "You told me not to use the guest towels."

"My kids, they make a mess."

"I'm not a kid."

"Arlene wants to know if we're having a Seder."

"Absolutely not! Next question."

My mom laughs. "You hear him?"

My family hasn't celebrated Passover with a traditional Seder in over twenty years. Sitting around a table full of food that you can't eat until you finish reading the story of the Exodus is not the easiest holiday for modern Americans with short attention spans and huge appetites. We're not religious anyway. We're what's called culturally Jewish, which is a misnomer since we don't really eat, wear, or do anything different from most Americans. My family's Jewish cultural activities consist of kvetching, kvelling, and reminding the children that They could come for us at any time. Besides, as a gay man, I'm vehemently opposed to any religion whose basic text abhors my being and mistrustful of any faith that tells me what I can and cannot do with my penis—especially one that commands me to have a piece lopped off.

When I was a kid, my parents, brother, and I would celebrate the holiday with my grandmother, my aunt Syl and Uncle Lenny, and my cousins Elliot and Tracy. Sadly, by the time I graduated from college, Syl, Lenny, and Tracy were dead, and Elliot and my brother Jack lived in different cities. My mom, seeing no point in going to all sorts of trouble just to cook for the four of us made the suggestion: "Ed, why don't you invite some of your friends over; I'm sure they don't all go home for the holiday. "

And so it started. The "boys," most of whom aren't Jewish, started schlepping out to my parents' house on Long Island to celebrate Passover. My mother was thrilled; they came with healthy appetites, grateful words, and the knowledge of what every fork was for. And my dad—he liked everybody, and everybody liked him. I'll always be grateful to have had such a sweet-natured father. And I'll forever appreciate the tender way that the boys—some of whom had never had their own fathers' approval—spoke to him, making sure to include him in the conversation as they spooned food onto his plate at his last Passover when he was suffering from Pick's Disease, a rare form of dementia.

My grandmother, housebound and in her nineties, loved the attention, and the boys got a kick out of her—particularly when her poor hearing made her asides at the dinner table audible to all. Usually I whisper loudly to my friend Joe, while gesturing to his partner Tony, "Is he a gay like you?" It's a joke that always kills.

For twelve years, Passover has been me, my mom, and as many of my friends as we can seat uncomfortably.

My mother hangs up the phone. "Ed, it's getting late. Why don't you get the dessert plates out and then you can go for your run?"

"Sure."

I know that no matter how hard I try to control myself, sitting around a holiday table for hours, I'll overeat and feel disgusting, my pants hurting me the whole way back to Manhattan. I've brought my running shorts and my iPod so I can pre-burn as many calories as possible.

I gingerly take the English cake plates and matching teacups and saucers out of the curio cabinet in the living room and place them on the island that separates the kitchen from the dining room-living room. Each setting is different—some adorned with flowers, some with fruits, a few with geometrical patterns, and one bearing the likeness of a newly crowned Queen Elizabeth II. The dainty collection is grandmotherly—literally—as most of the pieces can be traced to my mother's mother's mother, with a few going back even further.

On my run, I'm much calmer and notice the beauty of the suburbs in a way I never was able to as a kid. It's unsettling to contemplate that my anxiety over being different could have been so strong growing up, that it kept me from fully experiencing something as profound as spring. And so, I hurl my middle-aged bones down the streets under the promising yellow-greens of the awakening maples, oaks, and sumacs, doing my best to live in the moment and shed the feeling that I still don't belong.

Like a zillion other gay boys raised in the 'burbs, I knew I wouldn't go back there to live. I never let myself forget how lucky I am to have such supportive and accepting parents; far too many of my friends' parents have disowned them, cut them off emotionally, or condescended to tolerate them but not their "lifestyle." Even after my ex, Jeffrey, and I had been together for almost ten years, his father still refused to meet me. While it was a relief to be spared a decade of awkward Christmases and Thanksgivings—not to mention family weddings where I'd feel resentful and funerals where I'd envy the deceased—I saw how deeply his father's rejection hurt Jeffrey.

Even though I never seriously feared that my family would stop loving me, as a gay kid I was still a minority child raised by parents who weren't members of the same minority—a situation experienced by most gay kids and children in mixed-race adoptions. Long Island felt wrong, and I had to leave. I'd heard enough homophobic comments to prevent me from feeling at ease with a lot of my friends' parents or my parents' friends. The word *fagela* had been tossed out more than once by a certain Hebrew school teacher, and I can still recall my anxiety when my close friend Jill's mother—a beautiful and warm woman whom I love dearly—casually mentioned that she was relieved Jill's brother, Eric, had changed dorms because his roommate was a homo. Though it happened almost thirty years ago, I've never been able to entirely shake the feeling that, in this town I left behind, with its strip malls and identical houses, I'm despised by some and a curiosity to others—not a far-fetched assumption, given the hurtful and thoughtless comments I've read on the Facebook pages of old classmates who've friended me without bothering to read my profile.

I don't even have a foot in the closet anymore; I'm out onstage, on television, and in print. But coming out isn't something you do once. You have to do it every day—to people at work, friends of friends, relatives, your doctor, your dry cleaner, and the lady who sells you your bedroom furniture. It gets old. The process of assessing someone's opinions and comfort level, deciding how to broach the subject, answering all of their questions, and walking away still feeling unsure and unsettled is exhausting. Sometimes, it's easier not to bother. The problem, of course, is that it's a Catch-22. You can't expect people to get over their discomfort and accept you unless you're willing to get over your own discomfort in letting them know who you are.

I wasn't part of the gay liberation generation and missed the heyday of Christopher Street. Some in my circle were wild teenagers who ditched class to hop the train to Manhattan and hang out in the Village. Luckily, I was a geek, and by the time I was living in Manhattan safe sex was a well-established practice. In my twenties, I didn't know anyone who would even think about not using a condom.

My high school and college years coincided with the bleakest days of the AIDS epidemic. For my straight classmates, mostly unaware of the 'mos in their midst and not burdened with the desperate necessity of separating their sexuality from terminal illness, "gay" and "AIDS" started off as practically synonymous. Even today, to a majority of the straight people I know, AIDS is still someone else's disease and, therefore, easier to fear—or at least to feel nervous discussing. Despite the public's increasing familiarity with HIV and the formerly unimaginable progress the LGBT community has made over the last three decades, the existence of the virus has only made coming out more complex.

Given that my physician informed me that over half the gay men my age in NYC are HIV-positive, I feel lottery-lucky to have sidestepped "the bug." The pandemic is still, however, a big fact of my life. Dozens of my friends are infected. I've dated men who are positive, slept with more than a few, and, when a blue-eyed veterinarian I was in love with seroconverted, I even joined a support group for serodiscordant or "magnetic" couples in a futile attempt to save the relationship. My familiarity with the virus—and with men who have it but are leading life to the fullest—has even made me cavalier about catching it at times. Try explaining that to someone whose firsthand knowledge of homosexuals is based on their witty-and-sad hairdresser or an occasional flight attendant. With performing, writing, enjoying my friends, hitting the gym, keeping an eye on my mother, and teasing my partner Court, my life is too busy for me to ungrudgingly invest a lot of time and energy trying to bring people up to speed who, no matter how well intended, don't know my world. And though it is indeed important for me to get over my discomfort, it's also important for me to have better things to do.

Running through the verdant subdivision, I'm grateful for the day—even if it's the only one in the year that I'm able to bridge the gap between my hometown and my life in the city. My cell phone alarm, an irritating polka in a minor key, informs me that my hour is up, and so I pick up the pace, splashing through oily puddles on streets lined with surgically precise lawns and expensive plantings that I can't help but compare to the cracked, plastic flowerboxes full of weeds on my windowsill in Hell's Kitchen. I return breathless and overheated, hoping that I'll stop sweating by the time I get out of the shower.

My mother takes one look at me. "You're filthy!"

"Thank you."

"Say hello."

I turn to see Rita and Shelly, "The Penns," getting up from the blue floral love seat that I dread inheriting. They've known my family since 1969 when Rita and my mom started chatting on the checkout line at Waldbaum's. I couldn't have asked for better friends for my parents—or for better cheerleaders for me. Their enthusiasm for my creative endeavors routinely surpasses my own.

"Hiya, Edwood."

Hearing Rita say my full name in the familiar accent of my childhood is lovely and sad. She and Shelly are both fit and look younger than their ages, but she's in her seventies and Shelly's probably eighty or eighty-one. They, along with Elaine and Ed, "The Liebermans," are the only friends of my parents from my childhood who haven't emigrated to Florida and, except for my mom, are the only roots I still have off of the Long Island Expressway.

Rita steps forward to give me a hug. I lean in to kiss her but hold my body back. "I am filthy."

She puts her arms around me anyway. "Oh, please."

Shelly shakes my hand vigorously. "Sonny says she's been working you hard today."

"It's no big deal."

"You're a good kid," says Rita.

"I'm forty-six."

"To us, that's a kid."

"Speaking of kids, how are yours?"

"Everyone's fine. Shelly'll fill you in. Sonny, can I use your bedroom?"

"For something illicit?"

"I have to make a phone call."

"Go ahead. Since when do you have to ask?"

I wash my hands at the kitchen sink and then pull a bag of baby carrots out of the fridge. Arranging them around a tub of hummus on a platter, I hear Rita through the open door talking to her son, Craig.

"Hi, sweetie. I don't think we're going to make it up to Mamaroneck tonight…Daddy's not feeling well…No, just a little cold, but I don't want to take a chance…He is. I have him lying on the couch…I'm sure he'll be fine…We'll see you tomorrow at your brother's. Give Bonnie and the kids a kiss…All right, I will…Love you too."

My mom, standing over the stove, snorts and shakes her head at the soup she's stirring. "Shelly, your wife's too much."

"Hey, what our kids don't know…"

He dismisses the playful shame-on-you expression she tosses over her shoulder and takes a carrot as I set the platter down on the coffee table in front of him.

As his wife comes out of the bedroom wearing a look of complete innocence, Shelly informs her, "Rita, look, they have the good hummus."

"I love that you're blowing your family off for the holiday," I say.

Rita levels with me. "Look, I love my grandchildren, but all eleven of them at one time, I can do without."

"I get it."

For what I'm sure is the tenth time since I arrived the night before, my mother inquires, "What time is Court coming?"

"I told you, 7:30."

Shelly pats the sofa cushion next to him. "Edwood, you have almost an hour. Sit down. "

My mother checks the stove's clock. "He can't; he's got to pick the boys up at the train."

"What time is it?" I ask.

"6:20."

"I'm just gonna jump in the shower first."

"You can take one when you get back. You don't want to be late."

Though my mother gets great satisfaction telling people that her place is only two miles from the station, she always nags me to leave twenty minutes before I have to be there.

"I have plenty of time. It's five minutes away."

"Twelve."

Shelly responds to my look for help. "Sonny, stop it. He's not gonna be late."

"I know my son."

I quickly shower using the crappy deodorant soap my mother buys that leaves me smelling like laundry detergent, throw on my clothes, and wave to the three of them as I head for the door.

"Be back in a bit."

Sitting in the car at the station, I check out some men in the parking lot. They're obviously fathers waiting for sons or daughters coming from the city—or maybe from college—for the holiday. They remind me of my own dad and the welcoming kiss on the cheek that he suddenly started greeting me with five or six years before he died.

When the train glides to a stop and the doors open and the people flood out, I scan the platform but don't spot my friends right away. I focus my attention on the far last few cars, reasoning that's where they must be.

A rap at the passenger-side window jars me, and I turn to see Peter pushing back his glossy black forelock as he signals me to let him in. Gregory, Danny, and Mark are at the other doors.

"I didn't see you get off the train. How did you know where I was?" Peter answers matter-of-factly, "I recognized Sonny's car."

"Really?"

"It's the same one she always drives."

Apparently some people pay attention to things like that. I haven't owned a car in over twenty years and know absolutely nothing about them. To me, my mom's taupe Camry looks the same as half the vehicles on the road. Whenever I return to a parking lot, it takes me at least ten minutes of aiming the electronic key at four-door sedans to find it.

"What's in the bag?" I ask Gregory as he crumples his six-foot-four frame into the backseat. I know he always brings something delicious.

"I brought Sonny some coffee from McNulty's on Christopher and—you'll be proud of me—a flourless double-chocolate cheesecake from Moishe's Bakery."

"Yum! But don't be upset if she tells you to take the coffee home. She still has the bag of Brazilian blend you brought her last year in the freezer."

"She doesn't like it?"

"She likes it, but she can't be bothered brewing it for one. She's happy with instant."

"She'll eat the cake though, right?"

"Of course. Her arteries aren't clogged with celery."

Peter, who's in charge of publications at the Metropolitan Museum, has brought my mom a beautiful coffee table volume on Baroque architecture to add to the stack of art books he's given her over the years. Mark waves at me through the thriving fern cradled in his lap, which will soon join the long line of gift plants that never lived to see another Passover, and Danny blows me a kiss and giggles, leading me to believe that he's already dipped into the dime bag of pot he's brought along so that he can "walk off" the meal and come back stoned just in time for dessert.

"Did Sonny make her brisket?" Mark asks.

"Child, she better have!" Danny warns, channeling the sassy black nanny character that he does in his stand-up act. "And turkey, too! Lord, I love me some turkey!"

"Sorry," I tell him. "No turkey this year, just chicken."

"Then you best be turnin' this car around!"

Peter laughs, "I'm sure it's good."

"It is good," I assure them, "but make a bigger fuss over the other food. The chicken's from Boston Market. She told me it was just easier to order it."

Mark approves. "Good for her."

"I agree. It's a ton of work cooking for that many people."

"Who else is coming?"

"The usual suspects."

"Esther?" Peter inquires.

"No, Esther's got a boyfriend."

"So what? She doesn't eat?"

I shrug.

"But Rita and Shelly are coming, right?"

"They're already at the house."

Danny, now serious and sincere, " I love them. They're so sweet."

Mark concurs. "They are—and Rita's got a nice rack."

Danny howls. I don't know how it started, or which of them said it first, but apparently somewhere during the last decade of Passovers, one of my homo friends was seriously checking out the grandmother of eleven. Now, every year, someone always mentions it, and we all crack up.

Getting out of the car I remind the four of them, "About the chicken, nobody's supposed to know."

Though my knowledge of cars is abysmal, I immediately recognize Jaffe's heap in the adjacent spot, so I know that he, and Michael and Bob are inside. Opening the door, I'm struck by Jaffe's voice—part Woody Allen, part Joan Rivers—explaining to Rita and Shelly about his soulmate relationship with Buster, the adorable cross-eyed, snaggle-toothed Japanese Chin in his lap. "He's wonderful and he's so smart. He really gets me." He buries his nose in Buster's neck. "Right, Busta? You're such a good boy. What a teddy bear. You're so delicious, I could eat you up."

Bob and Michael exchange looks. I can see that a grade-A mock-out has already formed in Bob's head, but know that he won't use it since Jaffe's infatuation with Buster completely mirrors the feelings he and Michael have for their beagle-basset mix, Bozzie.

As the hellos start, we discover Andrew's arrived as well. He's managed to get out of this first night of Passover with his family by promising them that I'll come and join them for the second night. I love the idea that my mom's annual tradition of eating brisket in the company of entertaining homosexuals might catch on, and I imagine that by the end of the century the Seder Gay (affectionately known as Bitter Herb), will be a Passover fixture in every Jewish household.

My mom kisses each of my friends on the cheek and then hands me the fern. As I set the plant down in what will be its final resting place, Jeffrey comes out of the bathroom.

"Hey!"

"When did you get here?"

"Five minutes ago. Andrew picked me up at JFK."

His smile and the bear hug he gives me bring home how much I miss him. It's been over fifteen years since we moved in together, seven years since we broke up, and six since he changed jobs and moved to Portland, Oregon. For two years while he was hurting, he didn't come for Passover. But even at the bumpiest points in our history, we both trusted that the other was screaming and slamming doors with respect and affection, and we knew his absence wouldn't be permanent. Knowing my mom's already informed him, I tell him again for effect, "Sonny's made you meatballs."

"I know. It's the first thing she said to me."

Jeffrey has celiac disease and can't eat gluten, so there's always a batch of meatballs without breadcrumbs and a small pot of soup without matzoh balls just for him. His mother died of an aneurysm when he was only ten, so Jeffrey's relationship with my mom is very special to him.

"Where's your fiancé?" he asks.

"Don't say fiancé."

"Why not? You are engaged."

"I know, but that word always sounds so silly to me, as if I'm a lovesick sorority girl gushing over a diamond and writing my married name over and over again in my diary."

"Okay then, where's Court?"

"He's coming after work. He should be here soon."

Someone calls out, "Jeffrey!" and we turn to see Mark stepping over the coffee table to get to us. Observing the two grown men hug, kiss, and giggle against the mostly male background, I think—certainly not for the first time—"My life is really gay."

It's true, and I love it. I love the enthusiasm that gay men have for imagination and the frankness with which they discuss sex. Getting out of the suburbs was one of the best things I ever did. Except for the strong possibility of an early death, when a generation of gay men perished, they took with them any expectations I might have had of what my life was supposed to be like. Already outside of the mainstream with no specific guidelines, my friends and I have had great freedom to choose careers that are meaningful to us and to establish the kinds of intimate relationships that work for us as individuals. I'm sure I'd never have even attempted stand-up comedy or writing a book without this confluence of circumstances.

Court pulls up in a taxi a few minutes later and I run outside. He's bright, affectionate, hunky, and as sweet as they come. I love him and am beyond thankful for the day two years earlier when chance put me at that bus stop on 23rd Street and 10th Avenue, just as he was walking by.

He gives Sonny a kiss and presents her with a gorgeous bouquet of lilies, roses, and irises so huge that the FTD Mercury would have needed jet engines rather than wings on his feet to deliver them. I hear her response before it leaves her throat. "Are you crazy? These must have cost a small fortune."

I roll my eyes and sarcastically correct her manners as if she were a child. "How about, 'Why Court, how lovely! Thank you for thinking of me'?"

She laughs, along with a few of the guys who're close enough to hear the exchange. Then she smiles fondly at Court, says, "Thank you, sweetie," and gives him a peck on the cheek.

This is the first time Court's come to Passover. Last year he had to work, and the year before, we'd met but hadn't actually started dating. He greets each of the boys with a hug and some cheerful words. When he's through, I bring him over to the sofa. "I'd like you to meet Rita and Shelly, The Penns."

Court's smile shifts into high gear. "It's so nice to meet you. I've heard such wonderful things. Eddie is constantly talking about the two of you."

I affect a serious tone. "Yes, constantly." Then I shake my head and let out a grunty laugh.

My future husband defends his assertion. "Yes, he does! He even wanted to name our cats Rita and Shelly."

A smile forces its way out of the side of Rita's mouth. "Jeez."

Shelly raises his eyebrows and accents the movement with a staccato nod of his chin. "That's quite an honor."

A loud and tinny clang comes from the kitchen, and everyone turns. My mother's knocked the lid to the soup pot off the counter. She takes the opportunity to address everyone, "If you'd like to sit down, dinner's ready."

At the stove, she enthusiastically ladles the soup into bowls, filling them to the brim. The scalding broth stings my fingers as I deliver the bowls to the table one at a time. Seated, Court starts with a string of compliments. "Sonny, everything looks and smells delicious! What a privilege to be able to share this tradition with you. I'm so grateful to be here. The tablecloth, the silver—it's all just so beautiful."

I can't take it. "And you're looking especially lovely today, Mrs. Cleaver. Is that a new dress you're wearing?"

From behind, I throw my arms around Court's neck and kiss the top of his head so he doesn't feel hurt by me mocking his Eddie Haskell-y manners. Despite my New York cynicism, I'm sure there's no ulterior motive to his politeness. He was raised in the South, and that's just the proper way for people to act there.

Back at the stove, my mother gestures with her ladle at a steaming bowl. "That's the special soup for Jeffrey"

"Got it."

"For yours, do you want one matzoh ball or two?"

I could easily eat half a dozen but know I'll regret it. "None, just the stock."

She tightens her lips slightly as she fills up the bowl with the clear liquid. With my thank you, I acknowledge both the soup and her silent disapproval. I know that not encouraging me to eat is difficult for my mother—probably more difficult than it is for me to not make a pig of myself. Back at the table, I raise my glass. "To my mom for all of her hard work in preparing this beautiful meal."

Andrew adds an obligatory, "L'chaim!"

Gregory asks, "Aren't you supposed to say, 'Next year in Jerusalem'?"

"At the end."

He turns to my mother. "Sorry, Sonny. What do I know? I'm a goy."

She waves him off, "There's nothing to apologize for."

I can see the satisfaction that the swirl of food being passed around brings to the chef's face—and I can see she's tired. Of course she is. Who wouldn't be after cooking dinner for fourteen people and working my nerves for twenty-four hours?

And so the eating begins, and continues, and continues. And, as she has every year, my mother enjoys—yet deflects—the compliments uttered by each guest as they taste each dish. As always, the brisket is a favorite. The platter is empty by the time it circles the table, allowing my mother, even though she's cooked two large cuts of meat based on its previous popularity, to say once again, "I wish I'd known you boys were so hungry, I would've made more."

And like every year before, as soon as someone praises the baked carrots, she challenges them to name the secret ingredient. The answer is nutmeg. Not only because she makes the same carrots every Passover, but because nutmeg is the only other ingredient— secret or otherwise—in the recipe.

I stick to eating protein and veggies until my mother notices. "Ed, you're not gonna have any noodle kugel?"

"No thanks."

"Since when don't you like my kugel?"

"I like it. I just don't want any."

"I wish I'd known you weren't hungry, I wouldn't have made so much."

Considering that at home I barely have the patience to nuke my oatmeal in the microwave for the full two minutes that the directions recommend, controlling myself at a table set with once-a-year favorites is a Herculean challenge. The slightest bit of pressure is enough to weaken my resolve. And so, to "make my mother happy," I have "just a bite" of the kugel—which is predictably followed by "just a spoonful" of the mashed potatoes, "just a taste" of the cranberries, "just a dollop" of the yams…and ends with "just another piece of cheesecake."

No matter how thoroughly the guys clean their plates, Sonny keeps at them until they take another helping. She picks up a half-filled bowl and calls it to the attention of the table. "There are still meatballs left."

Despite several no thank yous, she persists. "If I'd known there were gonna be leftovers, I wouldn't have made so many."

Although the guys think she's funny, Sonny's making me mental. "Leave them alone, they're adults. If they want more, they'll take more. It's like you're pushing meth!"

My comment's lost on her, and she continues, "Somebody eat them. There aren't enough to save. It's a shame to let them go to waste."

Finally, Andrew, used to appeasing his own Jewish mother, holds out his plate, "I'll take a few more."

After scooping out more than a few for him, my mother looks expectantly at the rest of the guests. "Who else? Mark, you're usually a good customer. Finish them off."

"Sure, why not? Thanks, Sonny."

"I could tell you weren't done. How about another piece of chicken?"

Mark smirks and flicks his eyes in my direction. "You know, I'll pass on the bird and just stick with your meatballs."

She doesn't push it. Those of us who know her secret easily detect the smug look on her face.

Danny pushes himself away from the table.

"Gonna take a walk?" I ask.

"For a little bit. Sonny, you don't mind do you?"

"No, dear, go. It'll do you good."

She has no idea how good. Jaffe gulps down the last of his wine. "Danny, I'll come with you; Busta needs to go out. Come on, Busta!"

The little dog gets so excited that Michael whispers to Bob, "Looks like Buster can't wait to light up either."

As they head out, my mother reminds them, "Don't take too long. We still have dessert."

With mouths no longer full, the table launches into conversation, and I head to the kitchen to get a jump on the cleanup. My mom, with a sense of maternal pride, fills Rita and Shelly in on Bob's new time-travel novel and Michael's latest musical. The discussion that ensues about the entertainment world is impressive, with the guys quoting old movies (along with each film's year and Oscar nominations), repeating scurrilous gossip about Hollywood legends, and offering knowledgeable opinions on theater, film, television, and literature. By the third Ethel Merman story, I can tell that the elders are just watching from the sidelines. From the sink, I call over my shoulder, "Shelly, ask Peter about the Yup'ik show at the museum."

Shelly, a retired archeology professor, eagerly follows my lead, and Bob, a huge science nerd who's spent a lot of time in Alaska, immediately bails on the diva dish to join the conversation about the indigenous peoples of America's fiftieth state. Meanwhile, my mother has turned her attention to Gregory, a CPA who's doing his best to appear as if he's listening to every mind-numbing detail about the job she has keeping the books for an interior designer a few days a month.

Rita and Jeffrey bring me the last of the dirty dinner plates. Though each offers to lend a hand, the kitchen's too small, so I send them back to the table. I don't mind washing dishes. It gives my mom a chance to relax. Actually, it gives me a chance to let other people answer her millions of questions.

Buster comes running in ahead of Jaffe and Danny who are both unmistakably mellower from their suburban stroll. With his wagging tail a blur, the pooch desperately works his so-ugly-he's-cute face looking for a treat. The urgency with which he pesters Court for scraps makes me wonder if the poor thing's got the munchies from a contact high or if Jaffe deliberately shotgunned smoke directly into the dog's mouth.

I take Gregory's coffee out of the freezer and arrange the macaroons and cheesecake on a funky '60s-style cake plate that my parents got as a housewarming gift for their first apartment. Court comes over to me. "Edward, what may I do to help you?"

"You could set out the dessert things."

Pairing up the delicate Aynsley and Crown Staffordshire cups with their matching saucers, Court remarks, "These must be very special."

"Sonny has about twenty more of them. One-third are set aside for my brother, one-third for my cousin Elliot, and one-third for me."

"They look like antiques."

"They are. Don't break any."

I stop my mother in her tracks as she approaches the kitchen. "What do you need?"

"I thought I'd give you a hand with the coffee."

"We've got it. Go sit down."

"You sure?"

"Yes."

I'm tired and cranky and know I'll completely lose my temper the minute she begins instructing me on how to make coffee.

As she returns to her seat, she shrugs at Rita who gives her one in return. "He's a good kid."

"They both are."

Over dessert, the conversation turns to politics, but since everyone present is basically on the same page, nobody needs to raise their voices except for Jaffe, who, when high, unleashes his outrage toward our government with a force and conviction to rival Emma Goldman's. Finally, the food and the hour hit everyone. Another round of accolades follow, and pleased that everyone's had a good time, my mom assures the guests that she always looks forward to having them. Danny, popping one last macaroon into his mouth, declares, "Sonny, this was so much fun. You should do it every week."

"You wanna kill me?"

As the laughter subsides, Gregory leans into Andrew. "Now?"

"Sure, go ahead."

He raises his teacup. "Next year in Jerusalem!"

The evening's been a success. It's a success every year—even when it's not—the triumph being the tradition.

Peter's convinced Rita to pull out photos of her grandchildren and she passes them around the table. Looking at a Bar Mitzvah shot of her oldest grandson, it seems impossible to me that he's already a teenager.

"That's an old picture," Shelly points out. "You should see him now."

Rita agrees. "He's a big kid. He's almost as tall as his father."

"He's not a kid. He's starting college next year."

I turn to Rita. "Oh, right, you're not a kid unless you're in your forties."

Just then, it hits me for the first time—perhaps because my niece Ella, my mother's sole grandchild, is only seven—that my mom, who's a few years older than Rita, could easily have adult grandchildren. Although I've noticed for sometime that she's aging, slowing down and even shrinking, in that instant, my eyes sharpen and my mom is old. Unlike my petite and timid grandmother who was widowed at sixty, became a little old lady overnight, and remained that way for the next thirty-five years, my mother, robust in frame, outgoing, and self-sufficient, went out and made new friends, traveled, dated, and did volunteer work after she lost my dad. I'm not used to thinking of her as elderly.

I ask if everyone's had enough dessert, hoping they have so I can eat the last wedge of cheesecake off the groovy plate as I carry it back to the kitchen. Clearing the English cups and saucers, I recall how I loved the patterns and colors when I was a child (the gold and cobalt blue is still my favorite). I wonder how many more Passover dinners there will be at my mom's—and if there will be any after that at all. She's in her late seventies, has trouble with her knees, and twenty-five years ago had a triple bypass that's no longer under warranty. My friends and I, I'm sure, would gladly serve up a feast in her honor if she should ever become incapacitated, but without her—and The Penns —I can't quite envision myself making meat-balls with grape jelly or bothering to set out the old-lady dessert plates.

The guys are great about lending a hand so that everything's back where it belongs before we head to the city. I can't sleep over at my mom's again—one night on her cruel sofa is my limit. Making sure she avoids any injury that she might sustain while putting glasses away on a high shelf is my number one priority. Making sure I avoid the guilt accompanying any such injury is important, too.

Shortly after we begin the final cleanup, Jaffe says his goodbyes and heads off with Buster to his mother's house two towns over, where he'll get stoned before dinner on the second night of the holi-day. Court grabs a dishtowel and, working together, we wash, dry, and put away the treasured cups and saucers while the guys disman-tle the table. In twenty minutes, everything's done. My mom packs up the coffee for Gregory and a care package for Danny, thrilled he's relieving her of the leftovers so that she won't be eating kugel for a week. Mark, Peter, and Gregory drive back to Manhattan with Andrew, who would rather trek back to Long Island again the next day than sleep over at his parents'. So that we can all make the 11:30 train, my mom chauffeurs Court and me to the station, and Shelly drops the rest of the guys off there before he and Rita head home.

Living on 10th Avenue, with the flashing traffic from the Lincoln Tunnel screeching and belching under my bedroom window for more than fifteen years, the static silence of the suburban night unnerves me. The roads, barely lit by intermittent streetlights, seem extraterrestrial. In the break from the darkness provided by the flo-rescent station, a group of rowdy, drunk teenagers screaming in the parking lot reinforces my conviction that—except for the shrinking woman sitting next to me—there's nothing for me out here.

Shelly isn't as cautious a night driver as my mom, and so the other guys are already waiting on the platform when we pull into the station. It's an hour past Court's bedtime, and though I can see that he's exhausted, his manners, as always, are in top form. "Sonny, thank you for making my first Passover so lovely."

"My pleasure, dear."

I unbuckle my seat belt and turn toward her. The sheen of street-light on her skin makes her seem less fragile than she did only an hour earlier. I kiss her goodbye. "Thank you."

My mom checks her watch and cocks her head toward the tracks. "Go."

She watches from a parking space beside the platform, making sure we're all aboard before the doors close. Through the illegible graffiti scratched into the window next to my seat, I see her waving at the train as if it's the school bus pulling away from the curb forty years ago.

CONTRIBUTORS

MARK AMEEN is the author of the poetry collections *A Circle of Sirens*, *The Buried Body*, and the writer and performer of the one-man shows *Seven Pillars of Wicca-Dick: A Triumph* (Duality Playhouse) and *Soul Suspended* (The Kitchen). His work has been anthologized in *Three New York Poets* and *Gay & Lesbian Poetry In Our Time* and has appeared in *Between C & D*, *The James White Review* and other publications. He is the recipient of New York Foundation for the Arts fellowships in Poetry and Creative Nonfiction.

PENNY ARCADE: A runaway at thirteen, a reform school graduate at sixteen, a performer in the legendary Playhouse of The Ridiculous at eighteen, and an escapee from Andy Warhol's Factory at twenty, Penny emerged as a primal force on the New York art scene in the 1980s. An originator of what came to be called performance art, Arcade's brand of merging high content, street-smart, punk rock showmanship and visionary theater has won over audiences internationally and has few equals. The author of ten performance plays including the international mainstream hit *Bitch!Dyke!Faghag!Whore!*, her work centers on the outsider and other in society. A political humanist and cultural critic, her work tackles racism, homophobia, and misogyny. The author of poetry, spoken word, and essays, she is also an interviewer par excellence in her long running video series with collaborator Steve Zehentner, *The LES Biography Project*, "Stemming The Tide of Cultural Amnesia." www.pennyarcade.tv.

CHRISTOPHER BRAM is the author of nine novels, including *The Notorious Dr. August, Lives of the Circus Animals*, and *Gods and Monsters*, which was made into the Academy Award-winning movie with Ian McKellen and Lynn Redgrave. He has also published a collection of essays, *Mapping the Territory*, and, most recently, a history of gay men's literature, *Eminent Outlaws: The Gay Writers Who Changed America*. He teaches at Gallatin College of New York University.

BRENDAN FAY is an activist and filmmaker. Founder and co-chair of St Pats For All, New York's inclusive St. Patrick's Parade, and founder of Lavender and Green Alliance, he helped form Irish Aids Outreach (IAC) to break the silence around AIDS in the Irish Community. He has testified in Washington DC and New York and has been arrested many times for civil rights. Brendan coordinated *Silence to Speech* a documentary series on being Irish and gay in America. He directed the film, *Remembering Mychal*, and co-produced *Saint of 9/11*, documentaries about Fr. Mychal Judge, the FDNY Franciscan chaplain who died in the World Trade Center tragedy. Brendan recently directed *Taking a Chance on God*, a film about gay pioneer priest John McNeill, takingachanceongod.com. Involved in the marriage equality movement since 1998, he and Jesus LeBron are co-founders of the Civil Marriage Trail Project. Brendan lives with his spouse, Tom Moulton, in Astoria, New York. They were among the first New Yorkers and binational couples to legally marry in Canada in July 2003.

THOMAS GLAVE is the author of *Whose Song? and Other Stories* (Lambda Literary Award Finalist), *The Torturer's Wife*, and the essay collection *Words to Our Now: Imagination and Dissent* (2005 Lambda Literary Award). He is editor of the anthology *Our Caribbean: A Gathering of Lesbian and Gay Writing from the Antilles* (2008 Lambda Literary Award). He teaches at SUNY Binghamton, and is a 2012 Visiting Fellow at Clare Hall, Cambridge University.

JEWELLE GOMEZ is the author of seven books, including the double Lambda Award-winning lesbian vampire novel, *The Gilda Stories*. Her newest play, about James Baldwin, *Waiting for Giovanni*, premiered in Fall of 2011. Follow her on Twitter @VampyreVamp or at www.jewellegomez.com

AARON HAMBURGER was awarded the Rome Prize by the American Academy of Arts and Letters for his short story collection *The View From Stalin's Head*, also nominated for a Violet Quill Award. His next book, a novel titled *Faith For Beginners*, was nominated for a Lambda Literary Award. His writing has appeared in *Poets & Writers*, *Tin House*, *Details*, the *Village Voice*, *The Forward*, and *Out*. He has received fellowships from the Edward F. Albee Foundation and the Civitella Ranieri Foundation in Umbria, Italy, as well as a residency at Yaddo. Currently he teaches writing at Columbia University and the Stonecoast MFA Program.

MARTIN HYATT was born just outside of New Orleans. He holds an MFA in Creative Writing. He is the recipient of an Edward F. Albee Writing Fellowship and The New School Chapbook Award for fiction. His stories have been published in such places as *Lodestar Quarterly*, The Electric Literature Blog and *Blithe House Quarterly*. His debut novel, *A Scarecrow's Bible*, was named a Stonewall Honor Book by the American Library Association and won the Edmund White Award for Debut Fiction. In addition, it was a finalist for the Ferro-Grumley Award, a Lamda Literary Award, and the Violet Quill Award. *New York* magazine named him a "star of tomorrow." His new novel, *Beautiful Gravity*, and his memoir entitled *Greyhound Boy, 1976* are forthcoming. He has taught writing at Hofstra, Parsons, and St. Francis College.

FAY JACOBS, a native New Yorker, spent thirty years in Washington, DC, working in journalism, public relations, and theater. She is the publisher of A&M Books, a successor to the legendary Naiad Press. Her first book, *As I Lay Frying—A Rehoboth Beach Memoir*, is in its third printing. A second essay collection, *Fried & True—Tales from Rehoboth Beach*, won the 2008 National Federation of Press Women Book of the Year for humor. Her latest, *For Frying Out Loud – Rehoboth Beach Diaries* won a ForeWord Reviews Humor Book of the Year, a Goldie Award, American Library Association Over the Rainbow nomination, and the 2011 National Federation of Press Women Book of the Year Award. Fay has written for *The Advocate, Curve Magazine, The Washington Post, Baltimore Sun, Delaware Beach Life,* and more. She lives in Rehoboth, DE ("Gayberry, RFD") with Bonnie, her partner of thirty years. Contact Fay at www.aandmbooks.com

G. WINSTON JAMES is a Jamaican-born poet, author, essayist, and editor. He holds an MFA in Fiction from Brooklyn College and is the author of the Lambda Literary Award and Ferro-Grumley Award finalist collection *Shaming the Devil: Collected Short Stories.* He is also the author of *The Damaged Good: Poems Around Love* and the Lambda Literary Award finalist collection *Lyric: Poems Along a Broken Road.* James is also co-editor of the historic anthologies, *Voices Rising: Celebrating 20 Years of Black Lesbian, Gay, Bisexual and Transgender Writing* and the Lambda Literary Award finalist *Spirited: Affirming the Soul and Black Gay/Lesbian Identity.*

MICHELE KARLSBERG brings a unique combination of skills to effectively carry out publicity/marketing campaigns for authors, organizations and film/theater professionals. She has worn many hats in her twenty-three year book-publishing career. She was recently presented with the Publishing Triangle Leadership Award. Along with Olivia Travel, she produced the first Olivia Book Expo on the Holland America Cruise Line. As curator of Outspoken, a nationwide gay and lesbian literary series, she helps new and established voices reach a wider audience. She is coeditor of *To Be Continued* and *To Be Continued: Take Two* (Firebrand Books). This is her first piece published in an anthology and she is quite honored to add writer to her list of accomplishments.

THOMAS KEITH has edited the poetry of Tom Crawford, Miriam Sagan, Jimmy Santiago Baca, and Dylan Thomas, and over a dozen titles by Tennessee Williams including *The Magic Tower & Other One-Act Plays* and *A House Not Meant to Stand*, for which he wrote the introduction. Keith is the co-author of *The Histories of Gladys* and *The Collector's Guide to Mauchline Ware*, the editor of *Robert Burns Selected Poems and Songs* and *Christmas Poems*, the co-editor of *The Selected Letters of Tennessee Williams and James Laughlin*, and has written articles and chapters for *American Theatre Magazine,*

The Drouth, *Studies in Scottish Literature*, *Tenn at One Hundred*, *The Tennessee Williams Encyclopedia*, *Robert Burns in North America*, and *The Oxford Companion to Burns*, among others. He teaches at Pace University

SHAUN LEVIN is a South African writer based in London. He is the author of *Seven Sweet Things* and *A Year of Two Summers*. His more recent books include *Snapshots of The Boy* and *Trees at a Sanatorium*. In 2004 he founded the queer literary and arts journal, *Chroma*, which he currently edits, and is also the director of Treehouse Press, a small independent publishing house.

AMOS MAC is a photographer, writer, and publisher. He is editor-in-chief and publisher of *Original Plumbing* (www.originalplumbing.com), the premier quarterly print magazine that documents the culture of transgender men, and *Translady Fanzine* (www.transladyfanzine.com), an annual fine art photographic periodical that features the words and images of one woman of trans experience per installment. He has shown his photographs in galleries and at events internationally and both his written and photographic work have been published in collaboration with *Italian Vogue*, *Huffington Post*, *CANDY*, *Out*, and other magazines. www.amosmac.com

DAVID MCCONNELL is the author of two novels, *The Silver Hearted* and *The Firebrat*. He is currently writing a nonfiction book on murder. His short fiction and journalism have appeared widely in journals and anthologies. He lives in New York City.

VAL MCDERMID escaped from a mining community in Scotland to Oxford University, where she came out at age nineteen. She abandoned an award-winning career in journalism for writing fiction in

1991 and has published twenty-five novels. Her bestselling books are translated into forty languages and her many awards include the CWA Gold Dagger, the *Los Angeles Times* Book Prize, Stonewall Writer of the Year, the Theakston's Old Peculier Crime Novel of the Year, and the Lambda Literary Foundation Pioneer Award. She is an Honorary Fellow of St Hilda's College, Oxford and lives by the sea in the north of England with her publisher wife, her son, and their dog.

REV. IRENE MONROE is an ordained minister, a *Huffington Post* blogger, and a syndicated religion columnist. She writes a weekly column in her hometown LGBTQ newspaper, *Bay Windows*. Rev. Monroe was chosen in October 2009 by MSNBC as one of "10 Black Women You Should Know." Rev. Monroe has been profiled in *O, The Oprah Magazine*, and in a Gay Pride episode of *In the Life* TV in which her segment was nominated for an educational Emmy. She appears in the film *For the Bible Tells Me So*, an exploration of the intersection between religion and homosexuality in the US and how the religious right has used its interpretation of the Bible to stigmatize the gay community. Her coming out story is profiled in the anthology *Crisis: 40 Stories Revealing the Personal, Social, and Religious Pain and Trauma of Growing up Gay in America*. www.irenemonroe.com.

RABBI ANDREA MYERS is the author of *The Choosing: A Rabbi's Journey from Silent Nights to High Holy Days*. She has also written for *Huffington Post* and *NY Jewish Week*. Rabbi Myers received her BA in neuroscience from Brandeis University, and was ordained at the Academy for Jewish Religion, an interdenominational seminary in New York City. She is a member of the New York Board of Rabbis, and has led congregations from the Rocky Mountains to the Borscht Belt. She is married to Rabbi Lisa Grushcow and they have two wonderful children, Ariella and Alice.

MICHAEL MUSTO writes the popular entertainment column "La Dolce Musto" in the *Village Voice* and the breathlessly opinionated blog La Daily Musto on villagevoice.com. He's a regular commentator all over TV, talking about pop cultural developments with sardonic glee. The *New York Times* calls him "the city's most punny, raunchy, and self referential gossip columnist." Said *Publishers Weekly*, his last book was "full of adulation, cattiness, and sexual innuendo...Musto's witty ridicule is pithy." His most recent book is *Fork on the Left, Knife in the Back.*

NICKY PARAISO is Director of Programming at The Club at La MaMa as well as Curator for the annual La MaMa Moves! Dance Festival. He has been an actor and vocalist in New York downtown theater and performance since 1979; a member of the international Meredith Monk/The House and Vocal Ensemble (1981-1990); an actor and musical director with playwright/actor/director Jeff Weiss and his partner Carlos Ricardo Martinez since 1979; has performed with Yoshiko Chuma and the School of Hard Knocks since 1988; and as a solo performance artist whose one-man shows *Asian Boys, Houses and Jewels,* and *House/Boy* have been presented at La MaMa, Dixon Place, P.S. 122, Dance Theater Workshop, and on tour in the US, Europe, and Asia. Paraiso's awards include a 1987 New York Dance and Performance Award, a 2004 Spencer Cherashore Fund grant for mid-career actors, and a 2005 New York Innovative Theater Award for his performance in Theodora Skipitares' *Iphigenia.* Nicky is a graduate of Oberlin College and holds an M.F.A. from New York University's Graduate Acting Program. Nicky thanks Thomas Keith for giving him the opportunity to contribute to *Love, Christopher Street.* He lives and works in New York City.

FELICE PICANO is the author of fiction, poetry, memoirs, plays, and other nonfiction. His work has been translated into sixteen languages and has received literary awards for many genres. In the US, Picano is considered one of the founders of modern gay literature; internationally as a noted postmodernist. Information on Picano can be found in *Contemporary Authors, The Cambridge History of 20th Century American Literature,* and *Wikipedia.com.* He received The Lambda Literary Pioneer Award and was an *Out* Magazine most influential LGBT person in 2009. His latest book is *True Stories: Portraits From My Past.* See www.felicepicano.net

CHARLES RICE-GONZÁLEZ, born in Puerto Rico and reared in the Bronx, is a writer, long-time community and LGBT activist, and Executive Director of BAAD! The Bronx Academy of Arts and Dance. He received a B.A. in Communications from Adelphi University and an M.F.A. in Creative Writing from Goddard College. *Chulito* is his debut novel, and he coedited, with Charlie Vázquez, *From Macho to Mariposa: New Gay Latino Fiction.* He is also an award-winning playwright and serves on the boards of the Bronx Council on the Arts and the National Association of Latino Art and Cultures. He can be reached at www.CharlesRiceGonzalez.com.

EDDIE SARFATY is a New York-based comedian and writer. He the author of *Mental: Funny in the Head,* a collection of humorous essays, and has appeared on *The Today Show,* Comedy Central's *Premium Blend,* Logo's *Wisecrack, The Joy Behar Show,* and in the documentar *Laughing Matters.* Eddie has written for *Huffington Post, Out, Metrosource,* the *Gay and Lesbian Review Worldwide,* and *LA Confidential* magazines. His work has been included in the anthologies *When I Knew* and *I'm Not the Biggest Bitch in this Relationship,* and he is the co-writer of the screen adaptation of his story, *Second-Guessing Grandma*.

JUSTINE SARACEN began writing fiction after careers as professor, opera manager, and editor. Trips to the Middle East inspired award-winning novels *The 100th Generation* (Egypt) and *Vulture's Kiss* (Jerusalem), dramatizing the dangers of militant religion. *Sistine Heresy*, winner of a 2009 Independent Publisher's Award, offers an LGBT backstory to Michelangelo's Sistine Chapel. *Mephisto Aria*, a World War II thriller with one eye on the Faust story and the other on the opera world, won the 2011 Golden Crown award (Best Historical), two Rainbow awards, and was an EPIC finalist. *Sarah, Son of God*, about a transvestite in Venice, ties in Stonewall New York, Venice of the Inquisition, and the Crucifixion. Her newest, *Tyger, Tyger, Burning Bright*, places us alongside Leni Riefenstahl, filmmaker of the Third Reich, and follows the struggles of four lovers in Nazi Germany. Saracen, who speaks German and French, lives in Brussels and loves scuba diving and opera.

BOB SMITH was the first openly gay comedian to appear on *The Tonight Show* and the first to have his own HBO Comedy Half-Hour. His first book, *Openly Bob*, won the Lambda Literary Award for humor. His first novel, *Selfish and Perverse*, was one of three nominees for The Edmund White Debut Fiction Award. His new novel, *Remembrance Of Things I Forgot*, was shortlisted for The Green Carnation Prize.

SHAWN SYMS has completed a short fiction collection and is currently at work on a novel. His fiction, journalism, reviews, essays, and other writing have appeared in *The Journey Prize Stories 21*, the Lambda Award–winning anthology *First Person Queer*, and over thirty other publications.

CHARLIE VÁZQUEZ is the author of the novels *Buzz and Israel* and *Contraband* and the bilingual poetry collection *Meditations: Bronx/Salsa*. He is the curator of the experimental HISPANIC PANIC! reading series and the New York City coordinator for Puerto Rico's "The Word/Festival de la Palabra," an international literary conference focusing on Latino and Latin-American literature. Charlie co-edited *From Macho to Mariposa*, a collection of twenty-nine short fiction works by gay/queer Latino men, with cultural producer and novelist Charles Rice-González. Charlie was born and raised in the Bronx, New York, and currently lives in Brooklyn with his partner John Williams. He likes coffee, books, and pretty snakes. Info: www.firekingpress.com

OCEAN VUONG was born in Saigon, Vietnam, and is the author of the chapbook *Burnings* and is currently an undergraduate at Brooklyn College, CUNY. He was a semi-finalist for the 2011 Crab Orchard Series in Poetry First Book Award and has received an Academy of American Poets award, the Connecticut Poetry Society's Al Savard Award, as well as four Pushcart Prize nominations. His poems appear in *RHINO*, *diode*, *Verse Daily*, *The Collagist*, *Crate*, and *PANK*, among others.

KATHLEEN WARNOCK is a New York City-based playwright and editor. Her plays have been seen in New York, internationally and regionally. She is curator of the Robert Chesley/Jane Chambers Playwrights Project for TOSOS Theater, and the Ambassador of Love for the International Dublin Gay Theatre Festival. Her play *Rock the Line* won the Robert Chesley Award and is published by United Stages. She is a member of The Dramatists Guild. *Some Are People* won the Arts & Letters Prize. She curates Drunken! Careening! Writers!, a reading series at KGB Bar in NYC (since 2004). She is series editor for *Best Lesbian Erotica* (Cleis). Her stories, interviews, profiles, and reviews have been published in *American Theater, Gay City News, New York Press, Bust, Ms., Metal Maidens, ROCKRGRL,* TelevisionWithoutPity.com, *The Dramatist,* and others. Website: www.kathleenwarnock.com; Twitter: @kwarnockny

ACKNOWLEDGMENTS

JOSEPH PITTMAN IS ONE OF the most determined and hardworking people in publishing. He has been characteristically persistent and motivating in his belief that I should undertake this project. I'm grateful to Joe for his friendship and for encouraging me to work with living authors on new books!

The individual contributors to this volume have gone above and beyond what was asked of them. I have been granted the good fortune to get to know some of you for the first time and with others to renew long friendships. Good sports, good eggs, good souls, and substantial writers all, thank you. You have my lasting gratitude.

My thanks also go to Christopher Bram who has been especially generous, not only contributing his discerning and warm introduction to this volume, but also granting permission to reprint his essay, "Perry Street Redux," originally published in *Mapping the Territory* in 2009.

For their kind advice, recommendations, and assistance, and for their friendship, my thanks go to Paul J. Willis, Michele Karlsberg, Martin Hyatt, Don Weise, Bob Smith, Carol Rosenfeld, David Kaplan, Amie Evans, Shaun Levin, Sarah Schulman, and Kathleen Warnock. I would also like to thank Victor Mingovits, Erin McHugh, Lou Pizzitola, Matt Nasser, and Jack Schlegel for lending their talents to the completion and publicizing of this volume. And I am always grateful to my dear friend David Bander, a man who should never be left out.

Finally I am happy to acknowledge the unwavering support of *mi corazón*, Arturo Noguera, and the finest inspiration, literary advisor, and arbiter of the outrageous and the sacred, my friend Jane Young.